Police Reform in Turkey

Contemporary Turkey, published in collaboration with the
British Institute at Ankara

Series editor: Ceren Lord

New and forthcoming titles:
Turkey and the Politics of National Identity,
edited by Shane Brennan and Marc Herzog
Police Reform in Turkey, by Funda Hülagü
Architectures of Emergency in Turkey,
edited by Eray Çayli, Pinar Aykac and Sevcan Ercan
The Alawis of Modern Turkey, by Hakan Mertcan
Gender and Education in Turkey, by Zühre Emanet

As our understanding of modern Turkish history continues to evolve, and
as the Middle East continues to change, a new generation of scholars are
exploring questions of identities, class, politics, diplomacy and religion. The
British Institute at Ankara (BIAA) is internationally renowned for its support
of new independent academic research in the region across various fields,
including archaeology, ancient and modern history, heritage management,
social sciences and contemporary issues in public policy, and political
sciences. *Contemporary Turkey* is a collection of specially commissioned books
published in a collaboration between I.B. Tauris and the BIAA, which focus
on the identity, history and politics of republican and modern Turkey. Authors
and contributors combine academic rigour and scholarship with extensive
first-hand experience in the region.

Police Reform in Turkey

*Human Security, Gender and State
Violence Under Erdoğan*

Funda Hülagü

I.B.TAURIS
LONDON • NEW YORK • OXFORD • NEW DELHI • SYDNEY

I.B. TAURIS
Bloomsbury Publishing Plc
50 Bedford Square, London, WC1B 3DP, UK
1385 Broadway, New York, NY 10018, USA
29 Earlsfort Terrace, Dublin 2, Ireland

BLOOMSBURY, I.B. TAURIS and the I.B. Tauris logo are
trademarks of Bloomsbury Publishing Plc

First published in Great Britain 2021
This paperback edition published in 2022

A catalogue record for this book is available from the British Library.

A catalog record for this book is available from the Library of Congress.

ISBN: HB: 978-1-8386-0412-7
        PB: 978-0-7556-3991-5
        ePDF: 978-1-8386-0413-4
        eBook: 978-1-8386-0414-1

Series: Contemporary Turkey

Typeset by Integra Software Services Pvt. Ltd.

Contents

Acknowledgements

This book is the most recent product of my academic journey, one full of ups and downs. It is the outcome of precarious working conditions, political despair and personal disappointments coupled with many good moments of solidarity, encouragement and inspiration.

Many people deserve special thanks. Had Prof. Dr Pınar Bedirhanoğlu not encouraged me to rethink my PhD thesis under the light of the last decade's political developments in Turkey, I doubt that I would have dared to revisit my doctoral dissertation, with which I have been in a love-and-hate relationship for years now. Many thanks, Pınar! Had Prof. Dr Annette Henninger not provided me with a warm solidarity in times of academic despair, I would not have had a chance to complete this book project. Prof. Henninger introduced me to the lovely department of Political Science in the Phillips University of Marburg, where I have been teaching now for three years. This has been the greatest experience of my academic life. Many thanks, Annette! I would also like to thank my interviewees who kindly shared their valuable time with me when I wanted to learn more about the police reform process and its gendered journey in Turkey. Without doubt, all potential errors are my own.

Finally, I would like to extend my gratitude to my amazing partner Berk who gave me unconditional support so that I could realize this dream of mine. I dedicate this book to my seven-year-old daughter, Defne Roza, without whose astonishing self-sufficiency, I would never have found the chance to finish this book on time.

Introduction

When the footage showing the clamours of Dilek Doğan's family, a young woman shot to death in October 2015 in her house during a police operation, was public, nobody could stay indifferent. The police raid, which took place in the Küçükarmutlu district of Istanbul, was conducted by a special police operations team. The perpetrator was the chief of the team. When asked about the shooting, the police chief told that on the day of the incident he had just come back from the state of emergency region in the South-eastern Turkey and that he was tired and had hurried to end the operation to go back home. He further declared that his conscience was clear, and that he did what the state told him to do.

The same year three more women were subject to lethal police violence (Şahin, 2015).[1] Some of these women were associated with politically violent left-wing groups. Police forces involved in the raids contended that the victims were armed. The only case which was brought to judicial investigation was the shooting of Dilek Doğan.[2] This was largely due to the public reactions to the video footage showing her, just a couple of minutes before her being shot to death, in her pyjamas, asking the police to remove their boots while entering the house. After this horrific event, pro-government media tried to prove that Dilek Doğan was a member of some outlawed left-wing groups. Her murder was *ex post facto* justified based on her alleged links to these groups. She was criminalized, as indeed all her family, so that the public discontent with the brutal policing politics of the government was alleviated.

Dilek was not the only female victim of the post-Gezi Protests 'authoritarian turn' of the state in Turkey. During the Gezi Protests in 2013, peaceful women activists and/or protestors were subject to gendered forms of state violence. Many were harassed, strip-searched and insulted by the police. During the rise of the armed conflict with the Kurdistan Workers' Party (PKK) in 2015, these gendered forms persisted marking the state violence. During the state crisis of 2014–16, when the coalition between the Gülenist bureaucracy cadres and pro-Erdoğan ones collapsed, the state violence continued producing heavily gendered outcomes. In each case, politically active women – whether they are protesters, activists or political fighters – were expressly targeted.

The murder of Dilek Doğan was realized under the auspices of a government that has been claiming to be committed to the moral dictates of human security, to the act of 'loving every creature because of the Creator'[3] and to a decade-long institutional transformation under the motto of 'Make human beings live, only so the state can long live'.[4] How is that a government that has presumably declared zero tolerance for police-led violence and trained a whole state apparatus from the police organization to the judiciary against gendered violence reverted or could revert to the opposite? How is that the so-called reformed police of Turkey under the Justice and Development Party (AKP, henceforth) governments brought unaccountable state action and brutal state violence back in? Were all the reforms done, all the deeds promised and all the international mentorship devoted to the police reform just cosmetic? Or was there something particularly specific in those processes that instituted the origins of the new round of *gendered state violence* in Turkey?

This book is an attempt to provide a critical interpretive framework, for the AKP-era reform initiatives taken by the state in Turkey in the field of internal security, especially of policing, a framework which can account for the coercive dialectic of the so-called pro-humane reform process. This study proposes that such a task can first be accomplished with the help of a feminist-materialist theory of the state. In a nutshell, the materialist-cum-feminist theory of state provides us with a methodological framework that posits the state form as a historical-relational structure, with deep-rooted gender selectivities. Materialist feminist theory's contribution is not limited to detecting the gendered nature of the state. It does also give us hints about the general transformation of the state in Turkey.

The main aim of this study is to understand the reform process by shedding light on the different agents and their struggles over the state with a focus on gender. For the making of police reform is a process of struggle, conflict and coalition among different agents of change, with different power resources, ideological commitments and practices.

In order to understand the seemingly paradoxical eruption of gender-based state violence after years of state transformation, first, the post-Cold War ideology of liberal of state-building and its agents who instigated the state/police transformation processes around the world should be delineated. In a nutshell, security sector reform (SSR) defines itself as a project of replacing the 'state security' understanding which shaped the state-society relations during the Cold War era with that of 'human security' (Chanaa, 2002). There is a global consensus on the definition of SSR as the reconstruction of the security institutions of the state after a human security-first understanding. But could the liberal sources of these reform processes, the very liberal geoculture of the post-Cold War era, have been real barricades against state violence? Or to what extent has the long-cherished liberal geoculture been truly conducive to a peace-prone state culture?

Second, this book delineates the Turkish security bureaucracy and especially the reformist police cadres who were behind the reform process from 2006 to 2016, and describes the making of those reformist police cadres and their peculiar moralistic philosophy in the job of policing. What were the defining ideological characteristics of their reform agenda? How have they devised the job of policing, with what kinds of motives, references and assumptions? In short, what is the philosophy behind the police science they tried to foster in Turkey? How gendered is this police science?

Third, this book assumes that to understand the root causes behind the escalation in state violence including its targeting of politically active women, we should also rethink on the political inputs of Turkey's progressive social forces during the so-called reformist era. Which struggles have been fought by the feminist movement in Turkey to create a change in the patriarchal state? How have the feminists and women's rights organizations interpreted violence against women in general and gendered state violence in particular? What kind of power relations have impacted on the feminist interventions in and against the state?

Fourth, despite the multitude of social, political and economic dimensions that characterize the latest era of state violence in Turkey, this book wants to illuminate the gendered dimensions of it and sort out the links that tie the so-called two phases of the AKP governments in Turkey: the reformist and the authoritarian phases. What kind of governance mechanisms do secure the resilience of the authoritarian regime in Turkey? Why have women become victims of state violence? As a matter of fact, why have *certain* women become victims of state violence?

All in all, this book is a feminist-materialist attempt to analyse the so-called authoritarian turn of the state in Turkey. It is a tale of three cities: the liberal international community involved in the reform processes, the security personnel leading the reform agenda and practice, and the feminist contenders.

This study detects that one curious concept creates a single thread among these different actors, that of human security: the idea that the fundamental human right an individual should be provided with – *by the state* – is freedom from basic insecurities. Explicitly or implicitly, directly or indirectly – as in the principle of due diligence[5] – human security has been commonly championed as the political programme to be adopted in order to prevent all forms violence including violence against women and the gender-based state violence. It became the common grammar of those who wished for the establishment of a democratic/non-patriarchal social contract between the state and society. Could a sincere adoption of the human security concept by the state in Turkey have prevented the authoritarian turn? Or what if the reverse is true? What if human security is paradoxically responsible for state violence?

To recap, this book reveals the main characteristics of the reform process, which *differ-while-remaining-identical* after the famous authoritarian turn. Those who wish to decode the violent nature of the AKP regime in Turkey should certainly revisit its liberal foundations.

The limits of the 'authoritarian turn' narrative

When the AKP came to power in 2002, the state in Turkey was in a deep legitimacy crisis. The wealthy classes, the political establishment and different international organizations like the IMF had all been in search for a meta-strategy to appease the accrued political conflicts and economic hardships. As a result, the newly founded AKP's proposal of establishing a 'conservative democracy' has been welcomed by different interest groups in and abroad. Despite the party's political Islamist roots – which would normally alarm the political fear-mongers of the post-9/11 world context – the then mainstreaming of the counter-hegemonic arguments on Islamophobia by the proponents of the liberal world order has helped the global forces including the European Union (EU) to cheer on the end of the crisis-laden coalition politics era in Turkey. The liberal enthusiasm about the possible ending of the legitimacy crisis in Turkey with the help of the AKP has led many actors within the civil society to closely engage with the ruling party to reform the state. Many EU-funded multi-stakeholder projects were designed to democratize the state in Turkey, by then characterized as 'praetorian' and 'corrupt'.[6] The AKP's willingness to engage in these projects as well as the welcoming mood of certain state cadres of the so-called democratic transformation – most of whom were Gülenist cadres – were taken as evidences for the beginning of a new political era in Turkey, where the human rights principles would be observed and where the state would be more willing to share power with the dissident social groups like the Kurds.

This liberal enthusiasm has also helped to reframe many of the political issues in Turkey with a methodological individualist perspective, whereby the political nature of a regime is generally defined with reference to the nature of the governmental comportments of the bureaucrats, military men and political leaders. The ability of the new reforms in terms of addressing the militarist political culture of Turkey's statecraft was insistently underlined. The lessening of the state-induced cases of torture, the amelioration of the relations between the police rank-and-file and lay people, the so-called open and libertarian visions of the security bureaucracy were cited as the strong points of a reformist political will in Turkey. This was an era of strong belief in the merits of inclusive liberalism.

By then, it took great pains for the political opposition to the AKP rule to display the anti-democratic character of it. Aside from a general critique revolving around a basic conception of neoliberalism, which was defined after the political economic processes like deregulation, privatization and flexibilization of the labour market, the not-so hidden transformations in the state form towards a privatized, personalized and non-secular political rule have been mostly discarded. This is also because the so-far excluded social groups of Turkey's capitalist social formation were very willing to benefit from the human rights reforms, codified by them as a historical political opportunity.

Even as early as 2010, when for example the then Prime Minister Tayyip Erdoğan confessed that he did not believe in the gender equality between men and women – as according to him, their nature is different from birth – during a consultation meeting he did with the progressive women's organizations, the liberal recasting of the AKP as a reformist party with a democratic ethos continued its discursive hegemony. As proof, it was stated that the AKP's reform projects were important as they were dragging even the reluctant democrats, therefore many interest groups associated with the AKP, into the game of democracy. In short, the reforms in the field of human rights, policing and citizenship rights were considered as the main instruments of a pragmatic process of 'democracy without democrats'.[7] It was assumed that even if the AKP was not sincere in its democratic promises, these reforms would make the AKP continue the game. Apparently, at some point, the AKP ceased to continue playing the game. This change has been generally known in the academic literature on the AKP governments' era as 'the authoritarian turn'. Since then, both the when and why of this change have been discussed with growing appetite in the academic circles and in the international media.

The existing explanations for the seemingly paradoxical results of the reform process in Turkey, however, generally do not depart from the liberal methodology of the previous era. Rather than rethinking the real character of the reform agenda and the accompanied state transformation, they stick to a reified analysis of political power as a top-to-down phenomenon. In other words, they perceive the reform process as a temporary progression, only pragmatically adopted by the AKP governments both to receive international recognition and to crack down the military tutelage in Turkey. They explain the authoritarian turn by basing on Erdoğan's lust for presidential power and his arrogant intentions to co-opt all forces of democratic transformation such as the Kurdish political movement to his agenda (Benhabib, 2013). Similar analyses have led scholars to argue that as the AKP lost the parliamentary majority in the June 2015 elections, the desire to hang on power accompanied a drastic rise in political violence (Esen and Gümüşçü, 2016). Others have also underlined the role of the July 2016 failed coup attempt as the catalyser of a violent search for securing the regime at all costs (Kaygusuz, 2018). Below are my main four reservations against this line of analysis:

First, these analyses are mostly gender blind. They tend to sidestep the centrality of the gender politics to the authoritarian state project of the AKP and indeed consider the gendered state violence as another symptom of Erdoğan's autocratic political domination. However, as also powerfully demonstrated by Deniz Kandiyoti (2016), the gendered state violence is not only symptomatic but also constitutive of the new state in Turkey. Moreover, had these analyses incorporated the gender lens, it would be easier to detect the continuities between the so-called reformist and authoritarian eras.

Second, despite their different explanatory merits, all these and similar methodologically individualist approaches tend to assume that the democratization steps taken by the government were democratic in theory and yet abused, tricked and/or mal developed in practice. That is to say, the liberal project of state transformation itself is hardly any rendered subject to a critical de-construction. However, the main of the argument of this book is that the post-Cold War liberal internationalist project, the hegemonic plan of building responsible and human-centred states capable of dealing with the humanitarian plights of their own populations, has itself been prone to generating non-democratic forms of political power. This argument is already a truism, especially with regard to post-conflict contexts, marred with grave human losses and severe economic deprivation.[8] However, even for a country like Turkey, which is considered to be a middle-income country with professionalized and rationalized state institutions, the violent unfolding of this liberal state-building agenda is worth considering. Onur Bahçecik (2015), for example, argues that the AKP era's human rights reforms in Turkey depoliticized the issue of state crimes and reconstructed them as technical problems and therefore failed to fulfil their potentials. However, even this critique based on a Foucauldian reading of neoliberalism as a specific technique of power dependent on de-politicization misses the illiberal and anti-democratic potentials of the liberal reforms themselves.

Third, the analyses that take for granted the periodization based on reformist vs. authoritarian eras mostly operate with a 'regime radar', a notion used by Morten Valbjørn (2012) to denote the scholarly habit of obsessively observing the political power, especially the authoritarian ones, as if they were operating in a social vacuum, with complete free check to choose their policies and political destination. This is not to say that in the authoritarian or not fully democratic contexts, people are free to express themselves and can easily intervene in politics. However, state power is always relational, even under repressive contexts. Relationality encompasses the formative power of the social forces. The struggles fought by the organized social movements but also by the non-organized ones, for instance those which manifest in the form of 'non-movements' (Bayat, 2013) put their prints on the state form in different ways. The Gezi Protests have displayed the formation of collective identities in Turkey in a noticeably short time. As in the case of the post-2011 revolutionary movements in many other Middle Eastern and North African (MENA) countries, during the Gezi Protests in Turkey, the political collective agency of women has become fully apparent and alarmed the political power. In short, women's movement in Turkey has become 'a movement that is organizationally ephemeral and in a constant state of flux and thus hard to suppress' (Hoodfar and Sadeghi, 2009: 215).[9] Therefore, each state analysis should be struggle-centred rather than merely power-centred.

The regression of struggle-centred power analysis is especially a burning methodological issue in the field of critical security studies, as also recently argued by many different researchers (Huysmans, 2008; Aradau and Blanke, 2010; Coleman and Rosenow, 2016). Although with differing stresses and from different angles, these perspectives criticize the existing critiques of security practices due to their exclusive focus on the question of 'how'. As in most of these analyses, the *how of power* precedes the *why of power*, the critiques of security obliterate the continuing centrality of the *Political* in the reproduction of the security policies of the (post-modern) state. The *Political* refers to the political horizons of structurally situated social forces and indeed to the question of 'what is a good polity?', which is either implicitly or sometimes explicitly endorsed by these forces. However, in the existing critical security literature, the emphasis on the sovereign as the ultimate enactor of political rules and/or of the rules of exception leads to an impoverished notion of politics, where the dialectics between the actual (political domination that tries to crush the political capacity of a society) and the potential (political capacities and horizons of the dissenting social forces) is collapsed onto a unilineal conception of power.

In short, the meta-critique of the critical studies on security maintains that neither the state power is activated through the single will of the sovereign nor does it act over a homogenous entity called people or, in the context of this study, women. It is a capacity constituted at the junction of clashing political horizons. For example, the gendered state violence in Turkey does of course target women-in-politics because they are *women* and try to reduce them to *sexualized bodies*, but also and indeed, this is inseparably so, these women are *in politics* and their opposition to state is not merely an act of gender but also a call *to the Political*. Therefore, gendered state violence is neither only about gendered outcomes (e.g. discouraging women from politics), motives (e.g. keeping the public field dominantly as a masculine field) and forms (e.g. using sexual harassment) nor only about silencing the opposition at all costs. It is activated at the junction of these two – women and *Political*. This intersection historically signifies a potentiality that the patriarchal-capitalist state in Turkey wants to kill in its early stages.

Fourth, these state power-centred authoritarian-turn perspectives end in *correctionalism*. They conceive not only the state violence, that is, physical violence caused by state terror, but also the everyday physical violence emanating from state neglect as symptoms of an excessive or weak form of state power – as if once this excess violence is taken aback, the democratic order would be restored or if once the state overcomes its infrastructural weaknesses, it will be able to fulfil its protective responsibility. However, it appears that the current era of state violence is of systemic character, in the sense that it expresses not only the evil or the fallible in the state but also its perpetual crisis under the conditions of neoliberal capitalism.[10] This latter perpetuates social problems (poverty, violence against women, human trafficking etc.), whose apparent solutions require a contradictory expansion of the administrative state power – also wished by a diverse range of civil society actors campaigning around single issues that call in the state to act.

However, this expansion does not translate into success. Although state policies are designed for eradicating social harms, these policies usually end in staying in theory or at best are inconsistently implemented because the states that are invited to act are also constrained by the force of circumstances. In other words, the voluntarism behind correctionalism obscures the simple fact that states are also structurally tied on the political economic realities. These realities are both global and national in scale. On the one hand, the states have lost their 'time sovereignty' (Jessop, 2002), for example, their bureaucratic capacity and capability to catch up with the rapid turn of events in global capitalism – financial crises, refugee influxes, global pandemics etc. On the other hand, their viability also depends on the social situation of sub-proletarian classes whose livelihood conditions constrain the states' political will and capacity to engage in cosmopolitan, internationalist or egalitarian policies.

Therefore, it is not a surprise to see that similar problems compel the states to enact very inconsistent or even self-contradicting policies within a limited amount of time. In countries for example where the foremost amount of the sub-proletarian masses is male, criminal justice decisions are always a matter of patriarchal negotiation between the men and the state. To illustrate, using heavy criminal/penal measures to deal with the expanding numbers of domestic violence might be used by the very same state which would also slip to – and/or co-use – non-punitive methods, that is, non-enforcement of law and/impunity provision to the male perpetrators. Both apparently contradicting measures make part of the same continuum of the administrative repertoire of the neoliberal states, pressurized both from below and from above. This is especially the case for the southern countries.[11]

Beyond authoritarianism: The making of a centaur state in Turkey

Keeping in mind these methodological problems related to the 'authoritarian turn' discussions, this study is also sceptical about the very concept of authoritarianism. Although it has become a common reflex to define neoliberal states around the world as authoritarian by their nature, the concept itself is hardly expressive of the peculiarities of the state form it wants to expose. Even if it tries to challenge the mainstream institutionalist idea of the early 1980s about the positive correlation between economic liberalization and democratization, it risks becoming another buzzword devoid of any real explanatory power. Plus, the discussions on authoritarianism are usually preferring to speak from within political regime analyses. Although the lines that separate regime-theoretical lenses from state-theoretical lenses are blurred, the main difference appears to centre on the research priorities. Whereas regime analyses prioritize the question of state power and its (il)legitimate deployment, state analyses prioritize the question of state form and its historical embodiments. This book follows this second road and contemplates from within a literature that tries to understand the major historical transformation(s) of the *modern bourgeois state form* in the twenty-first century.

This study comes up with the conclusion that Turkey's SSR in general and the police reform have provided the ideological and strategic means for the constitution of a *new state form* in Turkey. This new state form, though not fully consolidated yet, is de-rationalized, anti-*Political* and anti-egalitarian. It is thus *form-wise* different from the modern bourgeois state form where the state architecture was *ideally* built on the notions of rationalization (the institution according to which neither the state as an apparatus nor the outputs of state policies can be possessed by single individuals, certain privileged groups and for certain particular interests but do belong to the public; and the state acts for the public interest), on the aptitude to recognize political rights far beyond the civil right to vote and to be elected (the foundational principle that once state power gets privatized, the people have a right to pursue dissensus politics)[12] and on the potential to procure formal equality for all (the principle that everybody under the jurisdiction of a state should be provided with similar treatment irrespective of that person's ascribed status in a society).[13]

By way of an explicatory analogy, the new state in Turkey can be termed as a *centaur state*. The studies of Loic Wacquant, a prolific scholar in the field of critical criminology studies, obliquely picture the centaur state as a qualitatively different state form from the modern bourgeois state. And this is even more so despite the deployment of similar oppressive policies, in short similar mechanisms of state power, by both forms of the state. My personal exegesis from the writings of Loic Wacquant is therefore that what really differentiates this post-modern state form from the modern state form are not the specific policies developed and used vis-à-vis the social but rather the political foundations upon which these two state forms are erected. The centaur state is *post*-modern because it deviates from the republican, anti-monarchical and abstract but nevertheless egalitarian foundations of the modern state. The new state-in-the-making is 'liberal at the top and paternalistic at the bottom, which presents radically different faces at the two ends of the social hierarchy: a comely and caring visage toward the middle and upper classes, and a fearsome and frowning mug toward the lower class' (Wacquant, 2010: 217). In other words, the post-modern state can govern at one and the same time by and through different political regimes (i.e. both liberal and illiberal), each specifically tailored for different social classes (i.e. for those fully integrated to the market society and those who try to survive on its margins).[14]

Centaur is a half-man/half-horse creature from the Greek mythology. Loic Wacquant deploys it as a counter-image to Leviathan, a pervasively used analogy to visualize the modern state power. Although, analogies such as Leviathan and, in the case of this study, centaur always carry the risk of masking rather than illuminating the workings of state power by personifying the state, I stick to the analogy here due to its potential to capture the essence of the main historical change we are experiencing in the modern bourgeois state form: a transition from the claim of being the neutral legal arbiter of social conflicts, before which everyone is apparently equal, to the idea of a hybrid executer, before which nobody is equal to other. Differential treatment is the standardized functioning of the centaur state.

Wacquant does of course develop this allegory of the centaur state mostly based on his observations and field research conducted in the advanced capitalist countries which have undergone a thorough neoliberal transformation in the fields of work and social security. Although the neoliberal transformation has been global in reach and as deep in terms of its restructuring impact as it was in the capitalist core, the main architecture of the centaur state appears to be different in the Global South. For the centaur state in Turkey appears to be functioning very selective vis-à-vis the social classes, groups and sections it deals with – as are the states in the advanced capitalist core – and yet this selectivity is determined not only after social class hierarchy but also and indeed at the intersection of social class, ethnic background, sex and *political affiliation/ intention/activity/militancy*.[15]

For the selectivity of the bourgeois state in its treatment of population is nothing new. It is known that the criminal justice systems of the bourgeois states have always under-criminalized the criminal acts committed by the wealthiest sectors of the society, and also over-criminalized those committed by the poor and subaltern classes (Weis, 2017). Moreover, it is also known that this selectivity has always acquired an intersectional character in the sense that it operated at the intersection of the co-constituting forms of inequalities (based on class, gender and 'race') (Aguilar, 2015). Besides, the very category of citizenship has been from its inception a category which differentially incorporated men and women (Waylen, 1996; Babül, 2015; Kandiyoti, 2016).

What appears to be new, however, is that the centaur state is hardly any shy about displaying its differential treatment of citizens and indeed by way of this, it closes down the huge but beneficial modern contradiction between the ideal (the promise of universal equality) and the actual (differential integration) to the detriment of the dependent social groups and classes. It ceases to function after the promise of formal equality/abstract universality.

It operates by segmenting and profiling, by developing different administrative capacities corresponding to different layers in societal hierarchies. And this know-how is hardly hidden. On the contrary, it accuses poor and single mothers for raising potential criminal children in the absence of the fathers; it portrays the middle-class women who ask for their right to abortion in public hospitals as murderers; it depicts the disenfranchised black men as potential rapists; it accuses secular women of being puppets of the Western powers; it codes women agents of political violence as victims of male-dominated terrorist organizations, etc. This selective operation and valorization system are put into state practice, legitimated through various material and discursive strategies, and even legalized. Therefore, selective deployment of citizenship rights is not an aberration or a practice that diverges from the ideal due to various reasons, but it is itself the new ideal, the new post-modern template of state power. In short, the centaur state is the state whose modern contradictions are offset in disfavour of the dependent classes and groups, including women.

This book tries to demonstrate how the liberal reform process has created the centaur state in Turkey.[16] The following are the sub-arguments which are further developed in the following chapters.

First, it is maintained that the liberal state and peace-building processes have been built on certain ideological postulations, which have determined the practice of the international epistemic communities and state cadres alike. In relation with this, the first transformative element of the state in Turkey in the AKP era has been the ideological and practical inputs accompanying the globally induced liberal police reform processes which prioritized human security as a guiding principle. When, however seen from the perspective of materialist-feminist state theory (explained further below), the principle of human security meant nothing but some nebulous form of populism (promoted as the anti-dote of an impersonal distant state) and localism (promoted as the anti-dote of Westernism/Weberian statism). The translation of these two new foundations for the re-legitimation of the state monopoly of coercion into the context of Turkey has happened with a taxonomic dichotomy posited between the militarist-Kemalist state of Turkey and the 'property-owner modest man' who is oppressed by it. Although there have been pro-gender equality interventions of the feminist agents of the international epistemic community in this newest state-building process of Turkey, the universalist appeal of their interventions hit against the walls of populism and localism. This has been also unfortunately facilitated by the behaviourism marking the feminist engagement with the 'men in the state'.

The second process which has further given shape to the making of a centaur state in Turkey is the Turkish-Islamist incorporation of these two principles of populism and localism into policing. This moralist policing philosophy propagated by the reformist police cadres has been based on a conservative ideal of harmonious society. Accordingly, the society in Turkey has been harmonious by its nature. Most of the criminal problems of the social formation in Turkey are coded therefore as problems emanating from the fallacies of the militarist-Kemalist state. Hence, it was reasoned that the police should become reformed after the ideal of this harmonious society with a stated aim of restoring this society to its morally superior origins. Relatedly, for the reformist police cadres, the basic aim of the police reform was to restore the honour of the 'property-owner modest man'. Minimizing the judicial power of the police and augmenting its administrative powers have been set as the best practice. Accordingly, judicial policing tended to criminalize 'poor men'. However, for the moralist police science espoused by the reformist police cadres, administrative policing is an opportunity to improve the protectionist mandate of the state. This philosophy has had very controversial results for women. Although the reformist police cadres have developed a specific policy for the integration of women into the new state, women were integrated only as 'victims' in need of masculinist protection.[17] Moreover, the centrality of the 'property-owner modest man' (sometimes also recast as 'poor man') to the moralist reform project has contributed to the self-legitimation of impunity – the discretionary police powers about the selective non-enforcement of law.

The third process which has inevitably contributed in the making of the centaur state has been the feminist interventions in and against the state in Turkey (see further below). Although different from each other in terms of strategy and priorities, the three main veins of feminist interventions in the state, the equal rights feminism, the governance feminism and the peace feminism, have been referring to a common concept of human security – state responsibility to protect its women citizens from physical and male violence. On the one hand, this had provided the feminists with the ability to pressurize the state to take pro-gender equality steps. On the other hand, it has prevented them from realizing the resignification of these seemingly pro-gender equality projects into the service of the AKP's centaur state.

Finally, the Gezi Protests in Turkey have become the ultimate catalyser which prompted the continuity of these processes with a new intensity. The reformed state, endowed with a plethora of new techniques of political domination, including the gender, has brutally reacted to the social forces in opposition. Politically active women who opposed the neoliberal-neoconservative policies of the AKP have become the Achilles' Heel of the centaur state. Their presence has repeatedly pointed out the changing and evolving role of women, almost acting as a collective agent of resistance and transformation in Turkey. To govern them, the state deepened its *selective patriarchy*.

On the materialist-feminist state theory

To explain the main patterns that determine the character of the relations among the agents of reform process and to decode the machineries of the centaur state, I have mostly benefited from a materialist-feminist perspective. This theoretical perspective provided me with an expansive conceptual toolset, which has also facilitated my exclusive research focus on the making of police powers before and after the Gezi Protests within the broader global and local socio-economic developments impacting Turkey's gender order. Before proceeding with explaining the basic methodological and theoretical premises of such a perspective, I should inform the reader about the specific trajectory I have taken to come up with a materialist-cum-feminist state theory.

From the very start, it should be stated that by materialist-cum-feminist state theory, I do not refer to any systematic school of thought. In other words, the theoretical perspective that I try to promote in this study is a relatively free and eclectic interpretation primarily of the critical state-theoretical inputs of Claus Offe (1994), Bob Jessop (2004), Heide Gerstenberger (2007), Elisabeth Prügl (2009) and Sylvia Federici (2009) among many others. But let me briefly discuss the reasons which have pushed me to navigate in such a complex set of readings.

The last decades have witnessed a lack of attention on the part of the feminist theories towards the state as an object of study. Based on the limited number of existing studies on the state and feminist discussions about it, it is possible to explain this lack of attention on two grounds. The first is the methodological disinclination to work with a unitary theory of the state and the second is the feminist political will to go beyond being captured 'in or against the state' dilemma. The methodological caution resumes from the post-structuralist investigations which warn against conceiving the state as a monolithic bloc and as a unified structure acting with intentionality. This stance argues against defining a unitary theory of state (Rai, 1996). In her well-known article, 'Finding the Man in the State', Wendy Brown (1992) argues that the state operates as 'an intricate grid of often conflicting strategies, technologies and discourses of power'. Accordingly, the state powers exist in plural and each state power has its *sui generis* domination strategies and technologies. For Brown (1992: 16), to look for a unifying thread among those different powers would repeat the class-reductionism of the Marxist state theory.

In close relation with this theoretical approach, feminist activism suggests that as states are multiple and contradictory grids of power, they are open to subversion and deconstruction and could therefore become arenas for making changes in gender regimes to the benefit of women (Kantola, 2006). In other words, in the presence of a non-unitary state, 'being in or against the state' is already an irrelevant and even false presumption, which might obstruct the recuperation of the state power(s) for feminist purposes. Moreover, historically speaking, state feminism for example has helped women to politicize the private field and broadened the public remit to alleviate the social reproduction burdens of women (Hatem, 1992; Waylen, 1996).

Despite the merits of these intellectual and activist perspectives, this study assumes that although the state apparatus – which is argued to be composed of legal, bureaucratic, economic, security dimensions (Brown, 1992) – is a non-monolithic body, each with different power resources and techniques (which in return can be exploited by the feminists), I would argue that the *historical form*, within which this state apparatus functions, possesses certain over-arching predispositions limiting or conscripting the subversive attempts to appropriate the state power(s). In other words, this section on materialist-cum-feminist theory argues that the different dimensions of a state, however contradictory they may be, share a historically and socially determined political direction and certain correlated limits of action disciplining the disparate state powers towards a common aim: the reproduction of the capitalist society in its entirety.

Relatedly, the materialist-cum-feminist theory basically argues that (1) the capitalist state acquires different historical shapes, which this study conceives as different historical *forms* of the capitalist state, for example, the modern bourgeois state form and the post-modern centaur from. These historical forms result from the condensation of temporally and spatially conditioned social struggles in certain institutions, rules and powers. However, social struggles are not fully free to determine the forms over and in which they struggle because the capitalist state does operate along certain (2) *socio-economic necessities* and (3) *political boundaries*. The socio-economic necessities, the political boundaries and their bureaucratic-ideological interpretation by the state cadres, which will be discovered further below, shape 'the gender selectivities of the state' (Jessop, 2004). (4) These selectivities, in return, condition the final form of the feminist interventions in and against the state. In other words, the impact of the feminist interventions in and against the state is filtered by these selectivities. (5) State forms are only temporary settlements of the social conflicts. If inequalities continue depleting the reproductive capacities of social formations, the states cannot be other but self-contradictory entities. But making a progressive advantage of these contradictions is not self-evident.

Let me briefly go over these five theoretical premises under the light of the socio-economic developments impacting the formation of gender order in Turkey.

States as historical and material condensation of social struggles

The making of the modern state form does not happen in vacuum but in relation to different external and internal societal dynamics and because of related political conflicts which in turn congeal in the form of legal changes, institutional bodies and state apparatuses. In other words, the modern state as the ruling public power in a territorially defined setting is the material and historical condensation of political struggles between different social forces.[18] These struggles are usually fought over political representation (who will be represented in the political field), economic redistribution (who will benefit from the public goods provided by the state) or identity recognition (which subjects will be accorded respect and place within the political order).[19] Historically speaking, different types of social forces struggle over these three overlapping and/or sometimes diverging streams of political demands.

These demands do indeed challenge 'the rules of entitlement' and 'the rules of identity' ingrained into the modern state form. According to the feminist political economist Elisabeth Prügl (2009: 178), 'the rules of entitlement' define access to material or non-material resources which give power to individuals to participate in political and economic life. States are effective and indeed decisive mechanisms of controlling this access. However, it should also be added that the very material apparatus of the state is itself a resource to which universal access is not granted. Who benefits, for example, from the state police and its law and order functions? Who has a real right to ask for protection from the police? Women's movements have been long struggling for the right to benefit from the state apparatus for the protection of feminine bodies from male violence.

'The rules of identity', on the other hand, define the dominant identity character of the social hierarchies and the political establishment. According to Elisabeth Prügl (2009: 178), both – the social hierarchies and the political establishment – empower, dis-empower or discipline individual bodies via different rules of identity. States have been using different rules of identity such as belief in the 'male superiority' and/or in the 'feminine domesticity' to govern different socio-economic conflicts. Therefore, social forces try to destabilize, circumvent, challenge and/or advance these rules of identity to re-empower themselves. Women's movements have been long struggling for the recognition of gender differences in the making of public policies.

Women's movements around the globe have had a thorough impact on the re-making of *modern bourgeois state form* since the late 1990s. The relation between these movements and the political powers has never had a uniform shape. However, it would also not be wrong to argue that the dominant mode of relation has been determined – among other things – by the transnationalization of women's networks, by the institutionalization and professionalization, and the issue-based NGO'ization of the feminist movement, which has culminated its efforts in *legal reform and gender mainstreaming* (Moghadam, 2008; Prügl, 2011).

In the late 1990s and early 2000s, as the crisis of neoliberal state policies has deepened the plight of the ordinary people with different gendered outcomes, reforms in the field of women's rights have been reluctantly adopted by states as one of the essential ways of crisis management. In the Global South, as Sakkia Sassen (2000b) argued, globalization (of the neoliberal capitalist relations) has caused the emergence of counter-currents of globalization, such as the forced international migration of impoverished women as care-workers, human-trafficking and pervasive domestic and public gendered violence due to the rise of non-traditional wars and conflicts. Transnational women's movement has been continually active and rapid in highlighting these developments and pressurizing for the making of a global gender regime which would in return help the national social forces to force their own states to comply with. However, it has also been observed that despite all of these significant struggles, which have left their marks on state forms via radical alterations in the rules of entitlement and identity, the implementation of these rules – if at all they are applied – has not been always necessarily to the benefit of women's liberation in general and of gender equality in particular.

Critical feminists like Nancy Fraser (2009) and Hester Eisenstein (2015) have criticized the relation of this professionalized feminism to the neoliberal project and argued that the philosophical and political assumptions of this mainstream feminism have facilitated rather than hindered the neoliberal counter-revolution. Accordingly, by co-opting the feminists the neoliberal forces could integrate women into the capitalist market without necessarily improving the hierarchical gender relations or transforming the oppressive gender norms. Other critical feminist scholars like Sylvia Walby (2002), however, proposed a different way of reading the relation of feminism and women's movements to the neoliberal era and placed at the centre the argument that the 2000s are in fact the first time for the women in the history of the modern state that there is something truly like a liberal democracy – a political institution always failing to live up to its formal promise of gender equality. In other words, some authors have argued that the neoliberal era has paradoxically provided the socio-economic background conditions via which women's movements could acquire a political opportunity moment to realize their own bourgeois revolutions (Federici, 2009).

In this study, however, I prefer to adopt a rather nuanced approach (neither full co-optation nor a sustainable bourgeois revolution) and argue that the overall impact of the feminist interventions on the modern state form in general and in Turkey in particular – especially via feminist advocacy and women's human rights activism – has been conditioned by the *gender selectivities of the state.*

Necessities of capitalism and the gender selectivities of the state in Turkey

Either historically materialized in a modern bourgeois state form or in a post-modern carceral form, the capitalist state is determined by the essential task of reproducing the social formation upon which it is based. It is also only as such that it can reproduce itself. But what does it mean to reproduce a capitalist social formation?

It means two simultaneous and *potentially* contradictory mandates: first safeguarding the labour force (and the daily and generational reproduction of it) and second ensuring the profitability for capital (sustainability of capital accumulation) (Pichio, 1992). In other words, the capitalist state operates in a world where human subsistence is dependent on means of social reproduction, which are not directly owned by labouring masses. The very *raison d'être* of the capitalist state is to sustain an environment where both the human subsistence and the private ownership of the means of subsistence can perpetuate.

This internally contradictory mandate forces the capitalist state to forge different rules of entitlement and identity. In fact, capitalist state is a conceptual abstraction which is helpful to explain the historical change and continuity between the different forms of modern state (including its post-modern variant), which also struggles to reproduce itself in societies torn apart with structural inequalities.

To sustain basic human subsistence, the capitalist state develops or adopts policies (e.g. the family wage) and institutions (e.g. the male-breadwinner family model), which basically serve to the ends of social reproduction. These policies and institutions, however, are not immune from contradictions as they necessitate the reproduction of certain gendered dependencies and/or privileges. These dependencies and privileges have historically been contested. To illustrate, to secure basic human subsistence the capitalist state has for ages leaned on the unremunerated domestic labour of women. This is still the case in the greater geographical parts of the globe and certainly in the MENA, including Turkey.[20] In Turkey, housewifization is still the common socio-economic process upon which the social (re)production of the labour force depends.[21] However, housewifization requires constant adaptation of the patriarchal gender contracts, as their continuity includes a process of constant bargaining with women – whose needs, desires and political agency also constantly change.[22]

On the other hand, in order to sustain the profitability of capital, the capitalist state is also bound to operate and navigate through systems of inequality and benefit from them so as to devalue and/or revalue certain forms of labour – thus certain forms of body, as labour cannot be conceived independent from the body which embodies it (Ferguson, 2016). More specifically, the capitalist state has always benefited from structures of gender and 'race' inequalities to contribute to the profitability of capital. It has also constructed new ones. The constitution of women as housewives whose domestic labour was sealed as valueless – on the grounds that it stayed outside of the market-based production – was historically possible by the devalorization of women's bodies in the first place. As the feminist author of the witch-hunts' historical legacy, Sylvia Federici argues that during the transition to capitalism the early modern state power contributed in the devalorization of women's bodies through both terror and law (Federici, 2005).

In short, the two necessities of the capitalist social formations (social reproduction and capital accumulation) condition the *gender selectivities* of the capitalist states. Bob Jessop (2004) defines the 'gender selectivities of the state' as a strategic action framework used by the capitalist state apparatuses located in specific socio-economic and political contexts. The gender selectivities of the state is an institutional, legal and discursive set of strategic practices trying to govern the gender relations between men and women, but also between women and women and between men and men. The state privileges certain gender groups over others, certain gender-based policies and certain gendered institutions/state apparatuses to others within the structural necessities of and the limits put by the existing regime of capital accumulation.

However, it should also be added that theoretically speaking these selectivities are not necessarily patriarchal. From the perspective of theory, any other system of inequality and gender hierarchy could well serve these purposes (Jessop, 2004). Therefore, it is methodologically wiser to think of the 'gender selectivities of the capitalist state' as an abstraction which would help to concretely detect the gendered nature of each state – whether it is a masculinist state or a public patriarchy, whether the activated state powers are anti-genderist/anti-feminist but also maybe feminist, etc.[23] For the gender selectivities of the state should be constantly reproduced in a time- and space-bound manner, they are not once and for all determined.

The massive reintroduction of the women workers into the labour market during the neoliberal era and their proletarianization were important developments that have necessitated the adjustment of state welfare functions, rules regulating work life and the general philosophy of social security. In Turkey, however, when compared to this global tendency, the neoliberal era has seen a growing but still very mediocre participation of women in the formal labour market. The relative highness of the male wages during the 1990s and the 'growth without employment' in Turkey implied a quasi-stable gender order (Karacan, 2012; Toksöz, 2012).

Moreover, the neoliberal Labour Law, enacted by the AKP government in 2003, did not incorporate home workers, paid domestic workers and those who were working as temporary or casual workers, most of whom are women in Turkey (Dedeoğlu, 2012: 220). Although the government by then paid lip service to the principle of equality in public personnel recruitment, as of 2019, only one of each ten personnel recruited in the status of worker to the public sector is female (Genel-İş, 2019). Moreover, the state has provided working-class women with very precarious working opportunities. Temporary jobs such as those within the auspices of the social assistance programmes implemented by the Turkish Employment Agency employ women via very short-term contracts without even assigning them the status of 'worker' (Örnek, 2019). More women than men have been employed in public service jobs such as gardening, cleaning, repair and renovation, and yet their labour is not even within the scope of law as they are considered as *trainees*.

The AKP governments have so far tried with different means – such as offering cash remuneration to aged women in return for taking care of their grandchildren and as dowry contribution to young women who decide for marriage before completing their undergraduate degrees – to revalorize women's invisible labour as part of a new patriarchal bargain they have desired to forge with women. Within the period of time this study problematizes the gendered nature of state, roughly from 2006 to 2016, the ruling party locked in women to family life as care workers and convinced them to do so via different kinds of remuneration and also with the help of clientelist relations (Kandiyoti, 2016). Nevertheless, these new disbursements have not been enough to alleviate the autonomy demands of the young generations in Turkey.

Especially the significant increase in the number of young women who attend tertiary education in Turkey has so far created an additional conundrum for the state.[24] This is mainly because the existing market structure of the Turkish capitalism and the presence of an already expanded reserve army of male workers push these young women outside the employed workforce (Toksöz, 2012). According to a recent study conducted by the International Labour Organization, 87 per cent of the female population in Turkey wants to participate in paid work and yet, nine out of ten women (and in total 11 million women) must stay at home due to the non-existence of public day care services (Kızıltan, 2019). The idea that paid employment provides emancipation is still strong among women in Turkey and the younger generations have even a more tenacious belief in the correlation between paid work and independence. Nevertheless, as of July 2019, the rate of employment for urban young women has hit 41 per cent (Çelik, 2019).

These hard facts further determine the gender selectivities of the capitalist state in Turkey. Especially since the failed putsch attempt[25] which has taken place in July 2016, the state in Turkey upgrades 'the patriarchal dividend' (Connell, 2009), it has always promoted, this time by openly attacking gender equality through different nativist justifications and populist means – such as shoring up an organized anti-feminist movement that calls women's rights defenders as 'feminazis' (Hülagü, 2019, 2020).[26] In short, different types of crises push the capitalist state in Turkey to exploit the existing 'gender divisions by fashioning political appeals and building social bases, etc.' (Jessop, 2004).

Obviously, the gender selectivities of the state do not *reflect* the necessities of the capitalist accumulation and related needs of and for social reproduction in an immediate manner. They are rather *refracted by the* bureaucratic personnel *and in* the institutional matrix of the state. In other words, the ways these necessities and needs are conceived and interpreted within the state apparatus and by the state bureaucracy give their final shape to the strategic gender selectivities. It is now an established fact that the ruling bloc in Turkey has been fostering neo-conservative policies accompanied with a religious perspective to gender justice (Ayata and Dogangün, 2017).

According to this perspective, if gender equality meant equality of men and women, as two different sexes, this would work against the *fitrat*, the divine division of labour for the two sexes. Consequently, 'man and woman' are different from birth and have different responsibilities and rights, all of which preordained by the divine order of things. Within this perspective of gender complementarity, men have the obligation to take care of women, especially women of their own household, whereas women must raise the future generations.

This perspective has been further and further advocated by the state in Turkey, which has so far also failed to find an effective solution to domestic violence, a phenomenon drastically working against the social reproduction regime of Turkey depending on housewifization. Indeed, domestic violence is a greater concern for the political power in Turkey as the excess of it risks destabilizing the patriarchal bargain that settles women as free domestic labourers.[27] And it also risks disparaging the family, the beloved institution of the nativist-conservative ruling bloc in Turkey. For the AKP governments, a healthy family is designated as the utmost security valve before the social question (Yılmaz, 2015). Thus, domestic violence is considered by the ruling power as a threat to the unity of family and relatedly to the general social order (Küçükalioglu, 2018).

Political boundaries and the gender selectivities of the state

As shown in the previous discussion, the gender selectivities of the state are conditioned both by the socio-economic developments and by the gender ideology of the ruling political power. However, capitalist states are not only socio-economically but also *politically bounded*. In other words, what makes a capitalist state, a capitalist state but not a state in a capitalist society, is its task to systematically exclude certain events from the historical repertoire of social and political relations. Claus Offe (1994: 109) names these as 'non-events'. The two *non-events* – events that any capitalist state at all costs and all times struggles to prevent from happening – which also determine the strategic gender selectivities of a capitalist state are (1) the responsibility of the capitalist state to prevent any structural transformation of the political order that would impede and/or radically harm the capitalist accumulation process, and (2) the complete closure of the political scene to the reformist demands, which would in return prevent the effective management of any form of crisis – political, economic or both (Borchert and Lessenich, 2016). Before proceeding with the details of these two non-events, it should also be noted that these non-events are not only watched by the capitalist states as singular entities, but they are also ingrained into the state project(s) of the post-Cold War liberal internationalism (see Chapter 1, 'The New Liberal Geoculture').

The first *non-event*, which I construe as the principle of *anti-Subversion*, conditions the gender selectivities of the state by crystallizing not only at the intersection of different social hierarchies – class, gender and 'race' – but also at the intersection of these social hierarchies with political affiliations/intentions/aspirations/acts. This permits the state, for example, to differentiate the 'good poor' from the 'bad poor', or the 'agreeable' women from the 'non-agreeable'. This later, indeed, is not a category created only because of the sexist and/or misogynist gender scripts of the male statecraft but also because of the conditioning power of the *non-event* over the capitalist state.[28] In other words, the revolutionary transformation phobia of the capitalist state is a structurally ingrained filter which pushes the state apparatus to make pragmatic and conjuncture-related strategic selections.

When applied to the case of gender, it is historically possible to see that this *non-event* has further conditioned the political domination strategies of the states. For instance, while in certain historical and political contexts some women's political violence has been depoliticized – also because women's engagement in violent politics 'decouples strategic violence from a naturalized masculinity' (Melzer, 2011) – and their acts are explained by reference to their 'poor psychological situation' and/or 'poor family environment' (see Chapter 2, 'Moralist Philosophy of the Police Reform'), some other women's conventional social roles are politicized and qualified as 'combative motherhood' (Molyneux, 1985). If certain women's politicization is perceived as subversive and against the existing gender order – which in turn sustains the existing capital accumulation environment – the state apparatuses join anti-feminist movements (Eisenstein, 1981). If certain women's politicization is perceived as contributing in the system-relevant gender divisions, the state accords to give further concessions.

This selective treatment is determined by how exactly the state bureaucracy and the dominant political cadres read the *non-event* and through what means (e.g. power techniques) decide to manage it. As conservative, moralist and/or political Islamist figures, the state cadres of the AKP era have been very agile in creating categories of and for differential treatment, which help them to better govern the subversive potentials. For them there is not a general category as women, but there are women who adopt either appropriate or inappropriate political stances, women who are either loyal or disloyal to the state. Such a meticulously *differentiated or selective patriarchy* helps the state cadres to prevent the non-event more effectively. They appropriate and produce gendered divisions indeed as a form of administration.

The second *non-event*, which I would call hereafter the principle of *anti-Failure*, forces the state to forge an encompassing, inclusive social contract. The capitalist state indeed needs to *make life possible*, both for the reproduction of the state itself – which can be termed according to Claus Offe and Volker Ronge (1975) as the capitalist state's institutional self-interest – and for the reproduction of the capitalist social formation in its entirety. Therefore, to prevent a full-blown systemic reproduction crisis, the state engages in fostering public contentment (i.e. through new rules of entitlement and identity).[29] How and through what means and ideological motives the state cadres engage in the provision of public contentment are also incredibly significant in forging the gendered selectivities of the state. This is however not only about social services and welfare benefits and the redistribution policies but also about the policies of crime and punishment a state endorses. Is for example the prevention of violence against women treated as a criminal justice or a social service task? Does the policing of the domestic violence centre on the victim or on the offender? Do the state cadres side by the victims or by the offenders? Who is the recipient subject of state protection? The principle of non-failure does not give specific responses to these questions but only forces the state apparatuses to deal with them – to prevent a state failure and hence a failure of the entire system.

During the long decade of political and economic crises which preceded the AKP's coming into power, the state in Turkey had completely lost its legitimation powers. Either in the South-eastern Turkey during the 'low-intensity war' – as the military by then named it – ongoing against the Kurdish political and/ or armed liberation movement or in the impoverished outskirts of the urban centres, where millions of working poor live, the state had by then become a lethal power, failing to make its citizens live. This process was gendered in different ways: the state violence instrumentalized women's bodies to discourage civil resistance in general and to particularly secure women's subordination to the existing socio-economic order. In fact, feminist or not, women who were politically active in resisting against the political and socio-economic order by then were considered as threats to the patriarchal credentials of the state. Their femininity was demonized and considered as disorderly.

When the AKP came to power, one of the essential political commitments was formulated by the party leader Recep Tayyip Erdoğan as 'to make human beings live'. He has propagated that a state will live on if it makes its citizens live (prosper). This was the basis of the social contract he promised to uphold. Indeed, his approach was very similar to that of the human security approach, again formulated, in the beginning of 2000s at the UN, in order to deal with the growing social problems in the Global South, where states were declared to be failing and indeed themselves as problems. The resonance of these two perspectives, beyond being coincidence, should be considered as a response given by the global powers around the world to the deepening crisis of the state and its deprivation of the most basic tools of legitimation.

During this era, developmentalism also advocated that the deepening oppression of women hampers the general wealth of the states. Thus, gender policies that would empower women's status and include them into the socio-political order were considered of central importance. The social contract endorsed by the AKP in the early 2000s also included women. Indeed, this was more than lip service paid to the dictates of global power centres like the EU or the UN but an in-design strategy to re-establish a sustainable political order in Turkey with the help of women. In other words, the making of a new social contract would not be successful if it excluded women, at least so was the reasoning of the lead figures of the AKP (Ayata and Tütüncü, 2008). However, the inclusion of women and a progressive gender perspective to the human security concept was not as straightforward as it would appear to be.

In other words, the social contract upon which the new state power would be based in Turkey, in short, the human security *alla turca* has produced new gender selectivities, specifically a *selective patriarchy*, which will be further explored in the following chapters.

Feminist interventions in and against the state

Elisabeth Prügl (2009) argues that the outcomes of the feminist engagements with the state in the neoliberal era yield to different power mechanisms. It is not only that the state cadres indeed the bureaucracy and state personnel who decide on the final shape of the outcomes of these interventions but also the very form and content of the feminist engagements might lead to specific results. For example, the feminist movements that prioritize the achievement of equal rights engage with the state in forms that might qualitatively differ from the feminist interventions which prioritize challenging the rules of identity of the state, for example, the hegemonic masculinity promoted within the institutional matrix of the state.

According to Prügl (2009: 178), the most common power mechanisms which are triggered in and through the feminist engagements with the state are refusal (complete denial of the feminist demands) and empowerment (codification of these demands into the political-legal apparatus of the state) and in between lays a plethora of other power effects from co-optation to compromise. Prügl's heuristic devices help to improve the empirical relevance of the *state as the material condensation of social struggles* theory.

In Turkey, the feminist movement has been occupied with the normative and political question of 'what the state should do?' to improve women's rights since the early 1990s. This of course has provided the movement with certain formative power over the rules of entitlement and identity the state had been fostering in Turkey. From the early 1990s onwards, different governments in Turkey had to accomplish pro-gender equality changes in the legal field. In the beginning of the millennium, the changes in the Civil Law recognized women's rights as individual rights within the context of family. Moreover, previously private deemed issues become public issues (i.e. 'the Law on the Protection of the Family No. 4320' enacted in 1998 obliged the State to prevent domestic violence and to provide necessary protective support to women who are under constant threat of domestic violence). Because of the revolutionary changes in the Criminal Law, gendered violence started to be conceived as a crime against the person rather than as a crime against social morality (see Chapter 3, 'Feminist Interventions in and against the State').

The feminist movement has also developed an additional strategy in order to assure the internalization of these legal changes and changes in the spirit of laws by the state apparatus and be sure that the state responsibility towards the women citizens does not stay on paper. Many feminists and women's organizations have started to develop projects for gender mainstreaming. The aim was to augment the state capacity and spur change of mind-sets within the public bureaucracy by providing them with the gender expertise of Turkey's feminist movement. Nevertheless, both the feminist equal rights and gender-mainstreaming strategies built on pressurizing the state and working with the state have left many issues relevant to the gendered nature of the state outside of the focus. They tried to change the rules of entitlement, the legal and policy framework that defines who gets what. But the rules of identity have stayed relatively untouched.

A third feminist intervention has partially tried to remedy this gap by problematizing the Kurdish question of the state with a gender perspective. This strategy aimed at making the *women's standpoint* but especially of the Kurdish women heard and taken into consideration during the resolution process the AKP initiated in the late 2000s.[30] Therefore the strategy primarily aimed at changing the rules of identity, the question of who is recognized and how, by empowering Kurdish women while remembering the state its responsibility to take into consideration the gendered outcomes of the violent strategies it pursued in Turkey's Kurdistan. Although different from each other, all three forms of feminist interventions have followed a similar strategy of pointing at the paradoxes of the state. They also tried to benefit from the contradictions of the ruling party by constantly remembering the state's failure to protect its women citizens (either against domestic violence or against gendered forms of state violence) despite the promises of the initial social contract the AKP forged in its ascendancy era.

It is today however a fact that the implementation of the laws (concerning women's rights) is sporadic, inconsistent, not guaranteed and indeed discriminatory. The preventive power of them is again dubious. For example, since the revolutionizing of the Criminal Code in 2004, sexual assaults realized by the security forces have been qualified as aggravated offences. Nevertheless, this does not prevent the state forces from using their gendered scripts during police raids and operations within the context of political policing cases and social protests (see Chapter 4, 'State Violence against Politically Active Women'). The women-friendly tide of the reform era is turned. However, was the reform era women-friendly? Why have the feminist interventions to the state failed to prevent such a turn of the tide? Could they ever prevent it? How have their interventions to the state been received by and within the state? The following chapters will try to demonstrate that in Turkey during the AKP era, the feminist demands have been resignified by and through the gender selectivities of the state.

Contradictions of the historical forms of the capitalist state

A final conceptual tool from which this study benefits is the notion of contradiction. As previously mentioned, the capitalist state has a contradictory universe of tasks: the necessity to reconcile the needs of human subsistence with the needs of capital accumulation. Although governed with the help of different rules of entitlement and identity, the contradictions are ingrained into the structure of the capitalist state.

In the modern bourgeois form of the capitalist state, the main contradiction displayed itself as the gap between the promise of abstract universals and the particularistic nature of state power deployed to advance the interests of the wealthiest and mightiest sections of the society. The construction of the state as a neutral body politic has been, however, not just an illusion/appearance, but also a historical reality. In other words, although the bourgeois form of the capitalist state has not been class neutral, it has been also separated from the private ownership of the wealthiest classes, hence its public character. Yet, the legacy of private patriarchy has continued shaping the modern state form, deepening the contradiction between the so-called public social contract and the sexual contract (MacInnes, 1998).

These contradictions have therefore created political opportunities for women's movements to further the public character of the state. In the beginning of the twentieth century, the first wave of feminism acquired suffrage by exploiting this very contradiction. In the mid-twentieth century, the second wave of feminism skilfully demonstrated the hypocrisies of the welfare state by pointing out to how the public has turned a blind eye to women's subordination by framing it as an issue of private matter. In the late twentieth century, however, as the feminist movement continued doing politics to unsettle the private-public division the modern bourgeois state was paradoxically upholding, the public power was taking a different direction and indeed ongoing through a radical and neoliberal transformation (Simon-Kumar, 2004; Coşar and Özkan-Kerestecioğlu, 2017).

For example, as the feminist movement has been successfully pointing out the hypocrisy of the monopoly of coercion, a foundational institution of the modern bourgeois state, by showing that the non-criminalized domestic violence is in fact a patriarchal deal made between the masculine state and the men – thus implying that the state willingly gives up its monopoly over violence to further the yoke of patriarchy – the state has been gradually losing its public character and indeed even affirming the neoliberal motto that 'the state is not the solution but the problem'. This is not to say that the late twentieth century's feminist movement could not make any gains. On the contrary and strangely, women could only profit from the institution of the monopoly of coercion only first after the 1970s (Walby, 2009). Until the 1970s, domestic violence was not even recognized as an attack against the natural rights of human beings. The state both ignored and benefited from private violence to uphold its rule via male household heads.

The abstract universalism of the bourgeois state form has always been discussed by the feminists in detail. The radical feminist analysis and movement of the late 1970s and early 1980s forcefully demonstrated that the bourgeois state form does not possess impartial view from nowhere but rather possesses the very standpoint of the white, property-owner men, and that it was ignoring less powerful voices (women but also men who fall outside the hegemonic masculinity) and excluding their concerns through a strategy of legitimation that supposedly differentiates rational from irrational demands (Nash, 1998).

This feminist politics built on playing to the contradictions of the modern bourgeois state has not been simply a position of rectification. It has indeed been putting into question the very functionality of public power, the relevance of a central political organization for human life and for human existence. From the very beginning, the feminist concern with the violence against women has also been an ontological critique against the state form. It has recurrently asked: 'what role does the state have in our lives if it does even not fulfil the basic promise it gives, to care for the physical integrity of human beings?' This has indeed been an ontological-political challenge against the monopoly of coercion as a historical and actual state institution.

However, today, it appears that the centaur state as a hybrid state form that can deploy seemingly contradictory legal and administrative measures in an intersectional manner, by cross-cutting class, gender and 'race', is less interested in a universal legitimation than was the case with the bourgeois state form. This indeed constitutes a real bulwark against the success of oppositional politics that is generically built on reminding the state about its public good duties. The centaur state acts more like a protection racket. In his cult analysis 'War Making and State Making as Organized Crime', Charles Tilly (1985) argued that it is possible to think the state as a racketeer because it first creates a threat and then charges for its reduction and calls those who oppose it as 'anarchists' or 'subversive'. After nearly a half century from this analysis on, it is possible to argue that although the state protection today has become more and more a form of undisguised racketeering, there are less and less 'subversives' who say no. The demand for state and for more of the same state is the most common form of opposition. Let me put it in a better way. The lack of imagination on what kind of a public power the opposition forces should build prolongs the life of the centaur state (Fraser, 2015).

This also creates a *state paradox* for the feminist movement, a predisposition 'to seek protection from male violence by and in the masculine state' (Brown,

1992).[31] But is it possible to overcome this state paradox? Can finding another fruitful contradiction help to prevent the cycle of state paradox? This book does not provide any definite answer to these two questions. Yet, omitting altogether these normative questions risks ending the analysis provided in this study in a 'so what?' exclamation. In other words, although this book follows a conventional exploratory method imbued in critical analysis, its transformative motivation should not altogether disappear.

The way out of state paradox is certainly not to give up feminist struggle in and against the state. It is true that all feminist gains and gains in the field of women's rights until so far have historically been fought not only through opposition and struggle but also through negotiation and strategic bargaining with the state (Rai, 1996). However, it is also true that the feminist politics 'in the state' possesses the tendency for deepening the state fetishism.[32] This risk, however, is even not mitigated by switching to an 'against the state' position. Because struggling both in and against the state can reproduce state fetishism in their own ways: either by thinking that the only solution for acquiring gender equality is appropriating the state apparatus – not the political power – or by thinking that the main reason behind the women's subordination is the masculinist state practices.

Is there a way out of state fetishism? As I already told, this book does not propose any easy solution. However, it is only a reminder about the limits of interpenetrating into the forms of capitalist state and transgressing their gender selectivities. This is not to deny the contradictions of state forms, which can be exploited by the progressive social forces. Nor to deny the need to resist against the *selective patriarchy* of the state in Turkey. But to display that the contradictions of the bourgeois state form – which hardly any exists in Turkey – do not necessarily turn into political opportunities for feminist politics.

Within the existing literature and among the feminist activists, the reformist era or the early era of the AKP governments is considered as a precious moment of *political opportunity structure* (Negron-Gonzales, 2016). Yet, it is actually historically recognized that the political opportunity structures from which women's movements and/or feminist movements strategically benefit hinder them from having a clear sight of the wider state restructuring processes that usually accompany these moments (Randall, 1998). Moreover, in the absence of a thorough ideological analysis that determines these moments, justifying engagement with the opportunity structures on the basis of diverse criteria such as the 'relative openness of the institutional political system', 'the permissiveness of the elite alignments' and 'the support from the elite allies' (Randall, 1998: 194) is facilitating rather than hindering the patriarchal restoration that follows these moments.

It is a final inference of this study that the conceptual baggage of the human security – the main instrument which by itself secured the ideological selection of the social groups with which the AKP could coalesce during the reformist era – has provided a common grammar between the political owners of the state transformation era and the feminist movement and thus has also provided the ruling power with the ability to resignify some feminist demands without necessarily being caught in the act of doing it. While the feminist movement was trying to benefit from the political opportunity structure created by the liberal geoculture, the reformist police cadres and the political power were appropriating it to advance their own administrative capacity and to forge the continuum of *selective patriarchy*.

It is true that today in all over the world, activists, opposition groups, civil society organizations or social movements, rather than forcing their own grammar on liberalism, have tended to recuperate the trendy artefacts of liberal internationalism. Have they been successful or to what extent this recuperation forced liberal internationalism into a beneficial change for its contenders?

The following pages include thus as mentioned previously a tale of the three cities: on the one hand, the tales of the liberal security sector reformists and the moralist reformist police cadres who have tried to reform the state along the notion of human security. On the other hand, the tale of the feminists who have tried to contest the state with the help of the notion of human security.

****

Before continuing the discussion with a detailed analysis of these three agents of state transformation in Turkey during the early AKP governments era, I would like to make a short final remark about the merits and limits of the research strategy I have followed while composing this book. For the data collection in this study, I have benefited from a plural-methods approach. I have conducted expert interviews, done ethnographic observation when possible, made a close reading of the relevant published materials, browsed essential newspapers, etc. This plural-method-research approach helped to broaden the theoretical insights I developed during this study. However, for the sake of clarity and precision in the main chapters of the book, some of these theoretical insights – especially those related with the contradictory implications of the human security concept in and for emancipatory politics – could only be presented in the concluding chapter as new and potential venues for further discussion.

I also had to make certain research ethics-connected choices when deciding how to label certain groups, agents and actors of political change and conflict in Turkey as labelling is itself a politically and theoretically controversial process. In most of the cases, I decided to keep the political groups' self-description and/ or self-naming intact. For example, in the case of women fighting in the ranks of the Kurdish armed movement, I used the notion of 'guerrilla'. Again, in the case of police cadres who were organized in the Islamist religious sect of Fethullah Gülen, I used the notion of 'police reformers', a self-identification one would also come across in the various publications of the police intellectuals associated with the Gülenist movement.

In the case of these police cadres, an additional discussion of political Islamism would probably enrich the research's findings, but I decided to stay within the limits of my main research problematique of sorting out the dialectics of coercion in between the two periods of the AKP rule – the so-called reformist and authoritarian eras. Nevertheless, it should be shortly mentioned that what I call as 'moral policing' in Chapter 2 is itself a political Islamist position. Further research via a comparative political lens on the role of Islamism in the transformation of the state apparatus in Turkey is certainly needed. Finally, it should be noted that during the writing of this book, I generously benefited from the general perspective I developed in my doctoral dissertation, completed in late 2011, on the role of the *international* in neoliberal police reform in Turkey. However, the gender scope, the theoretical framework and the writing style I used in this book are totally new. Much of the data I introduce to the reader is recently collected in accordance with the research focus of this book.

The new liberal geoculture

In November 2011, when I entered the newly established Security Sector Reform Department of the UN premises in New York, I was truly welcomed. The department was composed of an international team of experts, mostly of non-Western origins. My visit was motivated by a need to better understand how the practitioners of global governance were producing knowledge in the field of security governance; how they were devising their projects/programmes of state restructuring and what were the principles they were advocating during their state-building missions.

Security sector reform (SSR) was defined as a change in power relations and pictured as a messy process whose primary aim is to develop a new social contract between the ruled and the rulers in conflict-affected national contexts. Different from the immediate post-Cold War era's frenzy promotion of democratization, especially in the post-Soviet state-building contexts, the Security Sector Reform of the late post-Cold War era has displayed a post-colonial ethos, an envy to disassociate liberal internationalism from its imperialist and colonialist strategies. There were three common and notable points mentioned in the different interviews I conducted. The first one was the changeover from a democratization perspective to *good governance* during the promotion and implementation of SSRs. The second was the shift from a Western-imposed reform strategy and process to the principle of *national ownership*. The third was the change from a consultative to a participatory process, where the real aim is to engage *ordinary people* into the SSR process, engineer a common wisdom among them and create good motivations so that some social groups agree to lose power.

SSR was conceived as a non-teleological process of state transformation, where the ultimate objective was not replicating liberal democracy but finding local governance solutions – even if these are not in line with the norms of liberal democracy. When I asked about the popularity of this new approach among the different international agents involved in the SSR projects, I also learned that despite a general commitment to this new approach at the normative level, there have been different approaches to the SSR processes due to different regional focuses. For example, one of my interlocutors would illustrate, 'the United Nations SSR Department and the Geneva Centre for Security Sector Governance (DCAF) have different regional focuses, different historical mandates and indeed different strategies'. The DCAF is primarily involved in the post-Cold War reorganization of European politics in Eastern Europe, whereas the UN has been engaged in fragile states and primarily in Africa.

My research showed that Turkey was somehow linked to both security reform initiatives applied by these different actors, in these two different regional settings. Whereas as a host country it was mostly subject to an early post-Cold War-era style of SSR, basically interested in regime change, it was also open to the ideological baggage of the UN-led SSR efforts in post-conflict contexts. Turkey has been involved in many UN-led peacekeeping and peace-building missions and has sent various police envoys to these missions who have returned Turkey accompanied with a similar missionary vision of policing (Hülagü, 2016). But also, as the timing of the SSR experience of Turkey from early 2000s to early 2010s coincides with the post-colonial turn in the liberal geoculture, even the more conventional SSR actors such as the DCAF would possess for Turkey a reform perspective beyond mere regime change.

The meddling of these two state projects has had important implications for the case of Turkey. To understand Turkey's experience of the reform process, I first invite the reader in this chapter to have a look at the two SSR styles, see their differences but also commonalities, especially in relation to the notion of human security. To this end, the chapter follows a *synthetic* approach. In other words, following a political theory-based discussion about the notion of human security, the reader will be presented by a general portrait of the SSR in two different contexts. Rather than making an analytical presentation of each and every element of the SSR processes, this section presents the general outcomes of the SSR processes in different contexts under two important arguments: (1) the early post-Cold War SSR agenda has been a programme for advancing anti-statist *populism* and (2) the late post-Cold War SSR agenda has been a programme for statist *localism*.

Having presented these two main arguments, the chapter follows with the presentation of the SSR community in Turkey. These latter include international technical experts, transnational NGOs, academics and the resident staff of various international organizations. It will be shown that these reformers' referent subject for human security is still an abstract individual, albeit different from the generic individual of classical liberalism. It is slightly modified and adapted to their perception of society and politics in Turkey. The main subject referent is a *property-owner modest man*: an individual supposedly ignored and side-lined in the social contract that the Kemalist/militarist state in Turkey had maintained in general.[1] The women, however, are introduced as 'women-and-children', a perennial way of representing women as innocent and vulnerable creatures – in the very minor opportunities when the SSR community felt the necessity to refer to their own gender sensitivities.

A challenging and final task of this chapter, and a standpoint which substantially differentiates it from the existing critical SSR literature, is also to include the non-traditional actors of SSR in this analysis. In other words, the emergence and mainstreaming of the concept of human security have also been galvanized with the efforts of the transnational women's movement, which concentrated its efforts in the post-1995 Beijing Conference era to anti-violence struggles – and micro-credit schemes (Barton, 2004). That is why, I propose that the SSR processes should be conceived in a broader perspective than they appear at first sight. In fact, the police trainings to prevent violence against women were organized for about a decade by the United Nations Population Fund (UNFPA) Turkey, an international organization unlike the conventional SSR actors. Different from the populism and localism of the two SSR visions on the state, the UNFPA-led project adopts universalism, a call for equal introduction to state-sponsored rules of entitlement. Accordingly, the state apparatus is responsible for granting its women citizens the right to protection. Nevertheless, the fundamental philosophical difference between the populist-cum-localist horizon of the conventional SSR agents and the universalist horizon of the UNFPA-led project tends to disappear in practice, as the resistance of statecraft to change leads the feminist contenders to adopt a *behaviourist* strategy.

All in all, this chapter gives the reader a holistic perspective on the Security Sector Reform and the human security philosophy behind it. It argues for conceiving the SSR processes as an essential part of the post-Cold War era's *liberal geoculture*. 'Liberal geoculture' is a term adopted by Immanuel Wallerstein (2011) to depict the becoming of liberalism by the end of nineteenth century a globally endorsed common sensual meta-ideology.

According to Wallerstein (2011: 1–2), ideology is the sum of strategies adopted to resolve 'what prima facie seems a deep and possibly unbridgeable gap of conflicting interests' and liberalism is such a meta-strategy. It tries to reconcile the contradictions between the demands for popular sovereignty – of the radicals/

socialists/revolutionaries who ask for a rapid change – and the desire for the maintenance of elitist status quo – of the notables. To this end, liberalism set itself in the late nineteenth century the task to re-construct both sides and their political projects as *extremes* or, if we translate this to the conceptual luggage of this study, as two *non-events* the bourgeois state form should take care of. For Wallerstein (2011), liberalism has since then placed itself at the centre and become a centrist ideology. It mainstreamed itself by monopolizing the authority to define the extremes. In line with this way of reasoning, it is possible to argue that the liberal geoculture of the post-Cold War era is an attempt to redefine the extremes, the two non-events or the scope of possible that the capitalist state should embrace to secure the reproduction of the existing social and economic order.

From human rights to human security

Liberalism as a special meta-strategy to govern the main contradictions of the capitalist world system is in fact an ideology of state formation. In other words, since its early beginnings liberals were interested in finding the golden mean between the monarchical political classes who govern the international sphere through their inter-state clubs of privileged men and the proletarian internationalists who would like to dismantle the conservative classes' political power by way of dethroning the historical category of political class altogether. Liberalism, consequently, developed the doctrine of nation-state and self-determination. Accordingly, monarchical power would be replaced by national power and yet this latter would also constitute a barrier before the proletarian internationalists (Mazower, 2013).[2]

By the late nineteenth century, however, liberalism's focus switched from domestic developments to overseas. Colonial encounters shaped it deeply. Liberals started to argue against the universality of the principle of liberty. Accordingly, not every community would be able to adopt it as it necessitated certain civilizational prerequisites. To this end, following the First World War, liberals proposed the establishment of proto states, in fact protectorates that would supposedly tutor the 'barbaric' peoples and the 'savages' about the meaning of sovereign politics (Mazower, 2006). Interestingly at home as well, liberals like Woodrow Wilson were unwilling to grant political rights to non-white people and to women and argued for the existence of prerequisites for democracy – like the habits of self-control and self-discipline that these groups were not trained in (Hobson, 2012). The October Revolution, the labour and suffragette militancy which alarmed the Western powers in the inter-war era and the Second World War have all culminated in the embedding of liberalism in democracy or in 'the democratisation of liberalism' (Jahn, 2013).

By the mid-twentieth century, under the force of events liberalism had to endorse two governing human rights' principles: freedom from fear and freedom from want. The 'For Freedom from Fear' poster of the United Nations advertised in 1945 depicts a nuclear family composed of a mother, a father and a child. The family sits in an open-air recreation area. In the background there is a factory with its grey smoke coming out of the chimney. The child goes playing with his toys. He or she is safe and happy. The family represents the middle-class ideal of liberal internationalism, a worker family that becomes wealthy enough to get incorporated into the system and enjoy the non-work time in safety.[3] As early as 1945, freedom from fear was thus posited as freedom from want or as in Theodor Roosevelt's formulation securing welfare would also mean instituting an effective police power.

By the end of the Cold War, however, the liberal geoculture was in a *crisis of success*. Immanuel Wallerstein (1995) even declared the dissolution of the Soviet Union as the defeat of liberalism *per se*. According to him, the demise of communism also displayed the failure of the liberal proposal that the contradictions emanating from structures of inequality could be handled by a developmentalist state. Within two decades of time, John Ikenberry (2009), a prominent pro-US establishment neo-Wilsonian, asserted that the victory over the Soviet model could not help liberalism to restore the loss of authority emanating from the failure of the ideal of a developmentalist state. The liberals have started asking if the modern state form, including its developmentalist nation-state variant, had not been useful to govern the main contradictions, then 'what is to be done?' (Slaughter, 2009). As a result, two different sets of proposals – human rights and human security – have been put into practice to restore the authority of liberalism.

Starting from the late 1970s, liberal internationalists argued for the fostering of personal political rights in and by civil society – hence also curtailed down the expanded notion of human rights of the Rooseveltian liberalism. By the 1990s, it was argued that liberalism's main mission should be to propagate solely for freedom from fear since when coupled with freedom from want, the emergence of a harmful state power had been inevitable (Keohane, 2002). Human rights were defined as the grammar of and for political emancipation. The main objective was defined as revealing state abuses against political dissidents. This approach was reproached by radical figures, such as Naomi Klein (2007), who argued how this exclusive and impartial focus on abuses, though not ineffective at all at reaching immediate targets, helped the accompanying socio-political transformation process, namely neoliberalism, to escape from sight.

However, in the meantime there occurred a tricky transformation in this political abuse-priority perspective. Whereas 'freedom from fear' was by then posited as *a political right*, after the 9/11 it has been redefined as a *right to protection*. Whereas during the euphoric years of liberal victory, fear was discussed as a very material (i.e. corrupt police forces, state brutality) thing that prevents people from doing politics, since the 9/11 it has been redefined as a state of mind (i.e. feeling of risk and vulnerability before unforeseeable events) that prevents people from looking after themselves. In other words, whereas human rights approach of liberal internationalism focused on human beings as agents of change who do possess political will (but sidestepped the socio-economic needs), human security approach of liberal internationalism focused on human beings as victims of unpredictable events (and coded socio-economic needs as personal or communal vulnerabilities).

The notion of human security was offered by the then UN Secretary General Kofi Annan just after the 9/11 attacks as a new conceptual framework to make sense of the side effects of neoliberal globalization in the Global South. Building on the discussions of globalization with a human face, Annan tried to make the development agenda of the UN relevant to the United States which was still in trauma of attacks (Mazower, 2013: 372). It was implied that the global security depends on the development of human beings living below subsistence levels in the outskirts of the global periphery. It was assumed that extremism was a direct result of poverty and deprivation. In 2003, the UN published the *Human Security Now* report.

In the report, human security is defined as 'including the excluded', creating 'the widest possible range of people having enough confidence in their future – enough confidence that they can actually think about the next day, the next week, and the next year'. It is argued that reverting to a limited notion of state security would be fallacious and that human security would and should complement state security to prevent the dangers of war looming in the horizon (Ogata and Sen, 2003). This neo-Rooseveltian approach to liberal internationalism, which conceives improving the class status of millions and promoting them to the middle class as building a safety belt for world peace, soon became exceedingly popular in global governance.

Hence, the notion of human security paradoxically *obliterated political rights and in fact political emancipation*. In that sense, its conception of recognition had also differed from that of human rights. The human rights perspective of liberal internationalism, although still limited in its conception of politics, initially was also a way of responding to the rise of the 1968 Revolutions in the West and recognizing their political sway. The human security perspective of liberal internationalism, however, is at odds with *the Political* as such. It recognizes people only in their capacity to live bare life, a life that is defined with minimums and basic survival. Human existence is ontologically reduced to the field of necessities.

In fact, historically speaking, human security demands as demands of and for necessities were revolutionary demands. They were the engine behind the making of the modern state. The modern state power was in fact justified on the grounds of the protection of the life of the citizen (McLaughlin, 2016). Hence the late eighteenth and early nineteenth centuries' passionate demands for human security revolutionized the political field, dismembered the political classes, de-legitimized sovereign power and accorded legitimacy to the state on the condition of its being a security provider to laymen. However, in the post-9/11 era, human security demands re-privileged the state as the primary agent of change and presented the recipients as powerless masses. The administrative will of the state seemed to hold the key to social question reframed as a humanitarian problem (Marks, 2011).

Despite all of the fair and multi-layered criticisms against it, liberal humanism was once promoted with an emphasis on the idea that human beings do and should possess ethical autonomy, freedom and equality to develop their creative capacities (Brown, 2015). Seen from this perspective, the doctrine of human security is not even humanist. The political desires, instincts and aspirations that define human beings have been all dropped out of the intellectual box of new liberalism or post-liberalism, as David Chandler (2010) names it. Neither the basic needs nor the human aspirations to a better life are *Political* problems. The human of human security is not a *homo politicus*.

One implication of this has been that the security provision started to be conceived as a matter of *goodwill* and the recipient of protection as the ultimate victim. The security provision has been conditioned by victimization. This inevitably shores up paternalist tendencies and depending on the political and socio-economic structure of the specific context where it becomes active, it restores and/or renews patriarchal contracts. According to Paul Amar (2011), who empirically focuses on the case of Egypt, 'human-security states' try to bring back a respectable patriarchy by restoring the myth of masculinist protection.

Not surprisingly, however, in updated patriarchal states, not all victims are accorded protection. Human security restores, keeps up and constructs old and new social hierarchies. In other words, once a public good, security has been redefined as a status good. Once the security contract is redefined over goodwill, the security provider, the beholder of the goodwill, possesses a right to choose, to select the right victim without even recurring to any rhetoric of equality and universalism. He can lean on different philosophies of 'goodwill': moralist, theological and/or religious administrative rationalities to choose the 'right' recipient. Human security, therefore, as a liberal project is a post-secular or even anti-secular project.

Security sector reform and human security in regime change contexts

One of the primary implementation contexts for the SSR projects was Eastern Europe in the aftermath of the dissolution of the Soviet Union. The SSR was primarily designed as a police reform with the central aim of dismantling the old regimes from within. The process was sent in motion with the help of an anti-statist populist discourse.

The academic paradigm that by then most fed into the making of these early SSR reforms was the democratization paradigm, popularized after Samuel Huntington's (1968) thesis that the main bulwark against transition to democracy is praetorian political systems. The praetorian system thesis was suggesting that the states in praetorian systems are dictatorial states, lacking authoritative institutions that would mediate social conflicts. In short, the democratic systems that were posited as the antonym of praetorian systems were rather devised as effective, foreseeable and reliable mechanisms of conflict resolution. The military and/ or police apparatuses in the praetorian systems were considered as apparatuses, which although tied to the regime, were also intermittent threats to it, as was the Praetorian guard to the Roman Emperor Caligula. Beyond being helpful to conflict resolution, they were themselves party to the naked confrontations of different social forces. In line with this line of reasoning, it was by then commonly maintained that to decompose a regime, decomposing first and foremost one of its dedicated apparatuses would be the most efficient method.

It was argued that 'in post-authoritarian and post-Communist countries alike, the dismantling of regime policing and the establishment of democratic policing – policing that is professionally effective, accountable and legitimate – is an indicator of the consolidation of democracy' (Marenin and Caparini, 2005). It was additionally argued that during the Cold War era, 'government was too *remote* and *impersonal* to meet the needs of diverse communities' (Bayley and Sheaford, 2001: 25, italics added). The panacea to this obstruction has been found by the police reformers in increasing the popular appeal of the police units through community- and problem-oriented policing (Bayley and Sheaford, 2001: 26). Police reform therefore aimed at solving the legitimation needs of new state formation processes, like those in the post-Communist geography.

In the beginning of this process, during the transformation of the East European states, human security was not used as a driving concept. The common grammar was rather built on human rights. Reforming the police forces along human rights, however, was translated into practice through the principle of 'integrating the concerns of citizens and communities into every level of policing policy, management and delivery' (DCAF, 2009: 2). The reformers argued for a need to transform the state power philosophy from *a force* perspective to *a service* perspective. Indeed, police reform was portrayed as being about 'a fundamental change from police as "force" to police as "service", whereby a key objective of police reform is the reorienting of policing goals towards service to the community and responsiveness to its needs' (DCAF, 2009: 1). 'Servicing', though, did not necessarily mean an expansion in the *public service* functions of the police apparatus but rather a change in the *police attitudes* towards people who were by then considered as individual consumers of security (European Code of Police Ethics, 2001: 32). It was recommended that the ruling question of the police officers should be: 'How do individuals and communities experience security and justice?' (OECD DAC, 2009: 13).

In fact, reformers assigned a nearly sacred character to people, to the popular culture and reproduced a neoliberal version of populism. The old guards – Communist politicians and bureaucrats in the case of Eastern Europe – were posited as elites; the people were represented as their hostages. Reforming police would mean freeing the people and punishing the old guards. This SSR-promoted state project worked through easily operationalized and politicized dichotomies: authentic, original people whose tastes, habits and choices were disregarded by the corrupt regimes and/or incapacitated states. Police organizations have accordingly been devised as the new public relations offices of the states-in-the-making. In that sense, the job of policing has also been conceived as an emotional performance that demands effective commitment of the police officers onto what they do.

In the European Code of Police Ethics (2001), composed of a set of normative guidelines that were originally drafted by the OECD for the police reform processes in East Europe, the service function of the police organizations is stated as one of the main five properties and tasks a police organization should stand for in a democratic society. The others are public order policing, protection of and respect for human rights, prevention of and combating against crime, and crime detection. 'To provide assistance and service functions to the public' is presented as the newest component integrated to the remit of modern policing.

The 'vagueness' of this component, however, is also underlined in the commentaries additionally provided to better situate the code articles (European Code of Police Ethics, 2001: 21). It is noted that the service functions of the police shall not include extra components to their already existing workload but that they mean to be related to the amelioration of the police attitudes towards the public (European Code of Police Ethics, 2001: 22). These attitudes, therefore, need to follow some form of ethics, which are defined in the Code as 'a specialized version of habitual, every day, common-sense principled conduct' (European Code of Police Ethics, 2001: 14). However, what is meant by everydayness and common sense has been clarified neither in the Code nor in the commentaries provided with it. It assumes, thus, a relatively organic social tissue, a national space where everyday life is already regulated by common habitual ethical codes. This assumption is generally also the assumption held by the police reformers acting in the field. The general belief is to tailor police practice and conduct according to the most dominant form of behavioural codes within a society.

In the commentaries attached to the Code, it is clearly stated that '*in order to earn the respect of the public*, it is not sufficient only to act within the law, but to apply the law with integrity and respect towards the public; applying the law with a degree of "common sense" and never to forget the "public service" which is a necessary dimension in police work' (European Code of Police Ethics, 2001: 37). The risks this 'common sense' might constitute for different social groups and individuals within a society, including women, are not recognized. The only precaution taken in the Code is to continue the paragraph that starts, 'in order to earn the respect of the public' with a reminder on the role of the police to 'acknowledge that the public consists of individuals, with individual needs and demands. Vulnerable groups in society call for extra attention by the police' (European Code of Police Ethics, 2001: 37). Thus, rather than circumventing the potential political and social problems that might resume from common sense, adding the duty to care for the 'vulnerable' to it, deepens the paternalist potential of the new police ethics.

This populist perspective is also operationalized through a crude military-civilian divide, where the military- and/or the Cold War-type security state is blamed for all the fallacies of the incumbent and just thrown-out political establishments of the host countries. According to this perspective, the main impediment to a transition from a state-centred security understanding to a human-centred is both the institutional architecture and the political culture – of certain social classes – that ensure the continuing power of the military in politics (Hinton and Newburn, 2009). In such contexts, de-militarization of the security sector and augmenting the powers and independency of the police organizations were equated to civilianization. Parallel to the above-mentioned populism, civility and civilianness mostly referred to social groups and classes who were thought to or reconstructed as social groups who represent a political culture not yet contaminated by the effects of a militarized state-society complex. For example, in the context of the Middle Eastern and North American countries, including Turkey, the middle classes and some part of the intelligentsia were considered as dependent on the state and as militarist in their mentality (Waterbury, 1994). Again, for the post-Communist geography, the absence of a democratic culture mainly of democratic behaviour and attitude was conceived as the essential impediments to full-blown civilianization (Pantev, 2005).

Therefore, despite the so much underlined need for popularity and popular consent and trust, the particular social constituency that would support the SSR reform processes was carefully selected from within the national contexts. In other words, before fulfilling the promises of populism as reflected in the European Code of Ethics and reaching out to an imagined people, namely to the 'layman' who were supposedly excluded by the state-centred security of the Cold War era, the pro-regime change SSR processes prioritized empowering certain carefully nominated NGOs, civil society organizations and community leaders – who were supposedly not contaminated by the militarist culture of the middle classes.

Finally, within this context, human security was inserted as the protection of every human being from the counter-currents of globalization, meaning poverty, deprivation, human-trafficking, sexual and physical abuse of women and children, etc. SSR was meant to improve the policing capacity and methods to deal with these 'new threats', with which the military know-how would not be able to cope (Cizre, 2005a). However, this 'new threats' focus of the regime change SSRs stood rather under-developed compared to their preoccupation with democratization understood as expanding the civilian character of security institutions. In that respect, the concept of human rights was much more dominant in the SSR discussions in regime change contexts. The usage of this concept, however, was mostly narrowed down to bearing and paying respect to civilian people and individuals.

Finally, although political rights and their restoration have in theory stood at the centre of all SSR discussions, the SSR intelligentsia defined the political rights in a specific manner. They were indeed both conditional and procedural. They were basically reduced to democratic *behaviour and attitude*:

> From the point of view of behaviour, the democratic regime in a given territory is consolidated if no significant national, social, economic, political, or institutional forces attract considerable resources for attaining their objectives by creating an undemocratic regime or forcible detachment from the state. According to attitude, the democratic regime is a consolidated one when a considerable part of the society, even in the face of large-scale economic problems and deep disappointment with the government, continues to think that the democratic procedures and institutions are the most suitable method of government.
>
> (Pantev, 2005: 7)

All in all, during the new state formation processes in regime contexts, whatever belonged to the past, the old way of providing security was demonized to polish the existing reform practices. Whereas different social questions or social inequalities accompanying the globalization processes were paid lip service as 'new threats', citizens of the host countries were essentially portrayed as victims of a praetorian state or a state too much preoccupied with itself. In other words, the state was conceived as the problem and the civilianization was conceived as creating out of the old state apparatuses new policing institutions, which would act with a civilian ethos and as if they were themselves civil society organizations. Police forces who have kept pace with this process of anti-statist populism have been declared champions of change.

Security sector reform and human security in post-conflict contexts

Different from the SSR processes in the post-Communist geography whose priority was to dismantle the old regimes via populist police power, the Security Sector Reform in post-conflict environments has been working to empower the state institutions with the help of local forms of authority and/or through localization.

In the first SSR Concept of the European Commission published in 2006, SSR was presented as a process of institution building in post-crisis and/or stabilized environments in order to enable the state 'to protect citizens from threats of insecurity, including violent conflicts and terrorism, while protecting rights and institutions from being undermined by those threats' (European Commission, 2006: 4). Different from the democratization agenda of the regime change SSR, the driving idea behind the reforms in conflict-ridden societies was more of building resilient public authority institutions. It was assumed that getting rid of the state and defining sovereignty as the cause of all troubles would mean a bigger trouble for the liberal world order. Therefore, reformers reversed the 1990s liberal motto of 'sovereignty is the problem not the solution' to effective state-building processes (Fukuyama, 2006). They declared that states possess 'responsible sovereignty' which means that the institutional matrixes of the states should be constructed in such a way that there would be no more need for exogenous intervention to fill in the national and/or regional security vacuums (Chandler, 2010).

The advocacy for strong and responsible states to provide human beings with protection from basic insecurities has repeatedly and insistently underlined the need for 'national ownership' of the reform processes. In April 2014, the United Nations Security Council produced its first stand-alone resolution on SSR, where it was suggested that the primary characteristic of any SSR should be country ownership.

Before the introduction of 'country-ownership' as a well-established concept, state-building processes were dominated by an institutions-first approach. The dominant objective of the institutions-first approach was creating from scratch the Weberian legitimate monopoly of coercion in post-conflict contexts. The transnational community of reformers had by then argued that the disintegrated states and/or failed states suffer from lack of sovereignty and that they are deprived of the infrastructural capacity necessary for a central state to penetrate its territory. Therefore, the states were asked to create an effective inside-outside divide, a constitutional characteristic of the modern state system.

Nevertheless, as state-building processes failed to produce desired outcomes around the world, a fine-tuning seemed necessary in the reform logic. It was argued that the peculiar features of the post-colonial statehood, especially the fragmentation of the public authority, should be considered as the genuine ground on which to build a new state rather than deviation from the Weberian model (Andersen, 2012: 112). In other words, it was argued that the main impediment to effective and legitimate state rule was exogenous-driven state-building processes where not only the actors of change but also their driving set of assumptions on the nature of state and state-society relations were Western-centred. It was indeed implied that the lack of proper feeling of belonging and attachment among the populace to the Westernized state structures and accompanying notions of citizenship should be taken into consideration in the state-formation processes. Hence, this SSR phase transitioned from democratization approaches to post-colonial approaches, which underlined the lack of historical and social structures that would sustain modern state structures in non-Western contexts. In the MENA region, the discussions emphasized that in contrast to the statism hypothesis of democratization theory – that is put into effect to explain the resilience of praetorian states – the real problem lies in its non-existence. That people do not feel any kind of belonging to a centrally organized state prevents the institution of citizenship, which is a necessary precursor of modern state formation coming into fruition. The widespread reservations on the part of the individuals to membership in a state-centred political community are said to be the main impediments to the establishment of democratic modern states in the MENA context (Anderson, 1987).

The SSR implementations in post-crisis contexts have started thereafter placing at the centre the notion of building *locally* grounded social contracts. Different from the populism of the SSR concepts in regime change contexts, where NGOs and civil society institutions were conceived as the primary owners and constituency of the reform processes, the idea of country ownership aimed at including those sections and groups of the societies not necessarily adopting and/or embracing liberal values. In other words, it was argued that against the false and not working universalist assumptions behind the liberal peace perspective adopted during the SSR processes, the particularisms of the host geographies should be guiding the reform projects. It was argued that this would help to erect 'hybrid orders' that are 'better able to tap into local knowledge, to mobilize citizens and to generate legitimacy' (Paffenholz, 2015: 863).

Indeed, the SSR in post-conflict societies is defined as a main component of and for good governance rather than democracy. It is conceived as a new social contract between the state and society, where the participation of people to the processes of governance should not necessarily be framed after a normative ideal of a democratic state. The following sentences of the then UN SSR Lead Person Adedeji Ebo whom I interviewed in late 2011 are very telling in that regard:

We should use the word 'good governance' instead of 'democratization'. Good governance means participation, accountability, and transparency. What is important is the quality of 'social contract' in the recipient country. The notion of 'social contract' should lead the security sector reform. It means good division of labour between the rulers and the ruled. Social contract is key to SSR. When people feel they are part of the game, of the process … SSR thus should be contextualized.

(Ebo, 2011)

The notion of social contract is further explained as such:

SSR addresses different peoples (religion, tribe, etc). SSR tries to have a common history. SSR should be understood as a process of dialogue. Real SSR means a change in power relations. You have to give some people good motivation to make them agree to lose power.

(Ebo, 2011)

All in all, rather being obsessed with a Westernized state-formation conception which typically assumes that 'traditional sectional political interests are … corrupt and self-serving' (Chandler, 2006), it is argued that SSR necessitates involving informal and customary security providers and traditional justice actors in the state-building processes. Although this turn to local forms of authority as rightful bearers of reform processes sounds promising, it has also risked romanticizing the local and also muting and dissipating those other social forces who do not necessarily feel represented by the local forces who usually do have sufficient resources to reach political power and/or political visibility at the cost of others (Paffenholz, 2015).

Hereafter, as the Weberian notion of the state was declared unfit for non-Western world, human rights component of the SSR processes that have prioritized security of the political rights – of course in the limited sense of the term/the right to do politics within the limits set by 'democratic attitude and behaviour' (see above) – lost its chief position and indeed became irrelevant. Human rights were to a great extent replaced by the notion of human security, where 'threats such as hunger' and 'sudden and hurtful disruptions in the patterns of daily life' (Paris, 2001) were considered as the main security concerns of a legitimate and effective state.

The politics of human security, however – within such a post-colonial turn where the different components of modern politics were nearly declared to be exclusive Western constructs – has de-politicized local populations. It re-signified all the basic human needs (the essential needs of and for social reproduction) within the semantic framework of insecurity, as opposed to the classical liberal framework of freedom. And this reframing has had a pragmatic side because securitizing human needs appeared to be the only remaining tool to convince the political classes to care for the have-nots. Therefore, the politics of human security has turned into a strategy of sensitizing the ruling strata, imagined as reluctant and egoist sovereigns, to care for the well-being of local peoples.[4]

Especially in non-Western contexts, the politics of human security has turned into a patriarchal bargain, guaranteeing the sovereign its right to rule over as long as this latter acts through benevolence, secures its subjects' happiness and through it sustains order at home. To recap, human security has become a legitimation tool or as previously underlined an apparatus of and for racketeering to acquire the consent of the local population to state-building processes.

All in all, it is possible to argue that SSR is a process of characterizing the two *non-events* that should determine effective state-building in the post-Cold War order. The two non-events against which the two SSR concepts respectively try to sanitize the states are a revolutionary political turnover that would transcend the methods and horizons of procedural democracy (the principle of anti-*Subversion*) and a human catastrophe that would fail the local authority of a sovereign state (the principle of anti-*Failure*). The SSR concepts thus also redefine the notion of legitimate monopoly of violence and orient its locus away from the modern political field, that is, citizen, to the popular and local, making populism and localism the newest liberal or post-liberal centrist ideologies that would help the states to engender their new strategic and gender selectivities. But it does also affect the political horizons of the contending social forces or non-state political agents, who struggle to steer the state away from state security. Populism and localism have become the new ideological gatekeepers or new centrist liberalism which selects out which kind of other political ideas can participate into the mainstream politics.

Security sector reformers and human security in Turkey

The driving SSR approach adopted by the international epistemic community in Turkey principally overlaps with the SSR concept operationalized in the regime change contexts. Like it did in the post-Communist contexts, anti-statist populism inspired the style and mentality of pro-reform advocacy in Turkey. And yet, the needs for localization and for a new social contract were also mentioned. Therefore, it is plausible to argue that Turkey was one of the rare places where different SSR concepts have been put into practice in a mix. How exactly the international epistemic community in Turkey has imagined 'the people' and 'the local'? What kind of a social contract have they longed for? What kind of a state have they envisioned?

Turkish Economic and Social Studies Foundation (TESEV)'s security sector reform series: The absent presence of the referent subject

As a non-governmental organization closely interested in the democratization of the state structure in Turkey, TESEV initiated a research, publication and advocacy programme in 2004 in close collaboration with the DCAF (by then named as Geneva Centre for the Democratic Control of Armed Forces). Although aimed at the reform of the security sector in its totality, in its early era (until the early 2010s), the programme basically focused on civil-armed forces relations and on deepening 'the democratic oversight' of the military in Turkey. The first written product of this programme 'The Parliamentary Oversight of the Security Sector' was published in 2004. In the launching event for this handbook and the ensuing proceedings book, it is possible to follow a hot debate on the need to make the military in Turkey accountable for the decisions and actions it takes and to separate the defence and the security from each other, as two different mandates of a sovereign state (DCAF and TESEV, 2005). Again, in this debate, it is mentioned that whereas military should be entrusted with the defence mission of Turkey, so long as it does not usurp the notion of threats, the civilian face of the state should be responsible for security, which is envisioned as:

> When I am in traffic, I fear that somebody will just hit me from rear or front, that I will be overrun by a car even when I cross on a green light as a pedestrian. We have lost some very valuable people like that. Second, I fear that my wife or my daughter will be attacked and raped any minute. I see that I can be attacked and robbed walking in the dark, or my apartment can be robbed as it has been often happening in my neighbourhood recently.
>
> (Ergil, 2005: 57)

Thus, the idea that security should be basically defined as a policing task and as a question of human security came to the fore.

In a parallel ethos, TESEV set the main target as making civilians – civilian representatives, expert NGOs and media – involved as primary actors in the definition process of security threats (Cizre, 2005a). Followingly, the community engaged in TESEV's work on democratization defined 'the man in the society' as the main recipient subject of human security. The enthusiasm shining through these lines is self-revealing: 'Rather, it [security] comes down, touches day-to-day living, the happiness, welfare, peace of the citizens. Security of life means quality of life, security goes down to the level of the "little man", to the "man on the street"' (Cizre, 2005b: 68).

After these early debates, TESEV's priority in 2005–6 became offering further encouragement for widening the public debate on the transformation of the security sector in Turkey. It was by then argued that a main impediment to Turkey's democratization is the dearth of structured knowledge concerning the security apparatuses of the state in Turkey. To augment public awareness and sensibility in this field by fostering a culture of opposition/objection against the prevailing culture of acquiescence was defined as the principal means to foster accountability and transparency of the security sector, especially of the armed forces (Cizre, 2006a). TESEV thus started to expand the debate on the democratization of the security sector. It organized many conferences and workshops, which were considered as making part of a process of 'normalizing the debates on the democratic oversight of the security sector' (Aytar, 2008).

Normalization was sought as a discursive and political strategy to deal with the resistance of the military in Turkey to give up its custodian role in politics. Henceforth, TESEV prioritized abating 'state security' rather than promoting 'human security'. It is therefore arguable that the notion of human security was relatively underdeveloped in the publications and in the very mission of the TESEV. However, this very under-development was also the cause and the result of a fetishist interest in the military as the source of all bureaucratic paternalism and the main cause of robustness of the authoritarian state tradition in Turkey. Although used many times in different semantic formulations such as 'citizen-based security', 'individual-based security', 'human-centred perspective', the hollowness of the notion was paradoxically conducive to exploitation by different users of the term in accordance with their ideal referent subjects.

TESEV and DCAF's formulation of 'state security' as a problem of bureaucratic guardianship, that is *preventing full-blown individualization*, reformulated the SSR as the empowerment of civilian people against the militarized guardians of the state. The military's power was personified, and against this 'person' another type of personality, one that is supposedly representing the resisting voices of the peripheralized masses, was posited: 'the man in the society'. In short, the absence of the ideal subject referent was an absent presence. It was an abstract individual, but certainly assuming certain context-specific characteristics. It was assumed to be a modest property-owner man, a household head, anxious about the security of his property and the honour of her female relatives, struggling against the hegemonic men in the state.

UNDP Turkey's 'Improvement of Civilian Oversight of Internal Security Sector Project': From absent presence to full embodiment

The United Nations Development Program (UNDP) Turkey Office has been conducting the 'Improvement of Civilian Oversight of Internal Security Sector Project' since November 2007. The basic aim of the project which is conducted in close cooperation with the Ministry of Interior has been described as sustaining the participatory oversight of the internal security within the system of public administration and legislation and improving citizenship rights and providing them to be fully employed. The project openly refers to the notion of human security that it formulates as 'human-centred understanding of security', and supports the transition from 'state security' to 'citizen-based security' and from 'retroactive provision of security' to 'proactive provision of security' (Roché, 2010b: 23).

The project is also defined as an assistance to the zero-tolerance to state violence policy of the AKP governments, by way of enhancing citizen participation to the creation of security policies in Turkey. It is assumed that the participation of local actors in the development of local security plans will augment public trust in the police organization and in the state. Different from the case of TESEV, therefore, the subject referent of human security is clearly articulated. Although the principal addressees of the state violence and maltreatment in the late 1990s and early 2000s' Turkey were essentially leftist political activists, trade union representatives and fighters from Kurdish liberation movement, the referent subject of the human security encapsulated in this project appears to reside somewhere else.

The introduction of human security into the local governance plans is conceived as keeping the pulse of local people in terms of informing the state about their experiences of insecurities. These insecurities are mainly connected to demands for physical security/police protection. For example, some proactive security targets set in local security/safety plans – developed in cooperation with local stakeholders – include fighting against petty crimes like burglary and drug use or indeed controlling, for example, 'the increase of population in city centres during the month of Ramadan' (Akıncı, 2013). This latest demand was formulated in the Eyüp district of Istanbul, a pilot city of the project, and the local security directorate responded by increasing security measures, especially by raising police presence, augmenting the police controls and hiring private security guards. These measures taken to meet the so-called human security demands are in fact illustrative of the SSR logic adopted in Turkey. This process frames civil society participation as an issue of both public relations and localization.

The localization criteria adopted in the project work as a mechanism of advancing the governmental brotherhood among the local power holders such as *mukhtars*, local media and local police forces. One of the experts who participated in the project as senior international expert, Graham Ellison (Ellison and Pino, 2012) argues in his analysis on the SSR process in Turkey that the reform serves more to the ends of political control rather than to democratization. But indeed, this has always been the basic tenet of the SSR processes in regime change contexts: creating a new political field by getting rid of the old guards through populist measures.

The final report of the UNDP projects on civilian oversight reinstates this understanding by arguing that 'in democratic regimes the power of the state is also the power of citizens'. However, trying to create such a state in the context of Turkey with the help of a nebulous concept of localization is not problematized at all. Implementing a project without caring for 'who protects', 'who are protected' and 'who are punished' and indeed without asking 'who exactly are criminalized' or 'non-criminalized' and with an abstract notion of civilian participation, where the local is most of the time represented by the local male power holder and/or property owner (e.g. the *esnaf*) has gone unchallenged. Correspondingly, in their condensed analysis of Turkey's SSR from a gender perspective, Sabine Mannitz and Stephanie Reckhaus (2016: 8) conclude that 'the abstract plea for local ownership does not answer the question of whom exactly the reform process would best be "owned by"'.

Yet, as already implied, even the abstract plea is apparently not that abstract. In fact, the very 'Local Security Plans Pilot Implementation Booklet' (Roché, 2010b) prepared by the UNDP gives us a more concrete information about the background of local participants:

> By the end of the pilots most of the Local Security Commissions had a membership of around twenty members under the chairmanship of the deputy governors. Participants included: Public Prosecutor, Gendarmerie, Human Rights Board, Provincial Administration, Health Directorate, Zabıta (Municipal

Police), Chamber of Commerce, Bar Association, Artisans and Small Traders Union, Private Security Companies, Other Key Groups.

(Roché, 2010b: 20)

The booklet itself recognizes the limits of this populist participation method when it tells:

It was seen that sometimes the survey [security needs survey] results drew critical reactions from certain members. This was especially true regarding findings that touched upon culturally or politically sensitive topics, such *as violence against women* and other *gender-based groups* which stakeholders are reluctant to take on board.

(Roché, 2010b: 35, italics added)

In other words, the international epistemic community was also aware of the limits of the reform projects in terms of referent subjects but nevertheless reluctant to problematize this as a significant failure of the SSR processes in general. For example, Sebastian Roché said that the decision on who will be taking place in local security plans was made by the Ministry of Interior, out of a list prepared by the UNDP. But for Roché this was first inevitable as the Ministry of Interior was the main beneficiary and second it was in line with the spirit of the country ownership principle of the reform process (Roché, 2010a).

UNFPA Turkey and the project 'Partnering with Men to End Gender-Based Violence'

As was the case with the TESEV/DCAF duo and the UNDP Turkey, the years 2005–6 constitute the political opportunity moment for other international organizations to dynamize their reform agendas in Turkey. Although it is not a generic partner of SSR projects, I still propose that the UNFPA's gender-based initiatives taken in Eastern Europe and Central Asia are part of the liberal geoculture that defines the spirit of these projects. The gender mainstreaming efforts of the conventional SSR organizations include for example augmenting the number of female security officers, introducing regular gender training to curriculums of security sector personnel and/or establishing women's police units (Valasek, 2008). The UNFPA's efforts in the prevention of gender-based violence have a no less significant impact on deepening the notion of protectionist statism in the national contexts it has engaged in.

In the initial situation analysis of the UNFPA-led United Nations Joint Programme to Protect and Promote the Human Rights of Women and Girls (UNJP) in Turkey, it is stated that

despite [the recent legislative] changes, reaching gender equality and *full protection* of women's and girls' human rights remains a significant challenge for development in Turkey. Implementation of legislation, delivery of quality services, innovative approaches and projects and coordinated approaches to meeting the needs of the *most vulnerable women* are missing and/or are still hampered by low awareness and less than adequate capacities.

(UNFPA, UNFPA at Work: Six Human Rights Cases, 2008, italics added)

This emphasis on 'the protection of vulnerable women' has been the central feature of the gender equality initiatives developed in the post-Cold War era by the lead international organizations (Puechguirbal, 2010). Victimization of women and representation of them only in their capacities as caregivers and caretakers, and as peaceful beings who are alongside the children and elderly the ones who suffer most from the lack of a protective state have also been the leading gender concept of the internationally induced human rights programmes in Turkey (Babül, 2015). What is however as significant as this protectionist ethos-cum-statism in internationally led gender mainstreaming efforts, I argue, is the *behaviourist turn*.

This behaviourist turn – for further analysis, see Chapter 3 'Feminist Interventions in and against the State' – has resulted from the rightful frustration about the lack of effective implementation of measures of protection despite the introduction of a plethora of legal changes in national contexts. Indeed, it is possible to perceive that even the introduction of women in the status of victims of an ignorant/failed state – which would/could under ideal circumstances trigger the masculinist ethos for protection and paternalism – is not necessarily sufficient to cultivate the reflex for protection among the men in the state. The UNFPA's project 'Partnering with Men to End Gender-based Violence' can be considered as part of such a turn to further sensitize men in the state to gender-based violence and help them to develop *correct behaviours*.

The project defines its main objective as 'changing the perceptions of domestic violence among police in Turkey' and deliberately narrows down the topic of violence against women to domestic violence. However, different from the TESEV- and UNDP-led SSR projects in Turkey, which devised to include the allegedly so-far excluded men from the periphery as the country owners of the new state making era, UNFPA's intervention was more about changing 'apathetic' and 'resistant' men-in-the-state (UNFPA, 2009: 8).

The UNFPA project on police training started in 2007. One year before the initiation of the project, a team composed of representatives from the UNFPA and from the Directorate General on the Status of Women (KSSGM, its Turkish abbreviation) got into touch with the Training Centre for Crime Investigation and Research (SASEM) under the Turkish National Police Department of Public Order to prepare a nationwide training programme for police officers on the correct handling of domestic violence cases. The project design team was composed of six persons, a mix group composed of individuals representing these three main institutions. The training team was composed of eleven women's rights activists and feminists from Turkey's highly regarded women's organizations. The training materials were also composed by different contributors from these organizations. In the first two years, the team trained about 250 police facilitators, who then trained a total of 40,000 police officers in the field.

My in-depth interview with the lead manager of the UNFPA's police training projects in Turkey, Meltem Ağduk, further clarified the main objectives of this process. Ağduk (2019) said: 'We wanted them [the police officers] to do their job, fulfil their duties ... We wanted them to apply the procedures for victims of domestic violence, guide them, and inform them about the way to follow.' In other words, the aim of this reformist project was to convince the police that women subjected to domestic violence have a right not to go back home, and that domestic violence is not a private affair but indeed must be a concern for the statecraft. To also help to foster positive behavioural change, the project teams set some clear procedures and defined some guidelines which would help the police officers to find their ways when they face cases of domestic violence. Thanks to the project, a standardized spreadsheet that the police officers should use during the cases of domestic violence was developed and introduced into the intranet system of the Turkish National Police (TNP). Apart from the on-site training, the project also created a DVD so that the police facilitators could benefit from their peer training. Moreover, the project team wrote a short booklet including standardized guidelines for the police-rank-and-file. Ağduk underlines that these guidelines and all other relevant material were adjusted to the police world, including the choice of colours used in the materials. They especially cared for using an imperative language akin to the hierarchical institutional procedures of the police organization.

Ağduk also underlined the importance of the reformist police cadres, who during this process pushed for the establishment of a special police unit in the TNP for violence against women and were successful doing so. According to

Ağduk, it is through the UNFPA-led training that the germs of an understanding that perceive domestic violence as a form of violence and indeed as a crime were inculcated in the police trainees.

The second phase of the UNFPA-led police training took place in 2010–11. This second phase of the training was again designed as a training of trainers. However, the number of the trainers were limited to twenty, two third of which were male police officers. Ağduk told that the training was designed based on the Gestalt system and included film discussion sessions with leading academicians specialized in the field of gender studies. Trainings also encompassed sessions on communications methods besides other basic trainings on constitutional equality and fight against violence against women.

The project was owned by the reformist police cadres. Ağduk (2019) argues that during this process of the active UNFPA police training projects from early 2000s to early 2010s, they (the trainers and the project team) shared a similar language with the reformists. She insists, however, that this language was not a language of vulnerability, a discourse built on demanding compassion for the victims of domestic violence. Ağduk (2019) tells: 'We never did this. We never said to them "you should protect, you should care". She further elucidates that their aim was to teach them that their duty is to provide the proper service, the proper social service. Ağduk (2019) adds: 'We told them that "you are not brothers/fathers/relatives". This emphasis on redesigning policing as a social service from which all citizens – thus women citizens – should equally profit to thwart any form of discrimination that they meet in life is also a point underlined by Nazik Işık, one of lead members of the main project team. Işık (2019) tells that 'a state that accepts and fosters the perpetuation of discrimination is indeed a state that resorts to violence'.

Based on these findings, it is possible to argue that the human security notion embedded in the police training project of the UNFPA Turkey is different from the one which dominated the SSR discussions of the DCAF/TESEV and of the UNDP. Against the 'localism' and 'populism' of these projects, the UNFPA's project was more of a 'universalist' character. In short, rather than retreating, it aimed at redressing the Weberian rationalized/impersonal state. But to overcome the resistance of police cadres and/or statecraft to this universalism – as they were not necessarily recipient to a progressive vision of gender relations[5] – it appears that the trainers and the general spirit of the project transited to a strategy of cultivating the proper attitude. They had to say to the police trainees many times and repeatedly: 'You should do your duty. And the duty is this and this and this' (Ağduk, 2019).

Concluding remarks

This chapter tried to give a general view of the complex map of the Security Sector Reform terrain both around the world and in Turkey. The two main driving motives behind the SSRs, rising populism and expanding police power against the old guards and statist elements, and deepening localism and police power as the foundations of a new state form, have existed in Turkey in a mix. The international epistemic community involved in Turkey's SSR maintains, however, a poor notion of human security, where the subject referent ends up being nothing other than a slightly updated version of the abstract individual of liberalism (the white property-owner man): non-white or local/conservative property-owner man.

Centralizing this man's sensibilities and concerns to the state, augmenting his 'national ownership' is also devised as a political strategy to curb down the class basis of the old guards, for example the military, and to construct the social origins that would secure the regime transition in Turkey. Moreover, the participation of this man to the making of the new security understanding of the state, hence human security, is devised as a strategy to institute a fresh brotherhood between the statecraft and the civilians. This would, accordingly, restore the micro-legitimacy of the state's monopoly of coercion in Turkey and prevent the capitalist state's vulnerability before the two potential events, namely demands that transgress the political horizon of representative democracy and crisis of the reproduction of the entire system that might lead the state to explode in.

As against this background, the only game changer at first sight appears to be the inputs of the UNFPA-guided project to ameliorate the police behaviour to prevent violence against women. This non-traditional input to Turkey's SSR process potentially represents a significant challenge to the absent presence of subject referent by pointing out to women as the real interlocutors of and for human security. Nevertheless, the project still aims at working with the men and making a change in their conduct. In that sense, its vision is limited to behavioural change. It shares the police ethics conception of the post-Soviet SSRs over attaining positive police behaviours towards the public.

In that sense, it gets caught within the limits of the possible defined by the state projects induced through the SSR programmes. In the Turkish context, these new frontiers have not challenged the gender selectivities of the state to the benefit of women. On the contrary, they tried to replace the hegemonic men in state with supposedly excluded property-owner local men in the society.

This horizon has certainly facilitated the appropriation of the SSR by the police reformers to advance their own political project in Turkey. The behaviourist turn has indeed created a false cooperation between the reformist police cadres and the feminist agents. The use of a similar grammar, that of individual/community-centred security or the idea of statecraft in the service of people, masked the fundamental divides. The next chapter focuses on the cop side of the reform process in Turkey, on the populism, localism and indeed behaviourism of the transformation the reformist police cadres wanted to inculcate in Turkey. Gender, apparently, will only become an apparatus for bettering the effective police administration.

2

Moralist philosophy of the police reform

When I participated as an audience on 9 April 2010 in the Police Symposium that took place in the Police Academy premises in Ankara, I had a chance to make illuminating on-site observations. The conference was on police reform. The opening talks were listing various challenges before the Turkish National Police (TNP), ranging from Turkey's low rate of pro person police numbers to changing types of crimes in Turkey and the new profiles of criminals. The police violence was mostly formulated under the umbrella of psychological issues, and with reference to lack of adequate anger management skills of the police rank-and-file. Despite these problems, the opening talks were proud to announce that the TNP provided peace and security and that 'life, property and honour', these three values were entrusted to the police in Turkey. The new community-based policing projects were announced.[1] The introduction of the Mobile Electronic System Integration video-surveillance system was cherished.[2] In the opening talks, it was also argued that as a result of community-based activities the TNP got direct personal contact with more than 4 million people. In addition to local peace gatherings, these activities were mostly social events like wedding ceremonies and/or funerals to which police officers were invited by the local conveners. 'Even in Diyarbakir', added one of the presenters, 'police are invited to the weddings', implying that the public trust to the police augments even in the Kurdish populated cities of Turkey.[3]

In all these talks, the underlying and recurring theme was 'being close to the people', 'being able to give account to the people'. In one of the talks, the young police academy professor mentioned that 'the grounds of state legitimacy have changed around the world. Driving legitimacy [for state action] from statist interests has been replaced by the act of driving legitimacy from people ... Those [statecraft] who could not come to terms with this change have already decayed.' The young police intellectual was referring especially to the military forces in Turkey when he was talking about 'the decayed forces who failed to switch to people-oriented legitimacy'. He combined the two SSR philosophies, populism and localism, when he argued that 'the security services should be co-produced with people since security services should respect the sensibilities of the society'. His example was emblematic about his conception of 'these sensibilities': 'getting the shoes off during police raids'. This young police academic, a PhD holder from a US university in the field of criminology studies, illustrated his notion of people-driven legitimacy over the example of police officers' removing shoes when they search homes. He was indeed referring to the Islamic-Anatolian culture of privacy, which perceived entering home with shoes not only as an issue of hygiene but also as an act of disrespectfulness against that which is sacred, private and therefore clean.[4]

Had special police operations team members got off their shoes when they searched the family house of Dilek Doğan, would Dilek be still alive? I do doubt. The human security notion of this young reformist police hardly any included Dilek in his conception of society. Even though he argued for the need to switch from a 'holy state to a servant state', the list to whom the state should serve was certainly not all inclusive. This chapter argues that the reformist police cadres have designed the provision of human security as a job of moral policing and this has had two implications: it restructured the state as a post-modern patriarchal institution and second it shaped police power as an anti-Political task for the protection of an imagined harmonious society at all costs and against all. The moral policing adopted by the former reformers should be conceived in a dialectical manner. In other words, it contains within itself its anti-thesis. That is every act which destroys the image of ideal society adopted by reformers is a reason to kick out that person of the selective order they meticulously strive to build.

Moral policing here signifies a specific mode neoliberal policing adopts when dealing with the social question. It is also possible to perceive it as missionary policing. Historically, it refers to the police-led process of decomposing and recomposing the dangerous classes as creatures in need of respect, as denigrated human beings whose honour shall be restored (Neocleous, 2000). Against another neoliberal policing strategy, which is the over-criminalization of the poor, it champions the 'they-are-poor-but-honourable' strategy. Again, different from conceiving the poor as modern citizens, moral policing assumes a relation of dependency between the state and the poor and tries to make this dependency the basis for a new social contract. Accordingly, the poor are entitled to state services if they do *not* engage in the *political*, in political activity whose horizon surpasses the existing contract.

Such a populist approach to policing projects a harmonious society whose self-respect is hijacked by a non-authentic state, that is the Kemalist state in Turkey. This has helped the reformers to further operationalize moral policing during the regime change in Turkey. It has been used as an effective weapon against the old guard. For example, in line with the moral policing scheme, police reformers do warn against using criminalization as a policing strategy that exclusively targets the lower classes. They state that the police should use its authority against individuals from all class backgrounds and even if these are from upper classes, persons of higher status such as businessmen, military officers, civilian bureaucrats, media bosses and public intellectuals such as journalists and writers (Cerrah, 2011: 334). Moreover, they also argue that the police in Turkey should wisely use its discretionary powers and need sometimes to turn a blind eye to petty crimes. This is codified as a form of community-policing because it means non-enforcement of the law against the minor offenses to the benefits of ordinary people (Nalla and Boke, 2011).

In fact, for police reformers, moral policing had another mission as well: political policing in the service of an imagined harmonious society. By this latter, it is essentially understood coup proofing. It is first argued that 'the police serve democracy by inspecting and neutralizing the elements that are infiltrated to the state bureaucracy and armed forces' (Cerrah, 2011: 335).[5] It is added that police help democratic governance by preventing any kind of criminal organization that might paralyse the civilian administration and prepare the ground for military takeover. This latter widens the political mission of moral policing beyond coup proofing to decide on who is against the political order and who is not.

Indeed, the growth of the discretionary police powers during the police reform via two important legal changes confirms this expansive understanding of political policing: the amendments done in the Law on the Fight against Terrorism in June 2006 and the revised Law on the Powers and the Duties of the Police in June 2007. The first widened the administrative powers of the police organization and indeed squeezed down the notion of judicial policing. Administrative policing, which includes the preventive capabilities of the police, and judicial policing, which signifies the post-crime policing tasks, are neither in theory nor in practice separate in Turkey. On the contrary, the non-existence of such a separation works against developing a judicial understanding of policing, which under normal circumstance should focus on the act of crime rather than on potential criminals (Berksoy, 2013).

Not surprisingly, therefore, administrative policing in Turkey does not work in tailor with a conception of policing focusing on the act of crime but rather through a potential criminal radar. This is also in accordance with the anti-terror legislation. According to the Law on the Fight against Terrorism, the terrorist offender is

> any person, who, being a member of organizations formed to achieve the aims specified under Article I, in concert with others or individually, commits a crime in furtherance of these aims, or who, even though does not commit the targeted crime, is a member of the organizations, is defined as a terrorist offender. Persons who, not being a member of a terrorist organization, commit a crime in the name of the organization, are also considered as terrorist offenders and shall be punished as members of such organizations.

In the mentioned Article I, terrorism is defined as

> any criminal action conducted by one or more persons belonging to an organization with the aim of changing the attributes of the Republic as specified in the Constitution, the political, legal, social, secular or economic system, damaging the indivisible unity of the State with its territory and nation, jeopardizing the existence of the Turkish State and the Republic, enfeebling, destroying or seizing the State authority, eliminating basic rights and freedoms, damaging the internal and external security of the State, the public order or general health.

In both articles, the intent rather than the criminal act itself comes to the fore, pawing the ground for the extensive and arbitrary use of police powers. Moreover, according to the Law on the Powers and the Duties of the Police, officers may stop and search people in order to prevent crime if 'there is a reasonable ground based on the *experience* of the police officer and the *impression* he gets from the current circumstances' (Human Rights Watch, 2008: 57, italics added). This, of course, accords a great room for arbitrary decision-making to the police officers and indeed bypasses the rule of impersonality that defines the modern state apparatus, by way of bringing back the personal initiative of the security officer. The police officer obtains executionary powers that are not under judiciary control and any other form of civilian oversight.

However, according to the police reformists, augmenting the personal character of police powers is the main clue to the establishment of public security in Turkey as it secures the merging of the nation and the state, the unity of two bodies that have been kept separate by force because of the military tutelage. According to a veteran police-academic, police reform means uniting the mind (the state) and the heart (the nation), both of which suffer from an artificial separation and conflict with each other because of modernity. This police reformist, who also served as Head of the Turkish Police Academy between 2012 and 2014, maintained during the previously mentioned conference that police reform is about communication between these two separate parts. It means starting to greet people, making them feel safe. Accordingly, 'any greeting is also a sentence of good prayers, a message of peace'.

Finally, a focus on moral-cum-political policing should not detract attention from another crucial development within the police organization. Although hailed as the main cause behind the failure of the state in Turkey, militarism did not disappear altogether during the reform era. On the contrary, it achieved a new face and a new justification. The political power established highly militarized counter-insurgency units within the police organization. In the case of these newly refurbished counter-insurgency structures, it is arguable that the moral-cum-political policing has evolved into a kind of *virtuous violence*. In the modern state literature, virtuous violence 'means that they [the statecraft] are reliant on the possibility of a kind of violence that creates, sustains and exemplifies the lines between inside and outside, public and private, natural and artificial without which neither "state" nor "people" could exist' (Frazer and Hutchings, 2011: 69). However, in line with the centaur state conception I offer in this study, it is possible to argue that the virtuous violence of the Turkey's centaur state aims at setting a line not between the state and the people as two exclusive entities but rather between the authentic, virtuous state and non-loyal, defecting people. In other words, as moral policing meant for the police reformers removing the alienating borders between the state and society in Turkey, virtuous violence was one of the concrete embodiments of this so-called de-alienation. It does not set the boundaries between the state and society as exclusive entities but rather between the 'human' and the 'horse' parts that make the centaur state. Virtuous violence of the police organization, therefore, is a selective act of defining who merits the humane face of the centaur and who does not.

These three moral policing philosophies – patriarchal, anti-Political, selective – have specific repercussions for the gender order in Turkey. Moral policing selects out the 'modest' man as the one whose honour needs to be restored. Virtuous violence selects out the 'dissident' woman as the one who challenges the boundaries set by the political power. Moral policing (humane face of the centaur state) and virtuous violence (the brutal face of the centaur state) are differences in a continuum. They are each other's dialectical counterparts.

The following lines will try to substantiate all these arguments first by introducing the making of the reformist police cadres in Turkey, their political policing mission, the ideology of moral-cum-political policing they have been backing. They will also shed light on the gender and patriarchal selectivities ingrained within their new policing philosophy and practice. This chapter also illustrates the diversification of police powers, with a special focus on the rise of the Special Operations Department from 2011 onwards.

The making of the reformist police cadres

The reformist police cadres who make the centrepiece of this research are police intellectuals, majority of whom have been supported by the Turkish state as part of a security sector modernization plan, first introduced after the 1980 military coup in Turkey. The state has sent many police graduates to foreign countries as part of a state-induced higher education project initiated in the mid-1990s. The young graduates profited from scholarships provided by the Higher Education Council in collaboration with the Security General Directorate, under which the TNP is hierarchically organized. Many of them did their master and/or doctoral studies in the UK or in the United States. Once they returned, they were appointed either as academic researchers in the Police Academy of Turkey or they were employed as police superintendents or security directors in the local posts of the Security General Directorate in various cities of Turkey.

These police cadres acted in close collaboration with the AKP and helped the ruling party to establish its neoliberal-neoconservative political project by redesigning the state apparatus, especially in curbing down the might of the military and judiciary in Turkey. They were calling themselves as pioneers of democratic policing in Turkey, and as the young generation that would crack down the old and corrupt habits of the police in Turkey. Besides being very active in the field, such as organizing international security conferences, introducing new policing methods such as intelligence policing and community-policing, and developing new performance criteria to develop the effectiveness of police, these cadres were also interested in producing a new policing philosophy.

Nevertheless, the 'novelty' of these cadres should not direct attention from the fact that the Gülen Community has been long organized within the police and accumulated considerable power resources within the state bureaucracy especially since the military coup d'état of 1980 in Turkey. The military in Turkey had always wanted a stronger police force, more immune to the societal and political changes. This immunization against the societal changes meant in practice a police force especially capable of cracking down labour militantism and leftist activism. To this end, the ideology of Turkish-Islamist synthesis was purposively used.[6] The police cadres were chosen from the right and ultra-right ranks of the society and they were indoctrinated within the Turkish-Islamist ideology, which would presumably prevent the infusion of leftist ideologies to the police organization. Although quite successful in their aims, the military officers were also worried about the 'excesses' of this new police power in Turkey.

By the late 1990s, there was a widespread public discussion in Turkey not only on the extraordinary levels of police corruption and brutality people had to face in everyday life but also on the new political mission the police organization had adopted. Many newspaper columnists working in the mainstream media called out during those days that 'there is now in Turkey a Police Party'.[7] Not only the police rank-and-file was over-politicized but also the violent conflict in the Kurdish-populated regions facilitated the police apparatus to enhance its hierarchical status within the whole state apparatus. This was also a period when the police in Turkey were managing brutal operations in urban areas such as in Istanbul, and violently harassing leftist, poor and Alevi neighbourhoods. The 28 February 1997 intervention of the military into the politics was among many other reasons an attempt of the political establishment to curb the out-of-hand power of the police in Turkey and to re-discipline the whole organization by way of prisoning a few high-ranked cadres from within the police bureaucracy.[8]

The post-28 February period in Turkey witnessed a fierce struggle between the police bureaucracy and the military, whereby endless projects of police restructuring were released by different national and international constituencies.[9] Whereas the military aimed at taking over the direction of the special operation teams from the General Security Directorate on the grounds that it was getting beyond control and harming the state's struggle against 'the internal threats', the then freshmen reformist police cadres supported the anti-military stance of the police bureaucracy, who resisted against this takeover plan. The reformist cadres, however, also argued for the introduction of advanced techniques of policing, for example intelligence policing, as against the brutal methods used during the 1990s by that same police bureaucracy. Accordingly, information policing would help the police to get rid of the heavy load of brutal policing techniques, that is police torture. It would professionalize the security infrastructure and help in the popularity of the police organization, especially amid the capitalist classes, who were worried about the rapid loss of political legitimacy the state had to undergo in Turkey in late 1990s (Aytaç, 1997).

The 1990s were also the very years when the police rank-and-file in Turkey demonstrated against 'human rights', shouted slogans of hatred, distributed declarations of revenge, organized *Imams* to spread their Turkish-Islamist messages. By the late 1990s, the state needed to compensate its heavy loss of prestige in the field of human rights. Even several police managers famous for their hard-line approaches to policing started to pay lip service to human rights. In other words, the state was in a deep legitimation crisis and the internationalization of the state via the bid for European Union membership and associated adoption of the language of human rights seemed inevitable and necessary to the ruling classes. Several businessmen chambers wrote down reports asking for a thorough reform of policing in Turkey in line with the principle of human security. Some even introduced training programmes for the police, like the 'Human Being First' project supported by the Eczacıbaşı, one of the biggest capital groups in 1990s' Turkey.

Once the AKP came to power in 2002, within five years of the 28 February intervention, this reformist wing within the police organization quickly got promoted. They have fostered their reform plans, benefited from the European Union accessions process and joined forces with the technical staff sent by the EU, become the country owners of the UNDP-hosted police reform projects, collaborated with the international governmental and non-governmental actors, including TESEV and DCAF, founded research centres, devised special training units.[10] Some of them participated in the UN Peace-building Missions and/or OECD Police-Restructuring Missions for which Turkey contributed via police units. They published thematical books on 'fighting against terrorism', in collaboration with the NATO's public diplomacy division. These police cadres remained in office until 2014–16, when the coalition between the Gülen Community and the AKP broke down. Majority of them were dismissed from their jobs and/or jailed after the failed putsch attempt of 15 July 2016. They are accused of being part of the 'Fethullah Gülenist Terrorist Organization', presented by the state as the main actor behind the coup attempt.

The ideal of harmonious society and the birth of moral policing

According to these reformist police cadres, the solution to the legitimation problems of the state in Turkey could not and should not be sought in restoring the bourgeois modern state form. According to them, the modern era separated private and public and thereafter oppressed the private/individual in the name of a loose understanding of public. This separation also facilitated the establishment of 'security states', which operated on an enemy and friend differentiation (Arslan, 2008). For whoever challenges the security of the state is stigmatized as an enemy of public order. Against this, reformist police cadres have proposed a switch to a conciliatory understanding of politics from the confrontational style of modern politics. They argued for the establishment of harmony and peaceful coexistence. This harmony and peaceful coexistence, however, are empty signifiers in themselves as they tend to assume that every conflict is a constructed conflict. For the police reformers, whose imagination of politics also got inspired by political Islamism, once the modern state becomes displaced, the harmony will be restored to societies, when left to themselves they would naturally tend to live in peace.

The political Islamist origins of the police reformers however have also had a class background. Their political Islamism represents a petit bourgeois worldview, a political-economic attribute of the overwhelming majority of the political Islamists in Turkey.[11] It is therefore not false to argue that the 'male modest/pious property owner' is the authentic figure who represents their ideal of harmonious society. Nevertheless, this class background does not mean that the 'poor' are excluded from their vision of the enlightened society. On the contrary, for Turkish political Islamists, the poor, indeed the poor men, are the 'real Muslims' (Tuğal, 2002) and therefore the ones whose honour should be valued no less than the petty bourgeois men. As will be shown below, this conception will have a significant impact on the politics of policing pursued by the reformist police cadres in Turkey and on the making of their gender and patriarchal selectivities. But before proceeding with moral policing, let me further discuss the harmonious society imaginary of these reformist police cadres.

For the reformist cadres, the security bureaucracy in Turkey and particularly the military had vested interests that were refracted as national interests. The forces under the command of this militarized security bureaucracy were overgrown in terms of numbers – compared to the police – and yet they were still not able to improve the quality of life of those living under their jurisdiction (Cerrah, 2011). They were reproducing insecurity rather than security and by way of reducing security to a simplistic understanding of security of life and property, they were underestimating the post-Cold War era's expanded notion of security that indeed includes 'the security of life style(s)' (Cerrah, 2011: 25). The immunity of this militarized security bureaucracy including the military institution itself from civilian oversight is detected as the main impediment before the advancement of human security principle in Turkey. It is implied that the security measures adopted by these old guards were a constant threat to the otherwise normal and peaceful course of social life. For example, Ibrahim Cerrah (2011: 26) argues that 'the essential task of a civilian security force, indeed of the police organization, is besides protecting individual rights and liberties to help the perpetuation of *the already existing environment of peace and safety within social life*' (italics added).

For the police reformers, therefore, different than the Hobbesian conception of a war-like social condition where peace can be secured only through coercion, society is already an organic whole – a collective of humble people who live in peace with their identities, traditions, convictions and in solidarity with each other (Cerrah, 2011: 28) – whose inner harmony is put at jeopardy by the security personnel, in short by the state acting solely after its own security. It is underlined that the state must go beyond 'making bare life possible' by securing values deemed important by individuals and societies (Cerrah, 2011: 27).

In that sense, the *human* of human security advocated by the police reformers is conceived as a moral person, whose primary instinct is to live in harmony with the cosmos. It is argued that when security personnel do put emphasis on confrontation among human beings rather than on the potential for solidarity and cohesion, they miscalculate the security threats against this harmony as well as misconceive the security needs of that harmonious society. Cerrah (2011: 29) argues that a security philosophy based on a malign conception of human nature is destined to break the social harmony and, on the other hand, only a belief system that perceives human beings as harmless and innocent creatures from birth can advance human security. Police reformers postulate that this positive understanding of human nature not only is in line with the presumption of innocence principle akin to the advanced Western systems of justice but also can be driven from the very Ottoman civil code, *Mecelle* (Cerrah, 2011: 30).

In accordance with this conservative perception of social harmonious life, police reformers prioritize administrative policing over judicial policing. According to them, the core of the job of policing is to secure public order and prevent any harm to this order rather than reacting *ex post* and dealing with the criminal. The judicial policing is even considered as 'exceptional and incidental' (Cerrah, 2011: 30). Cerrah argues that this is also what constitutes the fundamentals of European Police Ethics. He illustrates his interpretation by pointing out to the very definition of the police duties within the first article of the European Police Ethics. In accordance with administrative policing, the very first duty of the police organization is to secure 'public peace, public order and rule of law', and Cerrah (2011: 31) adds that the very last component of this first article constitutes the most encompassing and fundamental definition on the essence of police duties in a society: 'helping people and being in the service of people'. Cerrah (2011: 31), as the principle author of Turkey's version of police ethics, feels himself also immensely proud. According to him, these rules reflect the native principle of 'make humans live so that the state lives on' because they accord priority to the protection of individual rights over the protection of public order.

Although it appears to be self-contradictory, on the one side a eulogy to a harmonious society conception and on the other side prioritizing the individual, the police reformers indeed try to translate the global regime of human security into the national context and indeed localize it. On the one hand, this is a move to dissipate the potential accusations of Westernism by the more trenchant figures of political Islam in Turkey. On the other hand, they do exactly what the 'country ownership' principle promoted by the SSR community (see above) asked them to do. A similar 'ownership' is also displayed by the police reformers in their conception of rule of law.

In a similar vein, the rule of law is interpreted by the reformist police cadres as 'the sanctity of what is just' [*Hak yücedir*] (Cerrah, 2011: 32). 'What is just' or 'Hak' in Turkish also means *Allah*, the creator. Supporting the supremacy of law thus also means applying the dictates of the just order, which is already ruling the cosmos. Police officers are, therefore, invited to act in accordance with law, because 'above all they are themselves human beings who should act with conscience' (Cerrah, 2011: 33). Conscience is used here as a theological notion – because human beings are 'the only creature who is responsible for his acts, about which he will also be interrogated' in the afterlife (Cerrah, 2011: 33). In the same spirit, the rule of law is portrayed as an instrument of a just state, a state that is not alienated from the already existing social and cosmological harmony – a state which obeys the rule of god.

For the police reformers, although it has been repressed due to the tutelage of the military during the Republican Era, the civilian tradition of the Turkish Police Organization goes in fact back to the Ottoman Era. Accordingly, as opposed to the lack of civilian oversight in the current phase, the civil participation tradition of the TPO goes back to late nineteenth century, to the establishment of *Zaptiye Meclisi*, a committee for policing, headed by a police superintendent but essentially composed of academicians and high-profile civilian bureaucrats who used to function as an auditing body (Cerrah, 2011: 51). It is argued that because of the civilian view and suggestions made in this committee, the performance of the police personnel ameliorated and so did the popular contentment. It is further implied that with the transition to the Republican Era, this civilian participation tradition disappeared. Accordingly, this prevented the modernization of police functions in Turkey as apart from the existence of a nationally centralized inspection mechanism (under the leadership of the Ministry of Interior); TPO was deprived of local participation and oversight and therefore of 'democratic governance' (Cerrah, 2011: 51).

Police reformers' bracketing of the modern era or the Republican Era in policing and screening a philosophical continuity between the Ottoman and the post-modern eras of policing is emblematic of the neo-Ottomanist populist mode of politics adopted by the AKP governments as well. Cerrah's ideal civilian participation done by people, whom he imagines as a harmonious pious community, as against the modern state elite which he accuses of running after its vested interests, is completely in line with the AKP-type neoliberal populism. This kind of populism, in fact, replaces the idolatry of the state with an idolatry of people.

This populist stance does also condition the perception of police reformers about the social question. As according to the police reformers, society by itself is peaceful and harmonious, any criminal problem that necessitates policing is indeed a transitory imperfection within the society, mostly triggered because of an inauthentic state. The mission of the police, according to this view, is to restore the authenticity and give back to people their stolen honour.

Moral policing and gender

Although the populist and indeed nativist or localist human security project of the police reformers in Turkey prioritize the 'modest property-owner man' and/or the 'poor man', the 'woman issue' has created important challenges for the project. Women's political mobilization has been of central importance to the electoral victories of the AKP in Turkey (Ayata and Tütüncü, 2008; Yaraş, 2018). Therefore, no kind of populism could have left them outside of the power equations. Moreover, the dependence of the capitalist (re)production in Turkey and of the entire public care system on the invisible domestic labour of women has forced the AKP governments to lead a careful patriarchal bargain with women, indeed offer them protection to receive their acquiescence to housewifization. This has signified above all making the domestic sphere bearable and liveable for women. In 2006, at the same time when the police reform took speed in Turkey, the government issued a prime ministerial circular on domestic violence. This circular held liable the police organization as one of the main institutions that should work for preventing domestic violence against women. The National Action Plan that followed the publication of this circular in 2007 detailed down the institutional division of labour that should be followed in this state-led campaign against domestic violence and assigned several internal-training tasks to the police organization (Kadının Statüsü Genel Müdürlüğü, 2007).

Moreover, besides modernizing the patriarchal gender order, the state in Turkey had to review its violence strategies. For the gendered state violence against women but especially against the politically active women (for further details see the following chapter) was for sure against the spirit of the new social contract that the AKP government wanted to initiate in Turkey. To recap, human security has been conceived in Turkey's SSR as a way of constituting new legitimation grounds for the state monopoly of coercion and gendering human security was especially considered important by the police reformers who strongly believed in the existence of a correlation between social exclusion and politicization. This correlation was also considered as the main threat against the security of the state. In other words, police reformers believed in gender inclusion as a state security strategy. The exclusion of women from the public sphere and their secondary status in society according to the police officers created a search for personal dignity and respectability whose void are easily filled in by 'terrorist organizations'.

In that regard, police reformers conceived women, whether 'militant women' or housewives, as victims of a mal-functioning social order. This mal-functioning social order, according to the police officers, precluded women from fulfilling their gender roles: in the case of domestic violence, 'women are prevented from fulfilling their duties of motherhood and wifehood' (Delice, 2013: 17); in the case of women active in politically violent activities, 'their gender specific psycho-social features are instrumentalized in order to make the terrorist organizations stronger' (Alkan, 2011).

The security bureaucracy has had a specific focus on women who were recruited to the ranks of outlawed leftist organizations and to the PKK. Deciphering the motives that lead women to participate in those organizations made part of the general strategy to drain the human resources of these 'terrorist' organizations. Although it seems to be separate projects at first sight, even the fight against domestic violence that was partially undertaken by the reformist police cadres during late 2000s was in fact an attempt to create a change in the social conditions of women that lead or might lead them to politicize and radicalize. The fight against domestic violence project of the police reformers is framed as a project of human rights/human security rather than a project of public order. The fight against recruitment project of the police reformers is framed as a fight against terrorism strategy by improving the human rights of general populace. In other words, both projects were framed with an emphasis on the need of a new statehood that steers away from state security. However, this humanitarian emphasis and position should not be taken for granted. For the populism of the human security project in Turkey – with its political Islamist background presented above – would create several uncertainties, inconsistencies and ambiguities within the police organization.

In view of their priority of restoring the legitimation channels of the state, the police reformers developed two policing methods in relation to 'women issue': one aimed to remedy the erosion of social values (i.e. by restoring male compassion-cum-protectionism) via policing redesigned as counselling and second aimed to de-radicalize women via policing redesigned as differentiated counter-insurgency. The two however are not mutually exclusive strategies. Indeed, they are internally tied to each other or used as each other's substitutes.

Policing as counselling and social servicing

In the very first place, it should be re-stated that the interest of the police reformers in the issue of violence against women was highly determined by their desire to gain appreciation from the wider community. In other words, the job of policing is conceived as a first contact between the state and the citizen, and thus police reformers aimed at improving police behaviour to improve the legitimacy of the state in Turkey. In the curriculum books used for official police education, this is even entitled as becoming 'men of society' (Hülagü, 2017). The new cadres are required to restore credibility of the state apparatus by way of tapping on the existing 'humane values that are rooted in the social traditions and belief system in Turkey' (Şahin, 2013: 5). This underlying urge to make the police appreciated by people has led the police reformers to perceive every social issue from a populist perspective. In that regard, struggle against violence against women was also instrumentalized for the purposes of regime change perspective adopted by the police reformers.

This has also led them to develop better contacts with women's organizations and benefit from their know-how. But these contacts were also conditioned by the gender selectivities of the state and indeed of the reformist police cadres. The feminist argument that the domestic violence results from gender inequality and persists due to the male violence which basically aims at securing the subordination of women could not and would not penetrate the policing philosophy of the reforms. Rather, a study of the cop-sided discussion on violence against women displays that male violence is seen either as a communication or a psychological problem, stemming from the socio-economic difficulties the men face in their daily lives. On the one hand this leads the reformist cadres to concentrate on the question of how to improve men's conduct; and on the other hand the bad male conduct is framed as the by-product of unfortunate socio-economic conditions, which are conceived as being beyond the control of the state. This leads the reformers to disavow the possibility to find a real solution to violence against women.

To recap, the police reformers have tried to get involved in the state-led efforts against domestic violence on the basis of three dictates: (1) reframe violence against women as a social question, (2) reframe the social problem as a matter of failure of men to live up to the higher moral standards of an authentic society and (3) reframe the police-cum-state responsibility in the prevention of domestic violence – indeed give aside the card of criminalization.

(1) Police reformers perceive violence against women as a social question, not only affecting women subjected to violence but their close entourage and specifically the institution of marriage. According to a police-led analysis of domestic violence complaints in Erzincan, violence against women is mostly experienced by married women and therefore says the cop-sided perspective, 'policies should rather concentrate on married couples' (Delice, 2013: 32). It is argued that the police organization has a first-contact responsibility in the struggle against violence against women. This responsibility is defined as the responsibility of an expert police officer who should follow some standards while dealing with the domestic violence cases: 'being supportive towards the victim; preventing women victims of violence from further anxiety they might leave in police stations; reporting the complaints in detail and informing women about their rights and guiding them with respect to possible paths they can follow, i.e. getting into touch with related institutions' (Delice, 2013: 36). These standards are also the standards advised by women's organizations. Therefore, at first sight their adoption by the reformist cadres looks promising. However, these standards are not necessarily seen as part of a state responsibility towards establishing gender equality. On the contrary, gender equality demands are trivialized and perceived as particularistic demands of women's organizations. The main aim is rather to reframe domestic violence as a threat against familial

unity. The following quotation illustrates this well: 'Even though the victims of domestic violence include elderly, women and children, as women groups are strong in exerting pressure during public policy making processes, the name of "woman" comes to the fore [at the expense of elderly and children]' (Çalı, 2013: 127).

The family-centred perspective of the reformist cadres aims to make both the victim and the perpetrator abide by their gender-specific roles and to prevent them from causing social harm to the existing gender regime. The police reformers, indeed, possess a certain idealized notion of the existing gender regime and condemn those who disrupt the proper functioning of it. The problem is not with the existing gender regime but with the lack of a strong morality and certain will on the part of people who fail to reproduce the correct gender roles. In that regard, contrary to the misogynist legacy of the patriarchal state in general that would accuse women for the causes of domestic violence, the new patriarchal state in Turkey rather puts some part of the blame on the 'men', who do not properly fulfil their familial roles.[12]

(2) Some studies conducted by the police reformers themselves within the police organization to judge the perception of the police rank-and-file on the issue of violence against women display that the police rank-and-file has a very biased view. The sample study shows that nearly 30 per cent of the police officers think that 'some women deserve violence' and that 44 per cent of them think that 'women exaggerate the domestic violence' and that 38 per cent believe that 'women and men are not equal'. Police reformers argue that these beliefs would prevent the police officers from being professional and showing 'zero tolerance policy against violence' (Kara, Ekici and İnankul, 2014: 15). They advise trainings as a way of teaching the police officers how to develop their empathy towards the victims of domestic violence. They argue that the police must be trained in such a manner because 'those who have been victims of domestic violence look for a safe haven, a place where they will be protected, their body and their life. A place where they can tell their story, get legal assistance, counselling, and proper steps taken to ensure it not happening again' (Kara, Ekici and İnankul, 2014: 18). Thus, it can be argued that against the patriarchal gender norms dominant in the police organization, the panacea is sought in fuelling protectionism, as a human security value. But there is a further and a particularly important twist in this protectionist ethos.

The human security-oriented perspective of the police reformers shall not be mixed with a notion of a welfarist state that pursues a rehabilitative understanding in the field of crime and punishment.[13] It is rather a perspective that underlines the need to upgrade social controls that would compensate for hard policing. For these social controls would and could be restored according to police reformers after removing all barriers before the realization of the imagined harmonious society that allegedly possesses values that would keep the marriages intact and free of violence.

In the case of violence against women, the police data mostly exposed in academic papers produced by the police reformers who work in provincial cities in Turkey as police chiefs or superintendents defines the young male (twenty-five to thirty-four) as the main perpetrator(s). These are portrayed as poorly educated men, mostly employed in low-quality jobs. They are assumed to be exposed to violence when they were children and it is argued that that is why they do not know how to solve conflicts other than by resorting to violence. It is mentioned that in many cases of violence against women committed by young men, perpetrators use knives. Indeed, these young men are detected as having the habit of carrying knives (Delice and Yaşar, 2013: 38). Reformist police argue that in order to decline the rate of knife crimes against women, besides augmenting sanctions against carrying and using knives, 'the trust towards government should also be developed' so that 'they [citizens] are less likely to solve their conflicts by using their own methods' (Delice and Yaşar, 2013: 387).

In line with their populist priorities, the police reformers do frame the male violence as demonstrative of the representation failure in Turkey: the state being the state of Kemalist elites rather than that of peripheralized communities. Accordingly, once the populace would feel itself represented in the political authority, male violence will also decline since the gap between the centre and periphery would wither away. The correlation established between the political form of the state and violence against women is indeed striking as the police reformers politicize the issue contrary to the generic characteristic of neoliberal criminal policing based on depoliticization and criminalization. The police reformers do not absolve the male perpetrators of violence against women from their crimes. On the other hand, they do not criminalize them as well, criminalization in the sense of solving social problems by way of using criminal justice procedures as the main solution. What they do is to put the blame on a certain conception of the political structure and thus also create an apology for the male violence.[14]

(3) Police reformers do many times underline the insufficiency of a criminalization perspective (Bayhan and Vural, 2013: 274) and indeed refrain from possessing any kind of an administrative ambition to eradicate the problem of violence against women. It is argued that criminalization of the

violence against women do sometimes reinforce violence rather than preventing it. Although very effective in many cases, it is argued that the judicial injunction decisions taken against abusive husbands do not prevent the cycle of violence in many cases as women, who ask from law enforcement agencies for temporary injunction decisions, do suffer from social pressure and/or pressure from the families of the perpetrator husbands or from husbands seeking for vengeance (Çakmak, 2013: 84–5). Consequently, the reformers rather imply that there are limits (i.e. low amount of complaints the police receive due to the private nature of the problem (Karakuş, 2013: 258) or the hesitant position of women victims of domestic violence to pursue their complaints) to a preventative state action, hence a full protection. In an edited storybook called *Bilindik Bilinmez Hikayeler*, published in 2011, it is possible to clearly see how police officers specialized in the struggle against domestic violence frame violence against women as a social question, caused by fallen men and portray themselves as powerless vis-à-vis this question.[15]

The short stories compiled in this book are mostly written by police chiefs or deputy chiefs. It is interesting to note that the stories usually are melodramatic and have heart-breaking ends. The stories mainly depict a kind of masculinity crisis, where men (in their roles as either husbands or fathers) cannot carry their gender roles properly and do tend to abuse their families (not only wives but also children and elderly) (Çelik, 2011). Furthermore, the stories contextualize the male violence within a wider web of social relations, where men do mostly come from decent working-class families yet themselves fail to sustain a dignified working-class life due to the complexities of urban life. The violence is depicted not only as a social harm but also as a self-annihilating process for men-in-crisis (Alagüney, 2011). The police who take part in these stories are rather depicted as witnesses of these unfortunate events and nearly figure as hopeless bystanders. The stories somewhat convey a sense of helplessness and despair the law enforcement agencies feel vis-à-vis the social question.

A similar mood of powerless-ness dominates the academic writings of police reformers. It is argued that the expectations from the police organization to prevent violence against women exceed the capabilities of the organization (cited in Demir, Fidan and Nam, 2013: 50). The lack of specialized police personnel and especially of female police officers is mentioned as essential barriers before the effective policing against violence against women (cited in Demir, Fidan, and Nam, 2013: 51). All in all, the vision of post-modern state propagated by these reformist cadres 'represents itself as pervasively hamstrung, quasi impotent, unable to come through as many of its commitments because "it is no longer the solution to social problems'" (Brown, 1992: 29). This disavowal of state power becomes, however, an effective strategy of governance.

Not so surprisingly, a kind of moralization immediately follows this confession of a lack of full power, or powerless-ness, and state capacity. The police reformers want to limit their roles to counselling, and indeed take refuge in populism, where an imagined traditional-cum-religious society, as the embodiment of ideal gender role models, is called into help. In other words, police reformers redefine the job of policing as a soft power issue rather than a hard power issue and yet as such paradoxically pave the way for the rise of impunity in the cases of gendered violence.

In some studies, again done by the police reformers, it is argued against the common profiling of male perpetrators as alcoholics, drug-addicts or psychologically unhealthy persons (Delice and Teymur, 2013: 244). It is also maintained that the police records display no direct correlation between education and violence. According to these police chiefs, the striking result in the police recordings is that contrary to the shared postulation, violence against women is low among people who have no formal education and who have only basic literacy. According to these police officers, the available data shows that violence against women is higher in families with one or two children as opposed to families with four or more children. Besides, it is argued that half of the male population who are involved in violence against women are professionally self-employed and lack regular income. In this context, women against violence is presented as a serious social and human rights problem. The police officers imply however that the traditional family structure is not the main source behind the issue of violence against women. They do indirectly point out to the relatively modern family, composed of male breadwinner, housewife and one or two children as the main culprit.

Underlining of modernization and its impact on family structures as the main reason behind violence against women is most detailed in the cop-sided research done on young female suicides in South-eastern Anatolia in Turkey. Murat Delice and Semih Teymur (2012) argue that as against the conventional perspective, the police data about the eighteen suicide cases which took place in the years of 2010–11 in the Batman province of Turkey shows that violence does not stem from social customs. They basically imply that the young women suicides are not related with the oppressive gender norms, mostly associated with the patriarchal structure dominant in the South-eastern region of Turkey. They maintain that out of eighteen cases only two can be discussed in relation to social customs (especially in relation to early marriage) but the others, they underline, stem from 'solitude'. These police chiefs claim that the feeling of solitude is rooted in the weakening of social ties caused by modernization. They argue that modernization fosters parent-child conflicts, inferiority feeling among juvenile girls and puts more responsibility on women. Although they underline the heavy care responsibilities the young women bear at home (such as doing chores and looking after their fathers, brothers and elderly), these are interpreted as problems of modernization. Because, according to these local police superintendents, these women lack necessary solidarity networks provided by their own communities.

All in all, in cop-sided studies done by police reformers, the violence against women is considered as demonstrative of a social crisis and therefore, rather than using hard policing approaches, they do foster what they themselves call as 'soft policing' approaches. Soft policing is portrayed as culture-centred policing, where it is argued that, there must be a strong correlation between the cultures of society the police provide services and the institutional culture of the police. For them, culture is a 'cluster of different wisdoms' (Teymur, Günbeyi, and Özer, 2010: 283). Hence, for police reformers, social crisis does not stem from the field of culture, that might very well include oppressive gender norms, but rather from the erosion of this culture and its constitutive power. Although they do not approve social harm that might be resulting from conservative beliefs such as 'women and men are not equal', they nevertheless perceive these as curable fallacies that shall not be equated with the local and authentic culture of the society in Turkey. A very conservative perspective to social change, these police officers have a moralistic perception of policing.

In that respect, they differentiate from the modern philosophy of policing that considers police as a 'necessary evil'. For them, police represent the good, the morally superior and integral institution. However, for the reformist cadres this does not mean that a rule of police should be restored over the society. On the contrary, the rule of police is not preferable for them because it would end in criminalizing all kinds of wisdom already existing in society. Thus, the golden mean for them would be to enhance policing as a moral job, where police are part of an ethical life, which compensates the loss of respect, integrity and honour. This is the police of Hegel, for whom, the independence of individuals from political authority or even self-policing would not compensate for the loss of self-respect they go through (Neocleous, 2000: 45–54). Accordingly, 'the police cannot provide a solution [to the social question] but can prevent the poverty-stricken class from becoming a criminalized and pauperized rabble' (Neocleous,

2000: 49). The police can prevent people from turning into 'mob', from losing their sacredness.

In a similar vein, the police reformers conceive gender-related violence as a symptom of a social question that makes people lose their sense of self-respect. Therefore, they try to restore the honour of men and women through shoring up the conservative social fabric. The culture is therefore imagined as by itself possessing the social control mechanisms that would prevent the transition to the rule of police. Culture is posited against the already existing state, whose central, secular and elitist characteristics, according to the police reformers, prevent the flourishing of the former. The police reform, therefore, is devised as a process of re-centralizing this culture – habits, customs and beliefs of a society that arguably stay in the form of being denied. Police reform process is conceived as a process of restoring the harmonious society, where men and women do remember the wisdom inherent in their culture and thus regain their lost honour.

Policing *as* 'deradicalization and disengagement'

Necati Alkan, the former head of the Strategic Planning Section of the Public Order and Security Undersecretariat attached to the Ministry of Interior, wrote a PhD thesis, published in 2011 by the Police Academy Press in Turkey.[16] In her thesis, Alkan (2011) tries to understand the reasons that lead women to join PKK. He focuses on gender relations within the PKK with the intention 'to provide scientific help for the making of the counter-terrorism strategy of the Turkish state' (Alkan, 2011: 22). Alkan uses a blend of feminist theory with sociological methods to argue that 'the PKK instrumentalizes women in its search for sustainability as an organization'.[17] He focuses on the relation between the PKK leader Abdullah Öcalan and women fighters and tries to prove his argument that the patriarchal relations within the Kurdish society cause the Kurdish young and ignorant women to participate in the PKK due their search for independence and identity. He adds that Öcalan benefits from 'the woman issue' by providing the women with a separate identity and thus securing his own primacy within the organization. Because, according to Alkan (2011: 88; 177; 200), women, who are treated as of secondary status within their social environment, tend to idolize Öcalan as the ultimate saviour who wows them with a status of goddess. Alkan argues to have conducted twenty in-depth interviews with former women fighters and bases his account on their stories. Although it is not possible to check the integrity of the information provided in the thesis, the motivation behind Alkan's thesis and the implications of this thesis for the concrete state strategies developed as counter-insurgency policies are essential for this study.

At the end of his analysis Alkan (2011: 216–17) provides a list of policy proposals for policymakers. The list is short but telling. He argues for the need to accelerate the modernization and urbanization processes to solve the 'woman question' in Kurdish social structure; promote the schooling of girls and solve the infrastructural needs of Kurdish people living in shanty-towns via exigent urban transformation projects; train women to raise their child-rearing capacities and integrate them to the urban culture; improve the status of women in places where the PKK is strong through establishing public centres for women and children; increase the number of the projects that prioritize families as their impact on children is bigger than any other public institution. Many of these proposals, which also display the making of the post-2006 bureaucratic mind-set regarding 'the Kurdish issue', invite further discussion. However, one essential point which is particularly revealing about the formation of specific gendered policing strategies of the reformist era is not included within this list of policy proposals but in the earlier pages. It is noticeable in the pages where the author discusses the 'instrumentalization of women' by the PKK:

> The women who took after the 1990s the tasks and roles mentioned above [acts of sacrifice such as suicide bombing; an abbatial life devoted to the national cause and becoming ferocious supporters of Öcalan within the organization] have become the essential force that *keeps the organization intact*. All women interviewees argue that if this force leaves the organization, 'the organizational structure would collapse'.
>
> (Alkan, 2011: 203, italics added)

Alkan adds that many women he interviewed argued that 'it would be impossible to keep men [guerrilla men] in the mountains if women were not there'. By these expressions, it is implied that the presence of guerrilla women encourages men to fight, creating a gender-based pressure over them. Alkan also notes that he made the interviews in 2009, curiously the same year when many Kurdish women politicians were taken under custody by the government under the pretext that they were supporting 'terrorist activities'. On 28 May 2009, one of the biggest trade union confederations in Turkey, KESK (Confederation of Public Employees Trade Union) was raided by the police and many women unionists including the general secretary Songül Morsümbül were taken under custody. In the aftermath of this incident, feminists argued that this move on the part of the state had been deliberately designed to destabilize the leftist and pro-Kurdish organizations by primarily attacking the women participants. İlknur Üstün, a veteran feminist activist, also stated during our interview that the state in Turkey has been targeting women activists to chipper out the organizations within which they organize their struggles (Üstün, 2019). Üstün argued that this is mainly because the state knows very well that it is basically women who are the backbones of these organizations (Üstün, 2019). Gültan Kışanak (2018: 45), the imprisoned mayor of the Kurdish-populated city Diyarbakır, similarly tells in her book that the main motive behind the April 2009 operations made against the Kurdish women politically active in different organizations aimed at dissolving the Kurdish women's movement, discouraging the political participation of women and rolling back the women's achievements.

It should however also be added that the security bureaucracy has self-contradicting perceptions on how to deal with the women in oppositional politics. On the one hand, the state does accept that these women are empowered by participating in politics and in the 'terrorist organizations' such as the PKK. Alkan (2011: 204) in his book mentions that the women's participation at the PKK fostered their self-confidence, developed their expressive abilities and filled them with a strong sense of female identity. On the other hand, the state insists on viewing these women as 'victims' of a wicked 'terrorist organization' that benefits from their gender-based vulnerabilities. Within the same book where Alkan concedes the agential power of women, it is also possible to read the following lines:

> Adolescents look for places where they are valued and where they are treated as adults because they lack these within their own familial environments. It is possible to argue that women meet with the PKK under such circumstances. Until it [the PKK] wins them to the organization, it is possible to observe that the PKK provides women with affection, respect and value they long for and once the women participate, it makes them pay the price for it.
>
> (Alkan, 2011: 132)

This logic follows such a reasoning: in the absence of strong families and supportive state policies, psychologically weak and desperate young women find condolence in terrorist organizations. Ersin Oğuz (2007: 271), a gynaecologist who works for the Ministry of Interior in the Medical Centre of the Ankara Police Department, tells that 'the family related negativities will increase the crime and terror tendency ratio in the child'. He adds that 'the introverted girls and those who want to escape from their homes have a separate value for terrorism' (Oğuz, 2007: 280). Oğuz (2007: 279), as does Alkan, argues that 'the lack of esteem she [a child girl] receives at home makes her vulnerable to manipulation. A terrorist leader can manipulate her with promises of an active, "heroic" role in a terrorist act.'

Thus, besides directly targeting women in oppositional politics, the TPO also operates on the basis of a perspective where women are portrayed as victims of 'terrorist organizations'. They contact the families of university students and/ or engage in counterpropaganda. They use sources such as the daily of Saliha Dagcı, a guerrilla woman killed during counter-insurgency operations. In the diary, it is allegedly written:

> I have missed my family. I wish to be at home. [If I were at home], I would lay down beside the hot stove. Then I would drink the soup my mother would prepare. The PKK was told to be quite different, but I have learnt about the despicable behaviour at the mountains, just after I went there. I never felt so regretful. Who am I, what am I doing with these people? I am so regretful to leave the university. Those two years I have spent at the university were the best days of my life. We had a happy life at the dormitory. Hatice, Aysun and Saadet, we were going everywhere together. Now they have finished school. Maybe they are all married.
>
> (cited in Alkan and Çitak, 2007: 292)

Because the lack of 'strong and healthy families' is diagnosed by these police reformers as the nodal point of Turkey's 'terrorism problem', they developed a policing strategy that relies on the integration of families into the policing activities. A nation-wide programme entitled as 'Information and Prevention Activities' has been put into practice during the late 2000s. It asked the police officers to establish contact with the families to ask their active help in disengaging their sons or daughters from 'terrorist activities'. This programme has been applied in different localities and pilot cities.

As discussed until now, whether 'agent' or 'victim', the motivations of women-in-politics are depoliticized by the police reformers. This depoliticization works as the background onto which the police reformers develop their human security mandate. It is argued that the 'Information and Prevention Activities' programme of the police organization increases 'the benefits of leaving the group as it provides the disengaged extremists with social and financial benefits to facilitate their re-socialization into community, including educational funding, employment, housing, healthcare, and other accommodations to maintain a normal life without further stigmatization and isolation' (San, 2018: 9). This process provides the state with the opportunity to augment its protectionist mandate and to restore its 'credibility' and presumably to augment the micro-legitimacy of the police organization among the populace. Through this strategy, the police reformers try to create *de nouveau*, the social basis for the legitimation of the state monopoly of coercion in Turkey. Yet, instead of grounding this legitimacy on citizenship, they ground it on clientelism. It is argued that by providing some entitlements to the 'militants', the police make them renounce their 'engagements'.

Clientalization of the politically active and/or violent women and men is also configured as a process of de-indoctrination, an attempt for switching their loyalties from their organizations to the state. It is argued that 'the humane treatment of the militants induces a cognitive opening' (Baştuğ and Evlek, 2016: 39). In that respect, the police reformers argue that the sincere personal encounters with the early recruits make them question their ideological commitments, which are essentially instituted on a hatred of government (Bastug and Evlek, 2016; San, 2018).

The police reformers' strategy of integration of families into the policing of women is further nuanced. Whereas in the case of conflict with the Kurdish political movement, the police reformers prioritize engaging families as the primary site of gendered social control; in the case of conflict with the urban-based outlawed leftist organizations, the approach slightly differs. For example, in the police studies done over the case of DHKP-C (The Revolutionary People's Liberation Party/Front), it is argued that the organization operates through and with the help of families. İsmail Yılmaz (2009: 21) argues that 'the [research] results showed that the DHKP-C uses families and relatives more than friends in recruitment, and that those who were recruited by their families and relatives had a greater involvement level when compared to those who were recruited by their friends and by other means (in prisons or by simply reading the organization's publications)'. Similarly, Salih Teymur (2007: 135), a police superintendent who wrote on the recruitment processes of the DHKP-C, argues that the 'destitution of a family can make the children ordinary criminals such as burglars; however, in the case of terrorism, the young people who inherit an ideological background from their parents tend to become involved with the ideological groups to fight for their destiny'. Thus, although police reformers benefit from the moralist mind-set in order to develop effective policing strategies built on strong families, they do also insist on applying differentiated strategies to different 'terrorist groups', 'extremists' and/or 'radicals' – all concepts interchangeably used by police reformers. Not all families are equally treated. Rather, differential integration of them is proposed as a policing strategy because according to the reformist police cadres, some families are appropriate vehicles for deradicalization whereas others are themselves instruments of and for radicalization.

There are two interim remarks I would like to do about the gendered nature and implications of moral policing, before ending the chapter with the analysis of the third style of moral policing in Turkey, namely the missionary policing strategies developed during the SSR era in Turkey. First, as seen in the cases of violence against women, the human security perspective in Turkey does not directly endorse the strategy of criminalization of male perpetrators. It rather indirectly supports impunity. That is first because the state is thought to be incapacitated to resolve the social question and second violence against women is not considered as a problem of gender inequality but a problem of failure to live up to the moral and cultural dictates of an authentic society. Within this background, although not willing to leave women to the detriments caused by a mal-functioning social order – which also proves a state failure to secure the lives of its subjects, and also a failure of the neoconservative project based on the sanctity of families and even a risk to alienate women from the social order altogether – the gender selectivities of the state continue to prioritize men – either by disavowing state power or by calling in the need to redress the moral order. Therefore, and second, the urge to look at the male perpetrators as the aggrieved characters of a false destinity, as the state-induced victims of a morally and spiritually poor social formation in fact fosters the tendency to accord the perpetrators impunity. In this perspective, women are not necessarily perceived as *Shahmarans* who with the help of their bewitching beauty cone the men and therefore need to be subordinated at all costs. On the contrary, they are mostly depicted as victims of a rapidly changing social order, of modernization. However, the protection accorded to women by the state is secondary to the honour provided to men and conditional on their re-entry to the patriarchal bargain – return to family, and indeed to the marriage. This conditionality becomes best visible in the case of cop-sided perspectives about the women in dissident politics.

In the case of politically active women and women who are agents of political violence, the human security perspective of the police develops on the moral critique of the social order and yet the political engagement is undermined to a child-like decision to rebel. In other words, in most of the cases women's agency is nullified, and they are portrayed as victims of a mal-functioning social order, whose cultural traits could or would if correctly operated help them to regain their dignity without feeling the need to join political groups and organizations. In that sense, the police reformers are also anti-Political. Besides perceiving the decay of the modern social order as a main cause behind women's politicization, they also consider the alternative imaginaries of the Political as aberrations stemming from or as reactions to the forces of modernization that hamper the inherent wisdom of the society. One and the most important modernization force that alienated society from itself according to the reformist police cadres was the militarist state – or the Kemalist, elitist, centrist state, all terms used interchangeably.

Policing as missionary power

During the reform process of the police in Turkey, the strategy of moral policing has had a different embodiment in different branches of the police organization. The reformist police cadres have seen essential to restructure the hard-policing legacy of the state in Turkey. To this end, they introduced a new missionary style of policing, which was mostly performed in the overseas United Nations peacekeeping and peace-building missions the Turkish police have been sent to and in the Kurdish-populated South-eastern regions of Turkey. This missionary mandate has also developed as part of the police training services provided to many Central Asian countries and to some Middle Eastern states. To this end, the reformist cadres founded the Project of National and International Police Training Centre (UPEM is its Turkish abbreviation). This centre was designed just after Turkey received temporary membership of the United Nations Security Council in 2009. It was also developed with reference to Turkey's National Program for the Adoption of the EU *Acquis*.

This missionary policing's political Islamist references have been more visible when compared to the policing as counselling and deradicalization. The reformist police cadres argued for example:

> These post-Soviet regimes [Central Asian states] should realize that the growth of Islam in their territories is not a threat but actually an asset to their countries … They must join forces with people of true Islamic faith to tap into the strength of Islam in fighting extremists and separatists … Finally, due to the fact that Islam has political clout in the world, they should continue to cultivate relationships with countries with large Muslim populations, like they have with Turkey, in which case both sides benefited economically, through tourism and in security.
>
> (Hançerli and Nikbay, 2007: 7)

The political Islamist tone of this missionary policing strategy was more transparent also because these missions have been accorded big importance within the remits of the neo-Ottomanist foreign policy of the AKP in the reformist era. Moreover, Turkey's missionary policing style was internationally supported on the grounds that for good governance to flourish in non-Western countries, the carriers of the reform processes should also be non-Westerners, that is countries like Turkey, which also by then was propagated as the 'model country'.[18] Third, missionary policing with more visible political Islamist motives has been conceived as a way of bypassing national conflicts with the help of a so-called common Muslim identity. This is especially the case in the reformist cadres' input in the South-eastern Turkey, where they tried to benefit from 'local traditions', 'local institutions' and 'religious culture' in the region to dilute the national self-determination demands of the Kurdish people (Hülagü, 2016).

This missionary or neo-Ottomanist style of policing first pursued philanthropic practices. It underlined the idea that the Turkish police are rightful heirs of an Ottoman past known for its protectionist policies towards the peripheral populations of the empire. It therefore included a policing strategy based on community-policing activities, where police cadres got more involved into the daily lives of the local populations, and indeed develop new state practices like tutoring children and adolescents after schooltime, organizing nation-wide excursions for them, cooperating with religious leaders, *imams*, to diffuse their word better, etc. (Hülagü, 2016, 2017). One of the most telling projects developed by the reformist police cadres within this context is the project of 'The future in Our Ideals: 110 Ideas, 11 Role Models' (Teymur, 2013). This project was implemented by the National Ministry of Education in the Southern-eastern Turkey in cooperation with the regional police centres. The stated aim of the project was to provide the Kurdish pupils with role models whom they can emulate in their own life paths. Of the eleven male role models, nine were male AKP politicians and the rest two were male celebrities who originate from the region.

The most significant gendered implication of this philanthropic modus was the cultivation of a protectionist masculinist sub-culture within the police organization. This protectionism was based on the victimization of 'women and children', a generic characteristic of human security approaches. However, this approach was not necessarily institutionalized in the police organization. On the contrary, it was an informal component. This informality is conceived to be the real strength of the missionary police practices.

Accordingly, it lessened the impersonal character of the state and improved the police behaviours. Many examples which make part of this protectionist missionarism are indeed cases of police officers and police cadres who 'fundraise among themselves', for example, to help 'needy Kurdish women who are left by their husbands who have gone to join the PKK' (Özel Harekat Polisinin Ağlatan Mektubu, 2012).

This philanthropic and protectionist modus of the missionary policing is however only one side of the coin. The other and complementary side is militaristic and expansionist. In fact, the neo-Ottomanist policy direction of the ruling party in Turkey was also a project about national borders and their flexibilization in the south-eastern hinterland of Turkey. The ideal of porous borders and the accompanied integration of the Turkish territory to the holy crescent were presented as the new historic mission of the Turkish State, and even as an innate requirement of the Ottoman past. This expansionist geopolitical stance of the state in Turkey brought about a reorganization of the state security architecture. New formal and informal security apparatuses have been built up. Existing ones have been adjusted to these new ambitious geopolitical missions. The Special Police Operations department (SPO) has been one of these security apparatuses, refurbished after years of relative downgrading within the police organization.

The SPO was founded in 1992 and vehemently used in the state operations against the PKK until the 28 February 1997 military intervention. The army officers decided on 28 February to seize the heavy armament of these operational forces and thereafter the mobilization of the police alongside with the military in the conflict with the PKK in South-eastern Turkey paused. The redeployment decision was made by the then Prime Minister Erdoğan in 2011. The decision was published after the killing of thirteen military personnel in Diyarbakır in 2011 during the violent clashes with the armed PKK members.[19] Once brought back into the higher echelons of the state security architecture, the number of special police operations troops augmented from 5000 to 7000 in 2012. Meanwhile, it was announced that the police would be reintegrated to the cross-border operations.

The government declared that the new special operations teams would be different from the ones that were in the past sources of insecurity for the nation. The then deputy head of the AKP, Hüseyin Çelik, contended that the new teams would not be like the previous era's types who used to wear pendant moustaches, symbol of the ultra-right nationalists in Turkey (Ünlü, 2010). The following events demonstrated that the training of the police special operations teams included a heavy dose of the religionization of the policing philosophy. Various team members who spoke to the conventional media about their fighting routines and motivations declared that 'we shoot for the sake of God, for the sake of the Prophet and of the Martyrs' (Özyurt, 2016).

Following this perspective, a new decade has started for the revitalization of virtuous violence in Turkey. The selection process of the potential team members and the training of the police recruits have included four guiding principles: 'voluntarism', 'patience', 'strength' and 'loyalty'. The recruits are asked to be voluntary to fight in special operations teams, to possess strong characteristics and be extremely loyal to the political power, but especially to Erdoğan. From the very first moment, both the political power and the SPO underlined the element of 'voluntarism' for those who join the special teams. In other words, the SPO members would not be conscripts; rather 'they will be voluntary individuals who can renounce their private lives to die for the sake of their nation'. The new SPO graduates cite their professional pledge in front of a setting where the Turkish flag, *Kur'an*, an M-Jig and a clove (symbolizing death) lay side by side on a table. The SPO members have some other key markers to describe themselves, their mission and their 'self-perception'. They define their task as 'intervening in the incidents that have gone out of control' and 'hunting down militants'. They define their 'preys' as people tricked by the dissident political organizations and are resentful to the fact that they have to fight against the 'women and children' [çoluk çocuk], who are according to them only fooled victims of the PKK (Sağırlı and Demir, 2011).

This fight against the 'victims', whom under routine circumstances they are asked to protect, certainly destabilize the police forces. For the inner-legitimation of a transition from a philanthropic-protectionist mode to militaristic-expansionist, however, is not that difficult for the ruling power. Besides very specific techniques to cultivate this transition among police forces, such as depriving the police rank-and-file from all basic survival needs so that they become more brutal, the ruling power has promoted some form of a jihadist hyper-masculinity – a sub-cultural mode of celebrating and desiring honourable death as a sign of masculinity, the reckless aggression against the infidels or heretics and the commitment to a faith brotherhood. The ruling power especially pumps up the talk of 'infidels' and 'heretics', with specific reference to human security. It depicts 'the infidels' and 'heretics' as those who are unfaithful citizens, who despite all efforts for state-led protection, care and support continue on being perfidious.

Concluding remarks

This chapter aimed at displaying the driving human security philosophy of the reformist era with a special focus on the ways gender has become central to the politics of policing in Turkey. It depicted how human security vision of the reformist police cadres primarily aimed at producing new legitimation tools for the state power. This legitimation lust has pushed the reformist police cadres to integrate the gender issue to their agenda over two topics. The first is developing police powers in the struggle against violence against women, but specifically in relation to domestic violence. The second is refining the policing of 'terrorism' in Turkey by knowledge production on the (gendered) motives of individuals and especially of young women who join 'terrorist' organizations. In line with the moralist conception of policing, which basically aimed at restoring the authentic character of the society in Turkey 'jeopardized by the militarist/Kemalist state' of the pre-AKP era, the state has developed new gender selectivities under the leadership of reformist police cadres.

These gender selectivities are contradictory in that the reformist cadres got caught in the middle of a social crisis/problem, in the face of which they oscillated to develop a real solution. On the one hand, they want to close the gap between the growing demands of women for due diligence. This is also important to prove the state capacity to sustain the new social contract promised by the AKP. On the other hand, both their neoconservative conception of society – based on healthy families – and their neoliberal avowal for state incapacity to provide full protection to women against domestic violence forced them to rather tilt the direction of the gender selectivity of the state towards men. This is further endorsed by their populist conception of men, as 'poor but honourable' individuals whose dignity is jeopardized by the elitist/Kemalist state. Plus, the neoconservative stance pushed them to grant protection to women based on two prerequisites: the protection of familial unity and especially of the institution of marriage.

This moral policing has also had direct repercussions for the women in politics, but especially for the women in opposition politics and/or agents of political violence. They are presented as victims of the organizations within which they are doing politics and of the decay of the authentic social order due to the forces of modernization. Their agency is recognized only in relation to their 'instrumentality' to the political or 'terrorist' organizations they join. The cure for these women appears to bring the family back into policing, either to 'deradicalize' them or to govern them. This is however not a uniformly applied policing strategy. Because some families, especially the urban and Alevi families who supposedly join illegal leftist organizations, are perceived as being the problem behind rather than the solution for women's 'radicalization'. Hence, the gender selectivities of the state get further and further refined in relation to class, ethnic and/or confessional identities. Relatedly, gender itself becomes a governing apparatus for the police. The knowledge production on the gendered characteristics of 'terrorist organizations' facilitates new types of policing strategies, that is attacking female members as a way of dismembering the 'terrorist organizations'.

Lastly, missionary policing further entrenches the dialectic of police reform, namely the sublation of human security (patriarchal protectionism) into a political Islamist hyper-masculinity. Indeed, it produces a form of a virtuous violence that is both resentful and decisive in facing the 'traitors', even if they are 'women and children'. It is resentful because women agents of political violence or women who are argued to be members of 'terrorist organizations' destabilize the gender stereotypes of the special forces braided for lethal policing with religious motives – in short, they are not peaceful women who waits for masculinist protection. It is pivotal because it needs to set the limits to show where the populist inclusion of this AKP-style human security ends and where it starts.

The prolific historical sociologist Michael Mann (1999) argues that what is done in the name of people and for people is historically not as innocuous as one would assume to be. Mann argues that the birth of democracy, which stopped violence working as the dominant form of doing politics in capitalist societies, was not due to people, if by this latter it is meant an imagined organic entity. For Mann, democracy was the product of a stratified society. According to Mann, stratification fostered democracy because of and due to the institutionalization of class struggle in liberal societies. That said the peaceful character of democracies for Mann does not ensue from being for and by people but rather from being by and through social classes. On the contrary, for Mann, large-scale social harms, political crimes, genocidal interventions have been committed under the name of people and for people. Thus, the moralist populism of the police reformers should also be reconsidered under the light of Mann's historical findings. The imaginary of harmonious society includes all sorts of gendered harms, done for the people and by the people.

3

Feminist interventions in and against the state

It is possible to discern that before the 2013 Gezi Events, women's organizations and feminist activists were mainly following two types of politics in Turkey. On the one hand, they were pursuing an *equal rights politics* to challenge the patriarchal discriminatory legal authority of the state. Changing the rules and legal codes of the state, hence the very form of the state would also help to confront the patriarchal practices in society. On the other hand, they were pursuing *gender mainstreaming politics* to build a women-friendly public power apparatus with which to raise the status of women in Turkey. Both strategies were basically aiming at providing women with entitlement to equal citizenship, to the state authority as a power resource that could and would help women to liberate themselves from the different shackles of patriarchal gender order, violence against women being the major and principal one.[1]

When asked about this period, İlknur Üstün, a prominent feminist and women's rights activist, explains that women's organizations in Turkey profited from the window of opportunity created by the reformist wave within the Justice and Development Party (AKP) and supported by Turkey's accession process to the European Union (Üstün, 2019). This 'window of opportunity' provided the feminist movement in Turkey with previously unconceivable happenstances, such as feminist-led trainings of the police on gender equality and domestic violence. Üstün, one of the trainers of the UNFPA Turkey's police training project commonly developed with the Turkish National Police (TNP), argues that 'even if the training we provided secured the safety of life of only one woman, it was worth doing it'. Üstün, I would argue, represents a generation of feminists in Turkey who have been struggling to install feminist ideas in actual legal-institutional state apparatus.

However, contrary to the cases of similar types of feminist engagements in the advanced capitalist countries, the feminists do not 'walk the halls of power' in Turkey (Halley, 2006). On the contrary, the feminist will for 'the governmentalization of feminist knowledge' (Prügl, 2011) in Turkey has not only hit against the walls of the centaur state-in-the-making but also got resignified by it. Although the main reason behind this resignification process is closely related with the gendered nature of the state in Turkey – hence its gendered selectivities rooted in the necessities of capitalism as shortly touched upon in the introductory chapter and patriarchal selectivities established by the moralist rationality of the Islamist-conservative bureaucratic state cadres as shown in the previous chapter – the feminist strategies have displayed their own weaknesses as well. The explicit focus on intervening in the legal-bureaucratic structure of the state to appropriate it for feminists' purposes paved the way for a *false cooperation* with the reformist cadres. This fallacious cooperation was mainly facilitated due to the common grammar of human security that was based on rectifying the misconduct of the state personnel.

It is true that during the SSR era in Turkey, when the reformist state cadres looked for solutions for closing the legitimacy deficit of the state, and for a professional know-how to govern the gender relations, they developed a strategic partnership with women's organizations and feminists. The specific social phenomenon which has forced the state cadres and/or encouraged the reformist police cadres to look for gender expertise has been the high numbers of domestic violence in Turkey. But this was not the only cause.

The late 1990s and the early 2000s were also an era of pervasive state violence in Turkey; the state-led torture and its gendered forms were such a daily reality that when the economic crisis in 2001 erupted even the social grievances resulting from this crisis were formulated with analogy to state violence. The small shopkeeper women who marched in tradesmen [*esnaf*] protests because of the hardships they were faced with after the 2001 economic crisis were complaining about their husbands whom they compared to the state: 'The state is masculine, and so is the police organisation and the husbands ... They are the state at home' (Demir, 2001a: 27). Therefore, the early 2000s fostered the political establishment to work on a new state project, which would also include women and reconcile them with the patriarchal gender contract. The statecraft considered that the feminist knowledge could be of a significant help. However, the previous chapter has shown that this knowledge could only be espoused when it is filtered by the moral policing agenda of the populist reformist cadres – prioritizing the 'honour' of the modest property-owner men, assumedly peripheralized by the state elite since the establishment of the Republic in Turkey.

This chapter aims at discussing this feminist determination to make a change in the conduct of the state towards women, with a specific focus on the notion of physical violence against women and how it is conceptualized by the feminists in Turkey. In other words, it aims at understanding the feminist interventions in the state and looking for the *internal weaknesses of these interventions*, which have hypothetically made them vulnerable to being distorted by the political power. To recap, the major weakness appears to be subsuming women's rights under human rights or, indeed, under human security – which is itself an extremely poor and controversial version of human rights. Therefore, the core of this chapter consists in understanding the governance feminism in Turkey, the feminist current which basically focused on gender mainstreaming in order to consolidate the women-friendly changes in the rules of entitlement, namely the women's entitlement to state protection. However, there are also two other issues which are dealt with in this chapter:

First is the birth and evolution of feminist struggle against the state concerning the violence against women. The governance feminists in Turkey are the heirs of a deep-rooted feminist tradition in Turkey. It would not be wrong to argue that from the 1980s onwards the women's organizations in Turkey have been implicitly referring to the notion of human security, as the public power's obligation to protect women from physical violence – and from other basic insecurities. They have incessantly underlined the state obligation to care for its women citizens and protect them from violence. However, there have been important changes and bifurcations within this continuity of feminist politics of violence prevention and recovery. In fact, it is only by the late 1990s that the issue of 'violence against women' has been reformulated as a question of women's human rights rather than a question of patriarchy and masculine domination. The theoretical links established by the feminists in the late 1980s and early 1990s between the gendered state violence and domestic violence started to disappear. The feminist struggle against domestic violence quitted the discussions on the patriarchal origins of the state – and the associated question of to what extent and in what forms the feminists should engage in the state has nearly fallen out of the agenda – and rather concentrated on making a behavioural change in the 'men in the state'.

The second additional focus of this chapter is concerned with the birth and consolidation of a third feminist strategy in Turkey, namely the anti-militarist feminism, which, different from *the entitlement* focus of the other two strategies, focuses on the rules of *identity*. Peace feminism tries to challenge the militarist masculinity that leaves its mark on state practices while simultaneously asking for the recognition of the gender difference of women. This strategy seeks empowering women, especially the Kurdish women whose peculiar needs are side-lined and/or shadowed by the two other strategies. This feminist intervention in the state refers to the notion of human security in a more explicit manner. It basically reconfigures human security as an ideological apparatus for challenging the gendered outcomes of different state practices in the South-eastern Turkey. Hence rather than focusing on the legal authority of the state or in the appropriation of state apparatus for feminist purposes, anti-militarist/peace feminism concentrates on a critique of the existing state security practices. But this focus re-associates it with other feminist strategies so long as the political horizon settles on correcting the statecraft's *conduct and misconduct* against women.

Despite their significant differences, all these three feminist strategies try to *educate* the state in Turkey, provide gender expertise on how to remedy the state failures emanating from falling short of abiding by the promises of a bourgeois state form: being true to the principle of legitimate monopoly of violence (to make the private violence a public issue and ask the state to monopolize it rather than making out of it a patriarchal dividend for men), being true to the principle of universalism (to consider women as human individuals with equal rights) and being true to the principle of rule of law (to punish the illegal acts of statecraft rather than granting immunity). Whether through the notion of gender equality as in the case of governance feminism or through the notion of gender difference as in the case of peace feminism, the feminist interventions in the state focus on the contradictions of a supposedly bourgeois state. This happens however at a time when the bourgeois state form undergoes a thorough change, not only in Turkey but all around the world and becomes 'antagonistic to ... the rule of law, formal bureaucracy and motives and cycles of democratic politics more generally' (Jessop, 2002).

Historical background: Gendered violence as a systemic instrument

When feminism emerged as a separate ideology in the late 1980s in the post-coup d'état Turkey, feminists questioned the separation of the public and private with a focus on domestic violence and its systemic functions – reproducing the patriarchal-capitalist gender order through male domination. Feminists possessed a holistic approach to the oppression of women. They were arguing that gendered violence is a systemic component of male domination and hence an existential issue of and for each woman, irrespective of her class background.

Put simply, feminists were underlining that women live in a sexist world where men do indeed subordinate them for their own common interests. For this second generation of feminists in Turkey, who raised the flag of an independent women's movement in Turkey after years of deep silence since the 1930s onwards, all institutions were primarily constituted by and for male domination, including the family and the state.[2]

The second-wave feminism in Turkey was against simplistic explanations of women's oppression. Neither the thesis that explains women's oppression with a focus on the so-called remnants of feudal social relations nor thesis of 'late and lame modernization of the Third World countries', which possesses a culturalist perspective, was for them enough or accurate to explain women's oppression. On the contrary, the modern capitalist society with its prevailing authoritarian state form was the main culprit. In line with this maxim, for these pioneer feminists gendered state violence and domestic violence were not different in character from each other. Both were tools to subordinate women to the private sphere, to keep them out of the political sphere and out of the labour market. Nazik Işık (2002: 42), one of the forerunner feminist activists who has been involved in the struggle against violence against women in Turkey from its beginning in the late 1980s onwards, points to the fact that the pervasive state violence following the 1980 coup d'état in Turkey directed many leftist women to discover different forms of violence women actually go through in their everyday lives. She argues that 'we could recognize the big similarities between the implications of this [state-induced] violence and the one in the private sphere' and adds 'what we have experienced in the domestic sphere was also violence' (Işık, 2002: 45).

Şirin Tekeli (1987), another pioneer feminist activist in Turkey, argued during her 8th of March speech that the domestic violence was one of most common forms of torture in Turkey and that it was however not problematized as much as those acts of violence committed by the state because of its 'private' character. In this same speech, Tekeli proposed a hypothesis about the inner relation between different types of violence. She argued that 'in a society, if violence within family against women and children is extensive and if that society is oblivious to that violence, it is normal to expect the violence among men and the torture implemented by the state actors to be very extensive'. Tekeli established by then a sociological causality between the private and public violence and invited those who prioritized the struggle against the state-induced violence to consider this hypothesis and widen their struggle to include the issue of domestic violence.[3]

In line with the feminist argument about violence as a mechanism for male domination, the very first campaign of the feminist movement in Turkey was the public campaign which took place in 1987 under the motto of 'No to Battering' [Dayağa Hayır!]. The campaign was stimulated by the refusal of a judge to divorce a pregnant woman who had been constantly subjected to spouse violence. The judge had by then justified his decision on the patriarchal grounds that 'you mustn't spare the rod from the back, nor the baby from the stomach, of a woman'.

Tearing apart the acceptability of 'battering' as a normalized heterosexual form of relation was presented by the feminists as one essential means of depriving men from their central tool through which they secure their everyday dominance. Moreover, as the feminists, who were organizing the campaign did not believe that the issue of domestic violence was an issue of backward social mores and/ or ignorance, they also did not believe that educating men in this subject matter would make a change. On the contrary, emancipation was thought to be a matter of women creating their separate political agenda and axis of struggle.[4]

Even the initial attempts of Turkey's social democrats, such as their declaration that they would be establishing a special Ministry for Women's Issues once they got into power, were considered as a suspicious move, a lip service to the demands of a slowly rising women's movement in Turkey (Ovadia, 1987).[5] The state and the political establishment were considered as the main responsible actors for the persistence of male domination, not because they were reflecting the so-called 'backward' social mores and relations but because they were constituting these 'mores' from scratch.

In early 1989, a very sophisticated discussion on gendered violence took place within the context of feminist struggle against the Article 438 of the Criminal Code, which granted a rapist reduced sentence if the victim is a prostitute. The law defined rape as a matter of crime only when the victim is a 'respectable woman'. Hence law assumed a certain notion of chastity and indeed categorized women as respectable and non-respectable. Feminists argued that such a definition encouraged rape. They added that the law de-criminalized rape and rather than punishing the offender it punished the victim. Furthermore, feminist writers underlined the fact that the law criminalized the prostitutes, who were in fact working via state permission and paying income taxes to the state. Thus, asked one press declaration: 'Should not these prostitutes, as every other professional, enjoy state protection?' The declaration openly targeted the gender selectivity of the state, its being a male dominance apparatus which governed women selectively. In the declaration, the judge members of the Constitutional Court who approved the law were openly criticized and argued to be ordinary male oppressors rather than supreme representatives of the rule of law and neutral enforcers of the principle of equality before the law. This declaration took place as part of a broader campaign by then organized under the motto of 'Our bodies belong to us! No to Sexual Harassment!'[6]

During the rise of feminist politics in Turkey, state violence against politically active women did not go unnoticed as well. In 1990, female political prisoners of the 1980 coup d'état started to raise their voice by sending open letters to the feminist magazines. They were protesting the sexual discrimination they faced in the prisons.[7] In January 1990, a feminist group read a public statement in the Sultanahmet district of Istanbul about the bad conditions under which political women prisoners had been trying to survive. In the statement, it is told:

> The state does not only imprison women, but it also imprisons them to their 'femininity'. Women political prisoners are forced to live under unbelievably bad conditions simply because they are women. The very fact that the prison management argues to protect woman's chastity, while in fact women are subject to sexual harassment and even rape during their interrogation periods, is pure hypocrisy.

Later in 1990, a group of women declared that they would like to initiate a group who would work as a 'Group for Monitoring Sexual Harassment during Administrative Processes'. In their press statement, they referred to the case of Saadet Akkaya, who was sexually violated by the police forces, who then annihilated all pertaining evidence; to the case of a Kurdish woman who had to go through a forced sperm test on the grounds that his spouse was a fugitive; to women members of a leftist music group who were subjected to virginity tests; and finally to the women relatives of political detainees who had to go through strip-searches just before their non-contact visits in the Ankara Central Closed Prison. In their statement, it was additionally underlined that doing strip-searches with the help of female police officers did not undo the fact of sexual harassment. The group added, 'the hands of these policewomen are also the hands of the state .... The sexual harassment aimed at discouraging women, humiliating, and shaming them but it does not work. Women are not ashamed of ....' The feminist voices underlined the need to expose the offenders publicly as a tactic of struggle against harassment and as a revolt against the general sexism in society. As a response to the gendered state violence, feminists argued for the need to prioritize violence against women in women's struggle for liberation. They argued that organizing women in this struggle and rising solidarity within the women's movement are a first requirement. Otherwise they believed that even the implementation of CEDAW (The Convention on the Elimination of all

Forms of Discrimination Against Women), which Turkey had ratified in 1985, would be impossible (Öztürk, 1988: 67).

All in all, in the early years of the feminist ascendancy in Turkey violence against women was not conceived as a simple human security issue – neither as a lack of state protection nor as a by-product of the prioritization of state security over everything else. It was conceived as an instrument of the male domination system, which reproduces women's subordination with the help of various instruments including sexual harassment but also the promise of heterosexual love. In many occasions, feminists underlined that the harm done to the individual woman through battering is less the focal point of their struggle than the systemic impact of battering. Naturally, they were not underestimating the individual harms women undergo but rather they were trying to decipher the systemic character of that violence. Therefore, even the individual measures suggested by feminists to women subjected to domestic violence, such as 'going to police and making them write your statement down; going to the justice centre and suiting a file' (Öztürk, 1988: 69), were framed as a political affirmative move for decoding the public character of private relations, for publicizing the private. Actually, 'going to the police' was suggested as an act of encouragement and empowerment in a society where the violence of husbands is normalized even by the battered wives themselves. It was part of the measures to remember women that it is not their marital duty to keep their mouth shut when they are battered. Moreover, these individual measures were devised as tools of the women's liberation movement at large. They were part of that bigger strategy: to reveal the inner contradictions of the abstract notion of equality; to keep a radical pressure from below over the public institutions which are allegedly built on the constitutional equality close. However, as already underlined, different from the exclusive focus of the 2000s on the state as both the ultimate cause of and solution for different sorts of violence – hence the notion of human security – this early era's feminist movement prioritized *the social* as the locus of all sorts of violence, including the state violence, and the cure against it.

Governance feminism and behaviourist interventions in the state

It is possible to argue that in the beginning of 1990s the feminist approach to the state in Turkey inherently dissociated two notions from each other: publicness and anti-statism. The former signified abolishing the protective shield before the private field, politicizing the private and challenging the discriminatory state practices towards women as a step towards women's liberation. The second signalled the need for keeping independence from the state and its corrosive impact, as well as preventing the creation of a public patriarchy or state feminism, whereby the power of the private sphere, hence of the patriarchal family, is replaced by that of the public power.[8] By the late 1990s, however, the feminist movement in Turkey distanced itself from this nuanced position and direction – if not in theory certainly in practice. The lack of popular women's organizations and the limitedness of women's small-scale or group-based organizations created a lacuna that was then partially filled by state feminism (Bora, 1996).[9]

In the 1990s, the state in Turkey was also seeking integration to the expanding global regime of human rights. The globally held developmentalist notion that states cannot develop without improving the living conditions of their women citizens also got some appeal among certain male members of the political establishment in Turkey. Like the early twentieth-century state feminist efforts in the Middle East and North African region, some political forces were conceiving women as indispensable to the 'image of the regime abroad'.[10] Being 'woman-friendly' was an international asset the Turkish Republic has benefited from in the international arena to differentiate itself from other classical patriarchal settings. After the bloody coup d'état of 1980, this strategy continued indeed. A not-less important pushing factor however was the demands of the capitalist market in Turkey for cheap and affordable labour.[11]

These had important implications for Turkey's gender order. The political establishment – at least the centre right and centre left figures – decided to meet the minimum of women's demands for dignity (hence to accord some patriarchal protection to women). This would, according to them, also keep the family institution in Turkey intact, guaranteeing the invisible labour of women at home so that the costs of social reproduction would not augment. The slow but augmenting rise of women's participation into the labour market was on the one hand permitting the capital with cheap 'nimble fingers' but on the other hand it was pushing the need for the state to overtake some of the social reproduction tasks women have fulfilled at the household – about which the neoliberal state was deeply resistant. These three factors – the needs of the capitalist market for cheap and sustainable labour power, the growing necessity for state prestige, and the proletarianization of women – have pushed the state to reconsider its gender selectivities and develop a new era of state feminism in Turkey. The first response was to establish a national machinery to implement certain global decisions in the field of women's rights.

The establishment process of the first national women's machinery in Turkey, *The General Directorate of the Status and Problems of Women* (KSSGM its Turkish abbreviation), following the 1990 Nairobi Conference, however, created a tightrope on which the feminists of Turkey had struggled to walk through. Whereas the establishment of such a public institution at first looked like being into the interests of women in Turkey, the accompanying ethos was very intimidating for the feminists. The political actor behind the establishment of this institution was the first neoliberal-neoconservative party of Turkey, namely the Motherland Party (ANAP). ANAP was trying to reconcile the growing needs of the market economy in Turkey with the social implications of the ascending marketization process. According to the Sixth Development Plan prepared by the State Planning Institute, which also prepared the policy background for the establishment of the KSSGM, the Turkish family structure was on the brink of decomposition because of the 'national and economic necessities women had to participate in working life' (Acuner, 2002: 129).

Hence, whereas the proletarianization of women was conceived as an inevitable necessity of the deepening capitalist relations in Turkey, the results of this process for the reproduction of traditional family structure were feared from. While one group within the neo-conservative political power wanted to further promote this transformation by supporting the individual rights of women, another group prioritized familial unity (Acuner, 2002: 130). The establishment of the KSSGM displayed the relative power of the more conservative constituents of the political power. The law establishing the general directorate mentioned that among many other missions, the directorate must guide the voluntary women's organizations and associations along a 'national outlook' (Milli Görüş, cited in Acuner, 2002: 139).

Although very vague in content and not explicitly defined in the law, the 'national outlook' had a very clear meaning in Turkey's political context: a religious-political movement initiated in the 1970s by Necmettin Erbakan and founded on an anti-Westernist discourse. Thus, although seemingly an advance in the architecture of state in Turkey, the gender selectivities forged by the conservative state bureaucracy and political establishment were demonstrating that the state in fact tried to take under control rather than promote the transformation of gender relations. On top of this, it was obvious that the state aimed to acquire more know-how and to benefit from the gender expertise of the feminists in Turkey. The initial bill, which founded the national machinery after some minor revisions, had stated that the aim of the machinery was 'acquiring knowledge on the activities and researches of the women's studies units of universities' (Kardam and Ertürk, 1999). Indeed, many feminists had by then analysed the establishment of such a public institution as a state practice to bring women back home, to 'lock them into the domestic sphere' (Koçali cited in Acuner, 2002: 141).

Despite the initial resistance to the establishment of such an institution on political and ideological grounds, the operation of the institution in a quasi-legal void and its institutional marginality within the state bureaucracy paradoxically helped some feminists to augment their formative power over the state. Reminiscent of the human security notion, these feminists possessed a strong notion of 'state responsibility towards women', also triggered and supported by the developmentalist ethos in the international women's rights regime of the 1990s (Kardam and Ertürk, 1999).[12]

It is within this general atmosphere that we see the emergence of an altered approach to violence against women in Turkey.

By the late 1990s, one of the founders of The Purple Roof Foundation and an acknowledged feminist lawyer, Canan Arın (1996: 306) defines violence against women as a practice for 'keeping the male dominant order up; ensuring obedience and preserving the power imbalance'. Violence, according to Arın (1996: 307), is one of the most effective ways to oppress women. However, Arın's reference to male dominance or her analysis of dominance is more culturally grounded rather than materially grounded. Arın exemplifies male dominance as the supremacy of male values within a society. Moreover, as a lawyer, she details down the legal philosophy in the Turkish Criminal Code and considers violence from the perspective of human person. Arın (1996: 307) makes the case that the Criminal Code in Turkey contains no specific references to domestic violence. She depicts how it is difficult for women to go to police to give a statement about it. The police accept as given the idea that 'nobody should intervene into the relation between a husband and wife', tells Arın (1996: 307). She adds that the 'leftist' stance of a fifteen-year-old child is even more notable for the police than the issue of domestic violence. Arın tries to exemplify the regular non-caring attitude of the police officers who try to dissuade women and who mostly invite the husband to the police centre to reassure 'the familial unity'. Thus, explains Arın, starts the new round of violence at home and this time even more intensive. This is the cycle of domestic violence where men behave along certain quite common and repetitive patterns: tension, violence, regret, apology, tension, violence.

Arın (1996: 310) believes that it is possible to prevent violence by implementing the principle of gender equality in every field and by showing no tolerance to violence. She gives some examples of 'zero tolerance to violence' policies implemented around the world, and she complains about the lack of political interest in violence against women in Turkey. Different from the late 1980s feminism in Turkey, Arın invites the state and the political power to take active measures against domestic violence. She translates the feminist voice heard during the taboo-breaking public campaign of 'No to Battering' into concrete demands for women's rights.

I would argue that what is lost and gained in this translation does matter to understand the spirit of feminist interventions into the state in the AKP era. What is lost is the feminist argument that restoring equality among men and women is not enough to realize women's liberation since there is a need for a radical societal transformation in the organization of production, social reproduction and in power relations. What is gained is the strategy of pressurizing the public power so that it keeps up its promises, even if these are abstract universals and even if these only foster formal equality. What is lost is the feminist warning that the singular measures that would be individually taken by women against domestic violence are meaningful only and as far as they make part of women's generalized solidarity to enhance women's liberation struggle. What is gained is comprehensive help and support to individual women subjected to violence – so that they can help themselves and know what to do and how to behave in times of aggrieve. What is lost is the feminist insistence that the state is itself an apparatus of and for male dominance and that male domination should be ended through women's own struggle. What is gained is the determination that men – either at home or in the state – can change their conduct if political power has egalitarian policies against domestic violence. The totality of these changes points out the birth of governance feminism in Turkey.

By governance feminism, I do mostly refer to the type of feminism which primarily aims to make a change in the state's attitude towards its women citizens, 'to conduct the conduct of men in the state' (Halley, Kotiswaran, Rebouché and Shamir, 2018). But I differentiate myself here from those feminist researchers working in the field of critical criminology studies and who tend to use governance feminism solely as a pejorative term to denote the full co-optation of the feminist project by the political establishment. In these debates, which mostly focus on the cases of human trafficking and prostitution, governance feminists are portrayed as liberal feminists who foster the administrative and therefore authoritarian capacity of the state by asking further criminal sanctions and penal measures against the women's rights offenders (Amar, 2011; Bernstein, 2012). In a country, like Turkey, where the general approach is to accord impunity to the offenders of violence against women and where the non-enforcement of the law is the rule rather than exception, accusing governance feminists with upgrading the carceral policies of the neoliberal state does not do justice to the political reality.

I rather want to concentrate on behaviourism as the *differentia specifica* of governance feminism in Turkey, the insistence on making a positive change in the *conduct of men* within the state such as police officers, religious leaders [*imams*], male teachers and judges vis-à-vis women citizens. Moreover, I propose to analyse the state vision of the governance feminism in Turkey, with the help of a state analogy pertaining to the eminent French sociologist Pierre Bourdieu, who depicted the modern state as a bureaucratic organization constituted by a strict division of labour between the welfare-oriented and the coercion-oriented apparatuses. The former are called as the 'Left hand' or feminine part of the state and the latter as the 'Right hand' or the masculine part of the state (Wacquant, 2010). This conception of the modern bourgeois state form is a good conceptual catch for understanding the state vision of the governance feminists, who with the help of such a dualist vision have cast-off the Right hand of the state, what it does and why it does, and concentrated on its Left hand.

The First Congress of Women's Shelters, which took place in 1998 with the purpose of bringing together various women's groups and organizations struggling against violence against women in Turkey, openly demonstrates the predicaments the feminists faced vis-à-vis the issue of working in and against the state. In her opening speech to the First Congress of Women's Shelters in 1998, Canan Arın (Mor Çatı Kolektifi, 2002: 34) asserts that the principal agent responsible for women's security is and should be the state and therefore women's movement should not forget to pressurize the state and make it acknowledge/comprehend its role in securing women's safety. Arın (Mor Çatı Kolektifi, 2002: 57) adds that the police organization in Turkey perceives itself as the owner of state. 'Therefore', she tells, 'one of the most important things that the police should comprehend is that within the context of human rights each [woman] in this room has as much right over the state as the police. Their duty is to prevent violence, without discrimination between men and women, not to create violence.

During the Congress, Nazik Işık (Mor Çatı Kolektifi, 2002: 70–1) proposes to widen the debate on state and the discussion on the best position feminists should take vis-à-vis the state. She says that not only the national machinery responsible for women and some other women-specific institutions within the state but the whole state should be kept responsible for. In other words, she argues that the entirety of women's demands, including 'the right to walk freely at night in illuminated streets', is an issue that the state should tackle with. Işık (Mor Çatı Kolektifi, 2002: 72) especially stresses the importance of pushing the state to reconsider its housing policy so that women who are economically dependent can also dare to face the post-divorce impoverishment.

In this exclusive focus on the role of the state, the growing fatigue and the feeling of isolation among the women's organizations were also important. In other words, whereas valuable in the short-term, the NGO'ization process during the 1990s, whereby the fight against violence against women became restricted to a struggle for women's special needs, demonstrated the limits of singular women's organizations in dealing with the needs of women. Hence, feminists started to ask and look for a more structured commitment on the part of the state.

Moreover, the difficulties that the feminist movement faced in this struggle – such as the fatigue and isolation – were also not sufficiently dealt with, keeping the agent of effective struggle against gendered violence non-defined or ill-defined – who should be the agent of change in the issue of violence against women?: the feminists, the state and/or grassroots women's organizations?

This lack of engagement with the question of agency was also visible in the final declaration of the 1998 Congress, where specific measures were suggested in the struggle to end violence against women. The proposed measures mainly relied on a welfarist notion of public power, where the state was conceived as a social state and women's protection as a duty of the left hand of the state. These measures, however, by keeping the agent of change anonymous and the demands prescriptive – as there was an exclusive concentration on the question of 'what the state should do?' – summoned the state to expand its stake in this matter rather than calling in for a broader women's movement to transform and challenge the state.

Thus, even if not used as a clearly stated concept, governance feminists of Turkey ended by the late 1990s in the notion of 'human security'. Despite the persistence on raising the 'women's standpoint', the feminist struggle against violence conceived as a systemic feature of male dominance got reduced to a focus on individual women and individual men, making a change in the lives of these individual women and in the conduct of those individual men.[13] The state paradox – asking for protection against men from the masculine state – was totally lost from sight and the notion of state responsibility started to be used outside the holistic framework of a women's liberation perspective.

Moreover, despite the early link established between the state violence and the violence experienced in the private sphere, the campaigns and activities of Turkey's women's movement in the 1990s did rarely display such a holistic perspective and the discussions and activities on state-induced violence, and violence against women got separated. This does not mean that the feminists, including the governance feminists, kept silent on the issue of gendered state violence but rather the conceptualization(s) of violence and the struggle against it was compartmentalized.

Training the 'men in the state': Feminist-tutors and police trainees

Once the feminist movement formulized its concrete demands in the beginning of 1990s regarding the issue of violence against women, the police centres became of central importance to these demands.[14] They were the first contact points for many women who were seeking refuge from domestic violence. Therefore, many women's organizations, in the leadership of the Purple Roof and the Women's Solidarity Foundations, started to consider the police services from the perspective of women who face violence at home. Feminists considered that women needed intermediate/guiding services so that they could reach women's shelters when they need. Police was one of the most important intermediaries; and therefore, there should have been a kind of awareness within the police to the issue of domestic violence. Police should be trained to help these women instead of sending them back home to sustain the so-called familial unity. In 1997, the Purple Roof Foundation collected 10,000 signatures to make an application to the General Directorate for Women's Status (KSSGM) with respect to police services. These demands found considerable echo in the KSSGM, which referred this application to the Ministry of Interior in the same year. In the application, the following grievances were listed:

1. The women's complaints are not put into process under the pretext of protecting the family.
2. The women subjected to violence are not directed to hospital for a health check under the same pretext.
3. Because of these *misconducts*, not only the aggressors are accorded impunity but also the women are victimized for a second time. (italics added)

Again in 1998, the KSSGM prepared a National Action Plan in coordination with different women's organizations. In the plan, the police training was classified within the training planned to be given to a plethora of other public officers including health officers, teachers, social service experts, psychologists etc. The main aim was to teach the police officers how to put a complaint about domestic violence into operation. Nazik Işık (1999), in her presentation entitled as 'The State and Problems of Domestic Violence Related to Police Services in Turkey', which she delivered in 1999 during a general Symposium on Police Education organized by the Police Academy, mainly lists two police misconducts that should be rectified: 'women cannot receive enough attention in the police centres when they go to make complaints'; and 'whenever women receive attention, the nature of this attention [police behaviours that are not citizen-friendly] works against women who could otherwise might have benefited from their right [for protection] and available facilities'.

Işık (1999) also makes some points about the reasons that impel police forces to stay inactive or irresponsible in the field of domestic violence. She basically argues that the police in Turkey do not consider domestic violence as a matter within the scope of their activity field and authority. This, according to Işık, is rooted in the lack of preventive policing philosophy and in the underdeveloped public service functions of the police organization in Turkey. Işık also mentions that policing as a job that involves force/violence is by itself not favourable for perceiving domestic violence as a problem. These points in fact have resonated very well with the initial arguments of the reformist police cadres within the TNP about replacing the force-centred policing with a policing redesigned as a popular service and as a counselling mechanism.

What differentiates, however, Işık's (1999) emphasis on the role of police from the arguments of the reformist police cadres is her general political framework, namely the vision of the state that animates her political stance and feminist advocacy. The following good governance benchmarks used by Işık (1999) in her presentation show how the inherent assumptions on the nature of (the imaginary) state as a social/welfare state bear their mark upon the feminist movement's approach to public power in Turkey: the expertise fields of the organization should include domestic violence; the police stations should accommodate social service professionals and police experts other than rank-and-file police officers. Second, Işık (1999) underlines an important factor that motivates the police to *act*: 'honour'. Accordingly, the police take a more spurting initiative to guide the women to the women's shelters when the complaints are related to cases of 'incest; forced prostitution (by close family members), etc'. However, adds Işık, police should also be trained in all matters pertaining to the violence against women and the training should spur their sensibility to the phenomenon of 'violence' in general.

Despite all emphasis on good behaviour and correct conduct, like is the case with every type of governance feminism, arguing that the feminist interest in the cultivation of a responsible public power for women who seek refuge from domestic violence contributes in the making of a carceral state in Turkey would be incorrect. Although the strategic selectivities of the state have been from the beginning conducive to internalize these inputs so as to empower the state's patriarchal logic – that is, to update the patriarchal protection so that the social reproduction system of Turkey's dependence on women smoothly continues – the feminists actually desired the installation of their ideas into the public power with a certain notion of public good in mind.

As one of the few pioneers who initiated the project of police trainings to improve the agency of police in the prevention of violence against women, Nazik Işık elucidates that her active interest in this struggle to prevent violence against women started just after the campaign of 'No to Battering' in the late 1980s, when as a small group of women they asked the following question: 'But where can they [the women who face violence at home] resort to?' (Işık, 2019).

Nazik Işık tells that when first brought to the fore, the idea of building some counselling/protective centres for women victims of violence was devised as a social service – and some feminists were not interested in and in fact critical of the idea. Işık perceives no paradox in the feminist drive to work in and with the state. Not because she is statist, but because she says, 'to work with the state is to ask for restoring equality before the law' (Işık, 2019). She thinks that involving the state in the struggle against domestic violence is in fact no different than the feminist campaigns pursued to make changes in the Civil Law and in the Criminal Code (see the equal rights feminism below). Protection, for Işık, is in fact the basis of any state. The state, she says, 'should protect me and my health even if I come to this country as a visitor' (Işık, 2019).

Hence, therefore, I would argue that the project of police trainings was framed by the feminists taking part in the project with reference to the image of a bourgeois modern state, whose monopoly of violence is thought to be the guarantee of the protection of each and every citizen living within its borders, hence a public good.

On the other hand, the fact that many of these police trainings were realized during the AKP era and that the feminists collaborated with the reformist police cadres who were an essential clique within the ruling bloc cannot be ruled out of the discussion on governance feminism. Indeed, one of the trainers, İlknur Üstün (2019), explained that the project was influential in making a change in the state conduct and told the following anecdote: 'The Police Chief [responsible from the police trainings in Diyarbakir] told [our feminist friend] that there won't be peace [making reference to peace in the Kurdish issue] as long as the violence against women does not stop.' Thus, adds Üstün, this shows that 'we were able to change some people.' Üstün implied that the training had an impact of widening the perspective of the police concerning the issue of violence. Thus, the police organization started to concentrate on the issue of violence not exclusively from the perspective of the state and only when violence targeted the state but rather from the perspective of human beings and their right to be protected. However, a close reading of the moralist policing project of the reformist cadres demonstrates that the populist gender selectivities turned this collaboration into a false collaboration. Reformist police cadres conceived mainstreaming of the feminist knowledge on violence against women as a way of governing through gender (see Chapter 2 'Moralist Philosophy of Police Reform').

Although this process shows that feminists in Turkey had a clear project of state in mind and found the political opportunity at least to put their foot within the state architecture to install some feminist ideas, the human security priority prevented them from fruitfully asking the following question: 'What happens to feminist knowledge when it enters mainstream organizational contexts?' (Prügl, 2011). This question is qualitatively different from the dichotomist problematization of the feminist struggle, whether to be 'in or against the state', which has been present in some feminist discussions on 'what is to be done with the state?' in Turkey (Akkaya and Demir, 2005; Bora, 2005).

Nazik Işık (2019), a proponent of working in the state and with the state, also warns against the risk of co-optation by the state and the risk of losing one's own intellectual independence. However, her critical distance, as well as the other feminists who have been critical of working in the state and with the state, has so far framed the risk as a risk of starting to think like the state. And yet, the centaur state has had another strategy, different from the perennial strategy of co-opting social forces through corporatist structures. That strategy is rather to learn how to behave from these social forces to better govern and to ameliorate the conduct of the men in the state and the know-how to govern through gender.

The reformist police cadres aimed at developing their 'reflex for protection' and attenuating their classical conditioning for 'public order policing' (Bayhan and Vural, 2013: 274–5). Işık also attests to this novelty in the state strategies and in the depth of the ideological fissure between the state led by the AKP and the feminist movement. She tells:

> What is more crucial than these debates [on feminists' relations with the state] are the conflicts today we have with the autocratic administration under the leadership of Recep Tayyip Erdoğan. As socialists back in history, we also had

serious clashes with the state … The women's organisations were dissolved as part of a bigger conflict within the state [Işık refers to the early Republican Era] … All the demands back then were demands in parallel with the modernisation process. There has never been such an ideological conflict. This is the first time that we go through such a period. The state today also fights against violence against women … Yet, this is made of love for the victim … not for the sake of protecting women.

(Işık, 2019)

It is therefore possible to derive from the experiences of governance feminism that their referential political horizon has been foundationally different from that of the reformist state cadres. Indeed, Işık says, 'in our [the feminist movement] past, there has not been this kind of a conflict'. Her words, for me, basically refer to the struggles of the feminist movement against and in the state before the authoritarian turn in the AKP era and underlines that there has been a qualitative difference between the past and the present in terms of the state form they are faced with.

All in all, it would be fair to say that the feminists' project to change the conduct of the men in the state as a method of bringing the state image (bourgeois state based on equal citizenship) and the state practice (adopt a women's rights perspective to the issue of violence) closer to each other has hit against the walls of a centaur state-in-the-making.

Equal rights feminism and legal interventions in the state

Equal rights feminism like governance feminism works with a vision of state that tacitly makes a difference between the 'left hand of the state' and the 'right hand of the state' to advance its cause of procuring more of the state legal apparatus for women's sake. It primarily aims at making the state authority recognize women as free and equal individuals before conceiving them with reference to their ascribed social roles, for example, mothers, sisters, daughters. When and if it has to focus on the 'right hand of the state', it also does with reference to an individual rights perspective, pushing the state to criminalize all forms of state-induced gendered violence causing harm to the dignity of individual women. In that sense, it tries to complete the 'bourgeois revolution of women' in Turkey.

As a strategy and form of intervention in the state, it focuses first on making progressive legislation as an essential means for appropriating state legal authority so that it works for women's interests and second on deactivating some forms of legal authority that works against women's interests. Nevertheless, despite the tremendous victory it has especially achieved through pro-gender equality changes made in the Criminal Law in 2004, the perspective of using the legal authority of the state to change the patriarchal practices in society failed to convince 'the men in the state' who have disingenuously argued – as in the case of reformist police cadres – that the social question in Turkey does not allow it.

In 2002, different women's and LGBTI+ organizations came together to establish a Platform for the Reform of the Turkish Criminal Code and founded the Women's Working Group on the Penal Code. The Platform published 'the Brochure of the Turkish Criminal Law from Women's Perspective' and organized an effective public campaign to sustain the cause. The campaigners lobbied, established supportive contacts in the Parliament and in the mainstream media, and exerted pressure on the Minister of Justice and on the head of Justice Commission in the Parliament, who were reluctant in the first place to make the proposed pro-gender equality amendments in the Criminal Code (İlkkaracan, 2007).

The Code was of core importance to fight against violence against women as it covered crucial issues such as 'honour crimes', forced marriages, sexual harassment, police violence under custody etc. The feminist lawyers who led the Platform's advocacy for a New Criminal Code also wanted to remove the existence of subjective terms such as 'consent to rape and abuse' from the Code, widening the definition of rape and sexual violence to include objects such as police truncheons, and removing the impunity (the reduced punishments) in the cases of honour crimes and the protective shield provided to the offenders of rape when they marry the victim. All these measures were in fact pushing the state to accept that women are not properties of their husbands, fathers and the society as such. Plus, the measures were seeking to lessen the culturalization of law and to prohibit the legitimation of violence against women under the rubric of social norms such as honour.

The existing Code was extremely limited in its conception of violence and archaic in its significance for the individuals. The spirit of the code concerning the crimes against women was very patriarchal, in the sense that it prioritized the reproduction of gender order under the pretext of preserving public morality. It was sticking to the patriarchal mode of gender valorization, according to which women's bodily integrity, physical and psychological well-being were valorized much less than men's – even if men were rapists. In other words, the patriarchal social values that grant men greater value in their roles as husbands, fathers, brothers and sons were considered in the existing Code as the legitimate threshold according to which the punishment should be designed.

It is therefore not surprising to see that many governmental figures including the conservative jurisprudence resisted to the feminist movement with the help of a similar patriarchal perspective – signed by class, as well. During the public discussions on the draft Law and on the reforms demanded by the women's organizations, the then chief consultant to the Minister of Justice professor Doğan Soyaslan argued against the proposed changes on the basis of the argument that they were against the 'realities of Turkey', echoing also other members of the government who were anxious about disrespecting 'the values of the Turkish society'. Soyaslan defended for example the Code's penal philosophy of according immunity to rapists when victims marry them by asserting that this in fact shows sensitivity 'to the social reality young women from lower classes with little education are facing in everyday life'. According to this logic, the young women can only survive the patriarchal terror if they marry their assailant. He indeed underlined that the article on the conditional amnesty to the rapists has had no relevance for women from upper classes, for example 'like his daughter' (İlkkaracan, 2007: 18). This stance of Soyaslan – although could not prevent the feminist revisions successfully brought in the Criminal Code by 2004 – continues today determining the gender selectivities of the state and explaining the huge gap between the legal changes and their poor enforcement in practice.[15] But before going on with what the intervention of equal rights feminism signified for the state form and state power in Turkey, I would like to touch upon two precursor feminist struggles, without which the success of the penal code reforms apparently would be impossible.

Honour killings: The late 1990s and early 2000s in Turkey were also home to widespread discussions on the so-called honour crimes. Many women have been killed in Turkey by their close families under the pretext that they did not protect the honour of the family – by transgressing the social rules concerning women's sexuality. But even the women who are raped by their male family members have been victims of customs dictating the 'erasure' of the crime by killing women. The Criminal Code was permissive of these so-called customs and many perpetrators were avoiding severe punishments by benefiting from the articles of the Code, such as the article on 'unjust provocations', which was foreseeing reductions in punishment in cases of customary killings. One of the reasons that were pushing the state in Turkey to accord such a permissive attitude towards 'honour killings' was also the political dependency of the state on the ethnic tribes – which have been strictly organized over kin-based patriarchal and hierarchical groups regulating social relations of appropriation and dispossession in the South-eastern Turkey – to administer the territories home to Kurdish people while fighting against the Kurdish liberation movement.

Kurdish feminists vigorously demonstrated how the state in Turkey benefited from the sustenance of the patriarchal relations in the region to govern the Kurdish population. Their standpoint, thus, underlined how in fact gender has become a form of domination in the South-eastern Turkey, facilitating the grip of the state over the Kurdish dissidents. Therefore, feminists asserted to perceive the honour crimes as political crimes rather than coding them as 'crimes related to the backward cultural habits', a dominant stereotyping public perspective. Hence, feminists were accusing the state with complicity in the so-called honour crimes and trying to show that honour is in fact the pretext for the under-criminalization of male criminals (Ertürk, 2015).

Beside their demands for deterrent forms of punishment, feminists were also asking for the implementation of preventative measures against the 'honour crimes'. The horrendous case of Güldünya Tören precipitated the feminist movement in 2004 to ask for active state responsibility and protection of the women. Güldünya, raped by one of her relatives, was seriously injured by his own brothers under the pretext of 'honour' but luckily brought to the hospital alive. Yet, his brothers found and killed her in the hospital on 1 March 2004. Not only feminists but a broad public opinion questioned the responsibility of the state and especially of the police in this murder. Yet, in response to allegations against the Istanbul Police Directorate, the head of the Directorate, Celalettin Cerrah, declared that the 'police had no omission in this crime' (Demir, 2004).

Women's organizations and feminists proceeded with different campaigns to pressurize the state to actively enforce the laws and provide women with protection to enjoy their citizenship rights. The campaign organized under the title of 'We want both nights and streets' was one such moment, when women from different organizations acting through the Platform against Violence against Women went on the streets in 2005 and asked 'the police to do their job immediately' (Demir, 2005).

Gendered state violence: After years of suffocating state suppression of political dissent in the aftermath of the 1980 coup d'état, 1990s saw a new wave of non-parliamentary street-based political opposition in Turkey. The neoliberal-neoconservative project of the post-coup government led by the Anavatan Party (ANAP) collapsed. Mass discontent became pervasive and the ensuing political crisis, accompanied by an economic crisis, ended in an organic crisis of the state (Önder, 1998). As a result, state violence and gendered state violence had become a daily reality in the Kurdish-populated regions of Turkey, and in the working-class and poor Alevi neighbourhoods of the big cities, especially in Istanbul.

The counter-insurgency methods of the state in 1990s included rape, torture and killings. Female body, and especially politically active women's bodies, became special targets for all sort of security personnel. Women were abducted, raped and raped through use of police truncheons. The bodies of guerrilla women, or of any other women affiliated by these guerrilla women such as the sisters, were mutilated. Women, whether politically active or not, were subject to chastity tests when they were taken under custody. Women's bodies were targeted to send a terrifying message to other women, especially to those young women who were joining the PKK in the 1990s and/or the Kurdish political movement in general. Women were sexually violated to force them to confess. The abused bodies of women became instruments of war to degrade the masculinity of the enemy warriors and/or to incite the patriarchal norms of the enemy group such as 'honour'.

During the second half of the 1990s, politically active women started to voice the violent experiences they went through to seek justice. The very fact that these women decided to speak up for themselves and to share their stories with the public was itself an immediate consequence of women's relative empowerment in Turkey thanks to the militancy of the feminist movement.

In the 1990s, many politically active women who were not necessarily identifying themselves as feminists were insistently pointing out that the state violence against politically active women was itself a state policy, a strategic policy to force women to go back home. They were arguing, for example, that even if rape was a torture method used against both women and men, women's vulnerability to state-induced sexual violence differed from that of men. Non-feminist leftist women were framing state violence as an attack against women's liberation. One of the leftist women who went to hunger strike during the protests against the F-type isolation prisons in late 1990s, Berna Ünsal, said, 'It is thanks to the women's popular movement, and by saluting it in my imagination that I started my hunger strike' (Demir, 2001b).

In January 2000, the Legal Support Office against Sexual Harassment and Rape under Custody and a group of women organized under the name of 'Women Worker's Union' initiated a public campaign against sexual harassment and rape under custody. Since late 1997, the Legal Support Office had already been giving legal aid and helping women who were sexually abused and/or violated by police. Overall, 85 per cent of the women who actively asked for help from the Office were politically accused women. The campaign received support from different women's organizations including the Purple Roof Foundation.

Eren Keskin, the feminist lawyer who led the project against sexual violence under custody, pointed out to a great omission in the Criminal Code of Turkey. The sexualized violence against women was not defined in the Code as a crime against human person (Koçali, 2000). She explained that the topic of sexual violence was taken care of under the heading of crimes against public morality and family. Furthermore, the wording of the Code had limited the sexual violence to harassment and the rape to aggression by use of male genitals. Keskin additionally underlined that the prosecutors did never put complaints of sexual violence in process.

The women activists of the campaign against sexual violence under custody maintained that 'the perpetrator is the state itself' (Koçali, 2000). This position was important to prevent the social and political tendency to explain these crimes as cases of rotten apples, hence as crimes committed by this or that corrupt police officer. Moreover, the politically active women who were subject to sexual violence under Custody and who decided to struggle against sexual violence as a form of state torture argued that sexual violence and the threat of it were used by the state against the revolutionary and socialist women because 'being a woman' was the most vulnerable part of these women – who despite their political consciousness were not immune to the corrosive impact of the traditional gender norms. They argued:

> The reason why rape created deep wounds even for socialist women [who are very aware of the fact that state violence and torture are everyday realities for revolutionaries and the people in the opposition] is the shaping impact of social values …. Even if they are revolutionaries, they sustain the traditional feminine roles without being cognizant of it. They ignore it. They silence it. In the absence of a conscious change and/or transformation, when subjected to certain circumstances [such as rape under custody], all these suppressed values, roles and identities resurface and passivize women … State is the biggest apparatus of male domination. Rape and torture are instruments of the state.[16]
>
> (Bu Süreçten Hepimiz Değişerek Çıktık, 2000: 17)

As previously stated, these two precursor struggles (the struggles against the 'honour crimes' and the gendered state crimes) cumulatively contributed in the success of the feminist-led Campaign for Reform in the Turkish Criminal Law. On 26 September 2004, the new Law got accepted in the Parliament. The changes in the Criminal Code confirmed a historical change: the sexual crimes are defined under the title of crimes against human person; the definition of rape is expanded, and the impunity provided to the offender of rape crime over marriage is removed. Moreover, rape within marriage became a crime. The public officers found guilty of torture and sexual violence during the torture would be punished twice, because of committing crimes of torture and crimes of sexual violence. Revolutionary-wise, domestic violence is brought under the title of torture crimes. The sentence reductions which were granted to customary killings are annulled.

It is possible to portray these changes as revolutionary and assert that the formal equality promised by the bourgeois state form became first time a reality for women. Nevertheless, the changes in the legal apparatus of the state, in the very form of the state, have since then failed to activate the state power to challenge the patriarchal practices that affect women in everyday life (Ertürk, 2015). In other words, as also experienced in many other cases of equal rights intervention to the formation of state rules, writing into law 'counter-hegemonic rules' (Prügl, 2009) does not necessarily help to fight the gender inequalities in social relations. Although the political establishment gave some compromises and accepted the counter-hegemonic feminist revisions, also under the pressurizing need for securing broader legitimation for the 'right-hand of the state', the revisions were hardly any internalized by the security apparatus. The resistance to internalization was due to the gender selectivities of the state in Turkey, the patriarchal-cum-capitalist fixation of the security bureaucracy that the social question in Turkey necessitates under-criminalization of men.

Peace feminism and anti-militarist feminist interventions in the state

In the late 1990s and early 2000s, about 135 young women committed suicide in the Batman province of Turkey. Batman, a Kurdish populated city, which was place to the most atrocious forms of state violence during the war with the PKK, and where fundamentalist and armed religious organizations also took refuge, became the graveyard of women who committed suicide or were forced to do so. Kurdish feminists argued for the link between these suicides and the post-war trauma and the socio-political conditions of the city. They argued that the mores or traditions which prevail in the Kurdish-populated regions of Turkey and among Kurdish population are not the only reasons behind these suicides and other 'honour killings', commonly deemed to represent the 'backward and feudal culture of the region'.

It was argued that because of the war and state's colonial methods in the region, the natural social development was hampered, and the society got more and more inward-looking. They added that this prevented the individual development of women as it resulted in the intense use of gender-based social controls. Plus, it was argued that after the capture of the PKK leader Abdullah Öcalan in 1999, which ended the war for about a half decade, women had also lost their chance to break away from social controls by joining the guerrilla forces. Accordingly, the status of women as private properties of men and of the society at large did not change but even got restored. Moreover, many women who were subject to domestic violence in the region were not essentially silenced due to their lack of education and/or normalization of everyday domestic violence but also and mostly because they were unwilling to air their grievances to an already violent state. In other words, Kurdish women were caught in a double fire: domestic and state violence at once, intertwined and co-constituting. The experience of Kurdish women was, therefore, according to the Kurdish feminists, differing from women in general, despite being subjected to a similar patriarchal oppression.

In Turkey, anti-militarist feminism is born to such a background with the aim of not only revealing the gendered consequences of war but also pointing out the controversial results of the war for Kurdish women, as they were not only victims but also active subjects who empowered themselves under the duress of the political conditions (Çağlayan, 2013). It also aims at the socialization of the peace demand because, according to the anti-militarist feminists, state violence continues in the Kurdish-populated regions of Turkey due to the lack of a society-wide anti-war stance. In short, anti-militarist feminism challenges the rules of identity endorsed by the state on three grounds:

First, it underlines the importance of women's standpoint. According to this perspective, those who are marginalized in the society do possess the most genuine insight about the system of oppression that binds them. When applied to the case of Kurdish women, this signifies that despite all cruelties, conditions of war helped them to obtain a special standpoint, from where they generate resistance. Accordingly, Kurdish women have been successful in refusing all nationalist and militarist sacralizations (e.g. fighting in order to protect the 'mother' nation) that tie them down to the patriarchal system and have started to become the agent of change in society (Günay, 2015: 177).

Second, it underlines the importance of gender difference. According to this perspective, women are peaceful creatures. Their peaceful nature is also their most important tool of resistance against the state. For the state is by nature a masculine and militarist construct. The participation of women in general – not only of the Kurdish women – to the politics of peace-building in Turkey is devised as a vital necessity since it is argued, 'women are peaceful also due to their nature' contrary to the masculine nature of the *raison d'état* (Günay, 2015: 179). Anti-militarist feminism underlines the fear of the political establishment and/or of the state from Kurdish women.

Third, it underlines the need to socialize the demand of peace. From the perspective of an anti-militarist feminism, the triple ideologies of nationalism, militarism and patriarchy constitute the main impediment before the rise of an extended anti-war women's movement in western Turkey. Despite their loss of children due to war, women of deceased soldiers are construed as 'martyr mothers', a social status that in turn locks them within the boundaries of this triple (Çağlayan, 2013). On the other hand, it is also argued that it is not impossible to build a women's movement that could and would bring and keep peace in Turkey, because women are more prone to choose peace over militarization.

In practical terms, anti-militarist feminism problematizes the gendered outcomes of the masculine state practices and asks for the inclusion of women into the peace-building process in Turkey. They try to create a 'better subject position' (Prügl, 2009) for (Kurdish) women, by concern of being left outside of the power equations between the state and other interlocutors of conflict, such as the PKK.

Practical demands of the anti-militarist feminism: During the peace/resolution process conducted by the AKP governments with the stated aim of solving the 'Kurdish Issue' of the Turkish Republic, many leftist, feminist women members of the Confederation of Public Employees' Union (KESK) were taken under custody. Some of them were also known to be active in the ranks of the Kurdish political movement. Although these women were not the only targets of the state-led oppression on KESK and many other male unionists were also detained, the feminist movement incisively evaluated this state practice act as a form of gendered state violence. They argued that this was purposely done to intimidate the women activists and to evacuate them from the public sphere (see also Chapter 2, 'Moralist Philosophy of Police Reform').

In August 2009, a group composed of individual feminists and different women's organizations protested the detention of the women trade unionists. In the close aftermath of this event, a new platform was established: the Women's Initiative for Peace (Barış için Kadın Girişimi). The main outcry of the Platform members was 'We [women] do exist!'. They principally argued that the peace should not be contracted between and only among men. Not only the arrests of women unionists but other state practices such as the establishment of the state-sponsored 'Committee of Wise Men' in 2013 composed of sixty-three popular and/or status-holding figures, majority of whom were male – so that they do spread the agenda of peace within the society – were denounced to be non-acceptable. According to the Platform, the Committee included only twelve women out of whom nearly none possessed a 'woman's standpoint'.

The first declaration of the Women's Initiative for Peace was published in late October 2009. *The Women's Initiative for Peace* underlined that they were neither an NGO nor a think-tank. They argued: 'We do politics for women and for peace. We are on the side of women' (Barış İçin Kadın Girişimi, 2013a). The Initiative put into front the idea that 'to be a woman under conditions of war is one of the most difficult positions for a woman ever to live under'. The declaration proposed specific measures that should be taken during the peace process including the 'dismantlement of the gendered, militarist and chauvinistic organizations' and 'the exposure of all war crimes committed against women and of the gendered face of the war'. The proposed measures also included 'trying the war criminals', 'freeing all jailed women' and 'putting an end to violent state operations'. Besides, the platform argued that the crimes of sexual harassment and rape should be considered as 'crimes against women'.

Like the governance and equal rights feminisms' engagements with the state, the *Women's Initiative for Peace*'s has desired to transform the state form, that is, the rule formations the state endorses in Turkey. However rather than appropriating the state apparatus like in the case of governance feminism or pushing for 'counter-hegemonic' codification like in the case of equal rights feminism; anti-militarist feminists have specifically focused on challenging the gendered identity of state practices. They have associated the state and political power with hegemonic militarist masculinity. For peace feminism, the state in Turkey and its security apparatuses represent the side of death, whereas women do represent the side of life.

The Initiative realized several visits to the South-eastern Turkey. During those visits, it was observed that the securitization policy of the state in those regions, which was 'paradoxically' accompanying the stated resolution process, made everyday life unbearable for women. It is stated that women complained from the heavy presence of security personnel in their hometowns. Accordingly, police forces were so everywhere that 'they [women] would even hesitate to get out and hang their washes' (Aşan, Uncu and Kutluata, 2014).

This breakdown of everyday life by the state has been conceptualized as an assault against the human security of women. One of the academician participants of the *Women's Initiative for Peace* Nükhet Sirman asserted that 'we [the feminists and women's organizations] should replace the approaches that prioritize state security with those that promote life' (Aşan, Uncu and Kutluata, 2014).

The growing presence of the state security forces in the Kurdish populated regions of Turkey, accompanied by the building of new military-style policing centres [known as *Kalekol* in Turkish], fostered the concerns of the *Women's Initiative for Peace* about the gendered impacts of this militarization. In a public statement, the Initiative presented its impressions after having visited those regions where Kalekols have been built. In this short document, the Initiative underlined the contradictions in the state policy of peace with the PKK and argued that

> the number of troops in the region augments. Kalekols mean lots of men who take everywhere under close surveillance. It is also because of this [surveillant male eyes] that women do not want them, and they are incredibly determined not to allow the construction of such structures. The people of Lice are under the impression that the state prepares itself for a war. Women resolutely act like shields between the region's youth and the soldiers.
>
> (Barış İçin Kadınlar Girişimi, 2014)

Hence, the declaration acknowledged the agential power of the Kurdish women who resisted the process and saw their active resistance as the only guarantee for these women to go out to the public space. Nükhet Sirman argued that 'women have been for years despised on the grounds that they conduct a politics of powerlessness but actually they speak the language of everyday life' ("Bakan Atalay Kürt Açılımını Kadınlara Sorsun", 2009).

The means of anti-militarist feminism: It is fair to say peace feminism continues the debates of the late 1990s on the nature of state violence and its gendered nature in the Kurdish-populated regions of Turkey. However, different from the late 1990s, it reformulates these debates by deploying the sterile and essentialist grammar of the post-liberal peace—building and SSR that treats 'women and children' as the most vulnerable sectors of the conflict and post-conflict processes. Thus, there emerges a hybrid stance, radical in its conception of the gendered nature of the state but more mainstream in the formulation of political tactics and demands. The reference to the UN Security Resolution 1325 eviscerates the radical feminist precedents from peace feminism and reignites the state that is found guilty of militarist sexism, to intervene on behalf of women. The existing statecraft and apparatus become the protagonists, who are asked to save the women. Let me briefly go over these arguments.

The Initiative proposes the UNSCR 1325[17] as a facilitator to intervene in the gendered outcomes of the war between the Turkish state and the PKK and to pressurize the government to make the necessary 'human security reforms' in order 'to guarantee the security of Kurdish women', 'to reveal the war crimes and punish the criminals' and 'to compensate women's losses due to war and to pursue gender equality policies so as to empower women' (Barış İçin Kadın Girişimi, 2013a). The Platform warns the AKP that the stated plan to rebuild state authority in the war-torn geographies of Turkey cannot be successful if it does not include women and women's separate concerns and needs. In the 'Women Take Active Place in the Peace Process' Conference, which convened on 4 May 2013 in Istanbul, the final resolution of the Conference reasoned that Turkey is one of the signatory countries of the UN Security Council Resolution 1325 and therefore should develop a 'national plan' accordingly (Barış İçin Kadın Girişimi, 2013b).

The Platform has also contacted guerrilla women. The members of the Initiative report that they informed the *Koma Jinen Bilind* (KJB), an umbrella organization for women involved in the Kurdish liberation movement, – about the UN Security Council Resolution 1325, as a means to ascertain women's qualified and equal participation in the peace negotiation process. The Initiative recognizes the hesitations of the guerrilla women about the resolution process as for these women laying down the arms without a significant change in the dominant gender order in the region could also mean a process of dis-empowerment. The Initiative thus argues that the state has the responsibility to protect those women.

Apparently, the sterilization and depoliticization of the radical feminist project is also detected by the guerrilla women. In the short-written account of the meeting the Women's Peace Initiative did with the Koman Jinan Blind (KJB), the guerrilla women are reported to say that their gender politics is different from feminism as this latter, according the them, ended up by being accommodated to the existing system and could not go beyond the horizon set by the Western-centred democracy and the limits of the patriarchy (Candan, Filiz and Kamile, 2013). The guerrilla women are also reported to say that to reach gender emancipation, one should go beyond the structural limits of a nation-state.

The state vision of peace feminism: Despite important contributions in the analysis of the continuities in the gendered state violence in Turkey, the feminists involved in the peace struggle have tended to focus more on the continuities and less on the qualitative changes the state form has underwent during the AKP era. In other words, their approach to the gendered state violence is conditioned by a very specific perception of the state in Turkey: a state that operates under the tutelage of the military which tries to hold its grip on political power by coercively excluding different social groups from the political sphere (Cizre, 2006b; Karakuş, 2006). Not only the state violence against women active in the public sphere and guerrilla women but also the domestic violence against women are, for the feminists involved in the peace process, basically conditioned by the militarist history, practice and ideology of the state in Turkey.

The lack of concern for the change in the state form (and for the evolving gender selectivities of the state in the AKP era) also looks like stemming from two main reasons. The first reason is that the line of continuity in the actual patterns of state violence is too obvious: targeting the body of guerrilla women and harassing the civilian women living in Kurdish-populated regions as a war strategy. The second reason is that the feminists who are engaged in peace and women politics as lead figures are purposely unwilling to focus on the state as a monolithic body.

Nazan Üstündağ, a peace feminist activist, tells that she does not want to be curious about the state. Because, she adds, 'when I am curious about the state, I feel that I am falling into an illusion: I start to think of it as if it is a human being, a single thing. In fact, however, the state is a fiction composed of many power nets' (Aşan and Aslan, 2009). As an academic by training, Üstündağ refers in fact to the Foucauldian approach to political power and rightfully warns the reader against the illusionary tendency to think of the state as if it was a uniform body. Üstündağ also sets the argument that 'you [referring to the civil/feminist initiatives] are less threatening [in the eyes of the state] when you are engaged with the state than when you direct your attention to the society'.

On the other hand, when seen under the light of the critical feminist discussions on the uses and usurpations of the UNSCR 1325 by the states and international organizations (see also note 17 of this chapter), this political choice about not theorizing the state harbours in itself a significant weakness. Independent from the noticeably short path it has undergone in Turkey, deploying the UNSCR 1325 possesses the risk of pacification by and due to the gender selectivities of the host states. Because, the UNSCR 1325 is itself a very statist resolution. According to Laura Shepherd (2008), the UNSCR 1325, and the spirit of the global gender regime that supports it, draws on an imaginary of women 'as morally superior, civil and aloof from the state'. This creates a convergence between the gender policies pursued by the conservative and populist governments (e.g. AKP's theory of gender complementarity) and the feminist critiques of war and state as masculine undertakings (e.g. anti-militarist feminism's gender difference approach). For Shepherd (2008), this convergence precludes the feminist conceptualization of alternative forms of political authority that might deliver the radical reforms that the Resolution and associated documents purport to seek.

Concluding remarks

During the so-called reformist era of the state in Turkey, feminists have also developed new strategies to put their marks on the state. The three main types of feminist engagements with the state respectively have been mainstreaming gender to state policies and practices, making legislative changes that would empower women in their struggle against patriarchal social relations and making the state recognize women's standpoint. The first two strategies have focused on transforming 'the rules of entitlement' that the state provides the women with; the last strategy has focused on changing 'the rules of identity' the state weaponizes against the Kurdish women.

The governance feminist interventions in the state were either *resignified by the state or refused*. The resignification was possible due to the common grammar of changing police conduct and behaviours. The reformist police cadres tried to fill in the legitimation deficit that the state was suffering from by tapping into the gender expertise the feminists could provide them with. On the other hand, the demand for the effective state protection of women from domestic violence was refused on the grounds that the power of the police is very limited, that is, that the police could not sustain the protection of women in the absence of broader welfare state functions. But the most important excuse that was determining the refusal of the security bureaucracy was stemming from the gender selectivities of the state, which were depending on a moralist reading of the social question in Turkey.

The pro-equal rights feminist interventions in the state were either compromised and resignified or refused. Whereas the feminist movement got successful in introducing the seemingly 'counter-hegemonic rules' into the legal apparatus of the state, the actual and systematic implementation of these rules has not been guaranteed. Besides the impact of political conjuncture and of the need for the neoliberal-neoconservative government to acquire greater societal acceptance, the growing gap between the societal gender norms that were dragging women back and the women's increasing assertiveness in the public life made it necessary for the state to readjust its gender selectivities to the benefit of its women citizens. Nevertheless, the same selectivities have also blocked the full realization of the new rules of entitlement. Seen from the perspective of the reformist police cadres, they were on the one hand for the re-integration of women as healthy members of a healthy family to the patriarchal gender contract and thus resignifying the feminist demands via their conservative-political Islamist society vision. But on the other hand, they were also against the criminalization, especially of the petit bourgeois and 'poor' men they considered as being so far peripheralized by the elitist state tradition in Turkey. In that sense, the state has displayed a self-contradictory and ambiguous attitude in its fight against domestic violence, up to this day.

The interventions of the anti-militarist feminism in the state followed a strategy of changing the identity rules and thereby empowering women but particularly the Kurdish women. Their strategy to challenge the state by showing that it indeed fails to live up to the moralist populism it promises, for example, disrespecting women's living areas/not protecting the dignity of women, has been either *distorted or refused*. In fact, despite the radical feminist politics pursued against the state, the critique based on the 'surveillant men in Kalekols' pushed the ruling bloc to distort these demands as a mean to further its neo-conservative policies and hence to profit from the multi-faces of the centaur state and the continuum of paternalism and violence within which it is embedded. Indeed, one of the reasons that have pushed the Ministry of Interior for an increase in the numbers of female personnel recruited as special operations police officers since then can be read as an idiosyncratic response of the centaur state to these demands (see Chapter 4, 'State Violence against Politically Active Women').

To recap, the gender selectivities of the state were very determining for the final character the feminist-inclusive reform process has acquired. First, the reformers were acting on the basis of the two criteria which have shaped their gendered selectivities: (1) the robust anti-Political conception of policing, which perceived politically active women – when of course these women are active outside and against the political establishment – mostly as victims rather than agents and (2) the populist conception of policing, which assumed the owner of the state to be 'property-owner modest men' who were supposedly excluded from the state powers in the previous eras. Second, the human security perspective of the reformist police cadres was embedded in moral policing based on an imaginary harmonious society. For the state apparatus, restoring the so-called honour of the fathers, brothers and other male kin from lower classes has been more pertinent than restoring the dignity of women from the same class. This is first because 'poor women' are even less valuable for the Turkish capitalism and second because the political Islamist political power should not alienate 'poor men' if it wants to continue ruling.

4

State violence against politically active women

Gezi Protests represent the ultimate moment when the state violence relatively dormant in the reform era has started to unfold in a very rapid manner. In other words, Gezi catalysed the full transformation of moral policing into virtuous violence, the selective act of defining who merits the humane face of the centaur and who does not. Gezi Protests have generated a political panic among the ruling bloc. It transgressed the political boundaries limiting the state. It proved the dysfunctionality of the populist and localist ideologies used for the legitimation of the state in the AKP era. Gezi Protests which started in the late May 2013 and the popular resistance that followed it during the whole June 2013 revealed the contradictions of the Turkish capitalism (Ercan and Oğuz, 2015). Millions of people protested the ecological, political and economic dispossession processes characterizing the restructuring of the state in the AKP era. The massive participation of women to the protests was remarkable.[1]

The Gezi protesters targeted the political horizon of the ruling bloc that had been limited to the 'property-owner modest man'. It is not a coincidence that one of the symbolic and widely embraced cult photos of the Gezi Protests was the photo of the 'lady in red', a peaceful woman protestor hastily tear-gassed by a police officer (Gürcan and Peker, 2014). Even before the Gezi Protests, women had already been protesting the conservative policies of the AKP government, which was gradually building a very intrusive politics of intimacy – propagating a three children policy for each women, criminalizing the demand and act of abortion, despising single life and advocating for marriage.[2] During the Gezi, women spontaneously exhibited a collective agency also showing the limits of the AKP's moralist policing based on mobilizing families to de-radicalize their daughters and sons. The contradiction between the respective political horizons of the reformist police cadres and the Gezi women became more apparent when for example the governor of Istanbul appealed to mothers to call their children back home. Instead of doing so, hundreds of mothers demonstrated in Taksim Square to support their daughters and sons (Canlı and Umul, 2015).

In the face of this resistance, the political power intensified its *selective patriarchy*, responding by deepening the schism of 'agreeable' and 'non-agreeable' women. While it put the 'agreeable women' over a pedestal as way of governing them, it declared the 'non-agreeable women' as the marginal, non-local, non-national women, who possess no attachment to the Islamist-Anatolian civilization.[3]

In order to discuss these arguments, this chapter will focus on three processes where it is possible to discern how the gender-cum-patriarchal selectivities of the state *differ* in terms of manifestation and intensity from but remain *identical* in terms of spirit with the reform era. The first process includes the gendered police violence during the Gezi Protests and the New Internal Security Law which came just after the Protests. The second process is related with the accelerated rise of the status of the Special Operations Department within the police organization. The final process is the post-Putsch era encounters between the politically active women and the state security apparatus. Before focusing on the implications of these historical turning points, the chapter further focuses on the notion of *selective patriarchy* with a specific reference to the state violence against women-in-politics during the authoritarian turn. The conclusion part widens the discussion on state violence against the politically active women to demonstrate the selective deployment of state coercion and its wider meanings and implications for the making of a centaur state in Turkey.

Selective patriarchy and its functionality in the post-Gezi era

The concept of selective patriarchy developed in this study denotes a governmental logic used by the state apparatus to manage – but also to construct – different gendered identities and divisions through distinct administrative apparatuses. It is a way of creating various categories of femininity (and masculinity) and proposing different methods of governance for each category. The Turkish-Islamist imaginary of the harmonious society constitutes the main reference point for this categorization.

Gender selectivities of the capitalist state are, as told in the introductory chapter, not necessarily patriarchal. There is no rule that the capitalist state is and should be dependent on male dominance. Or, there is nothing at the level of abstraction that pre-determines how the gender hierarchy will look like, on which kind of sex system it will be based. Nevertheless, the two foundational characteristics of the capitalist state – its dual mandate to secure contemporaneously the reproduction of labour power and the profitability of capital – force it to find ally structures and institutions within the social. To reproduce and control the labour power, the capitalist state has so far depended on the institution of family and heterosexual marriage. To facilitate the profitability of capital, it has contributed in the construction of different systems of valorization based on gender, 'race' and class status. During the original accumulation era, back in the sixteenth and seventeenth centuries, the de-valorization of women and the feminine body was also a way of devalorizing female labour, and the kinds of work mostly done by women. This has strategically helped to secure the support of the newly rising petit bourgeois to the capitalist market by eliminating women (e.g. craftswomen, midwives, women-farmers through Witch-hunts) from the competition (Federici, 2005). It has also facilitated the housewifization of women, whose invisible labour would reduce the costs of subsistence. To this day, this historical phenomenon managed to reproduce itself in Turkey. In times of economic crises, the capitalist states have benefited from gender, 'race' and class-based social hierarchical differences to revalue and devalue labour (Arruzza, 2016). In short, states are not passive consumers of the already existing differences.

It is possible to add to this picture that during economic and political crises, the states engage in the task of the revalorization of gender divisions since augmenting patriarchal dividends (accorded to certain men) during these moments might also help to widen the political support to the polity-in-crisis. And a patriarchal dividend does not necessarily take the form of a direct offer to men as such. It does also indirectly operate, for example, by eliminating (certain) women in politics. The fates of many women who took active part in the revolutionary/anti-colonialist struggles in the Middle East and North Africa, including the women who participated in the foundation of the Republic in Turkey, are historical cases in point.[4]

However, this method is today more contradictory for the state power than ever as the growing participation of women in politics is not seen by the general public as much of a threat as it used to be for example in the early twentieth century. On the contrary, recent surveys clearly show that the popular receptivity to women's participation in politics has been steadily and progressively enhancing for the last four years in Turkey (KHU Gender and Women's Studies Centre, 2020). Therefore, patriarchal selectivity or the differential treatment of the female population becomes even a more central but also more challenging task for the capitalist state in Turkey.

On the one hand, the limits of Turkey's capitalist formation (see Introduction) condition the gender selectivities of the state: the women are mostly required for the systemically relevant task of reproducing labour power or care work. On the other hand, the refusal of women to subscribe into this patriarchal gender contract – even if this refusal does manifest itself not directly as a political contestation of gendered domestic labour but also for example through the augmenting rate of divorces – pushes the capitalist state to find new ways of valuing the gender differences and divisions. Selective patriarchy does not only operate only along gender lines. On the contrary, it is constructed and operationalized at the intersection of various social hierarchies. The gender identities in Turkey are also dependent on class, ethnic/confessional background and indeed on political affiliation/intention/activity/militancy.

Within the requirements of Turkey's capitalist formation, the statecraft does propose new gendered identities and gender relations. Patriarchal selectivities, therefore, are such proposals. They are, however, not from top-to-down processed subjectivations. The fabrication of new gendered subjects and relations is a question of political and social struggles. They are indeed the manifestations of state power, in all its contradictory aspects. For the patriarchal selectivities are effective, forcible and moving but also contested, reversed, mal-functioning. All these power effects and their institutionalization in the state form depend on social struggles.

In the post-Gezi era, crystallizing divisions and forging new patriarchal selectivities have been imperative for the state apparatus because the neoliberal-neoconservative policies of the government which triggered the collective resistance of women in the Gezi were also controversial in terms of their socio-economic impact for the so-called agreeable women – women who are assumedly at peace with their *fıtrat*. To illustrate, the non-legal but official stigmatization of abortion in the early 2010s by the government further disempowered many women living under severe conditions of socio-economic poverty because the public hospitals in Turkey have started to retreat from implementing it.[5] The containment of these women, dispossessed from their existing rights, within the remits of the AKP's 'harmonious society', necessitated further gender-based divisions.

The ruling power has realized the limits of restoring a full-blown classical patriarchy, where women are oppressed over a gender ideology which constructed femininity as if it were by *nature* wicked, weak and in need of tutelage. It has rather tried to develop a patriarchal strategy of oppressing women by a gender ideology built on *nurture* (Hülagü, 2020). According to this position, women are not wicked, weak and in need of tutelage but rather are faithful, strong by nature and thus in need of special privileges. It is not therefore a coincidence for example that in early January 2015, the then Prime Minister Ahmet Davutoglu declared that the child-rearing mothers will be rewarded with gold coins as he told, 'Each mother will receive 300 Turkish Lira after giving birth as a gift from the state' (Buchanan, 2015).

According to the ruling power, women who do not procreate out of individual choices disobey their biological destinies and/or are not 'in peace with their femininity'.[6] Already in 2012, Erdoğan's raw comparison of the act of abortion to the military bombing of the thirty-four Kurdish villagers in Roboski/Uludere – smuggling cigarettes, tea and other packed material over mulls – crossing the Turkish border from the Iraqi territory was self-telling. He was complaining about the opposition forces' critique of this state-induced murder and rebuking that 'you always discuss Uludere, I tell you every abortion is an Uludere ... Abortion is an insidious plan to eliminate a nation from the world stage' (Prime Minister: "Every Abortion is Uludere", 2012).

The abortion discussions have had a marking impact on the gender selectivities of the state bureaucracy in Turkey. The state bureaucracy has speeded up the undoing of the previous contacts with the feminist movement and with the progressive women's organizations and a new generation of women's organizations, which give their open consent to selective patriarchy, has become the new partners of the state.[7] Besides, the ruling power boosted the support it has given to the government-organized non-governmental organizations, among which there are pro-natalist, pro-family and anti-divorce organizations upheld by the conservative and/or political Islamist groups.

In addition, during each heated political event which followed the Gezi Protests, the differentiated patriarchy of the state acquired a new face. Indeed, following the Gezi Events, in August 2013, Erdoğan has started to cheer crowds with the four-finger Rabia 'sign' in reference to his solidarity with the Muslim brotherhood in Egypt, and as a sign of his endearment for Asmaa, a young woman killed in Cairo by security forces who attacked the supporters of the ousted President Morsi (Bekdil, 2014). Erdoğan's Rabia 'sign' was a response to the Gezi protests and indeed to the millions of women who participated in the Gezi Protests. It was a way of communicating that the Gezi women were politically on the wrong side, that they were 'foreign to their culture, to the Islamic-Anatolian civilization'. This was also a first sign of the concrete political references under which the post-Gezi era's patriarchal selectivities would be materialized by and in the state apparatus.

Hereafter, the bureaucratic security apparatus started with a rapid, intense and violent enactment of the profiling/categorization initiated in the so-called reformist era. As displayed in the second chapter, during this era the reformist cadres were very much involved in developing policing as a deradicalization practice. The women who were politically active in the non-mainstream political parties and movements were of a special concern and even specialization. The specific police knowledge developed in each case – that is, the case of Alevite women living in the outskirts of Istanbul, the Kurdish women living in South-eastern Turkey – prepared the grounds for differential treatment. In other words, the state has not only enemized women who reject tutelage or protection, as clearly argued and excellently demonstrated by Gülbanu Altunok (2016) in her study on the anti-abortion politics of the political power, it has also done so in a class, ethnic/religious and/or political identity selective manner.

Gezi Protests and their aftermath: 'Women traitors' vs '*esnaf* policemen'

In the aftermath of the Gezi Protests, the ruling bloc assessed the event as an attempt for the violent take-over of the government. Within the state bureaucracy it was conceived as a revolutionary process and documented as 'a show of force against the state' (Göktaş, 2014). Thereafter, Gezi Protests have become a frame of reference for the security bureaucracy. Since then whenever political and/ or social scandals have erupted triggering social anger, the Ministry of Interior issued circulars warning the security personnel all around Turkey against the possibility of 'new Gezi Events' (Özdilek, 2016). This panic has re-conditioned the patriarchal selectivities of the state by sharpening the ones established in the reformist era. Young women who are active in the leftist/socialist politics, the university students and the working-class women from Alevite/Kurdish origins have been considered as the potential carriers of another 'Non-Event'.

Ceren Ünver, one of the Gezi protesters subjected to police violence during the Gezi Protests, tells that following the Gezi protests the police found the families of women protestors to warn them about their daughters (Koloğlu, Gençtürk, Kazaz, Mavituna and Şen, 2015: 322).[8] Another Gezi protester Arzu Demir underlines that the police violence she was subjected to in late July 2013 – during the police raids which followed the Gezi protests – was not only about implementing governmental orders but was rather demonstrative of a kind of feeling of vindication and revenge that was animating the police officers. She adds, 'They [the police officers] don't see us as human beings, I guess' (Koloğlu, Gençtürk, Kazaz, Mavituna and Şen, 2015: 260). Again another Gezi protester, Gonca Arslan tells that the police would shout them 'You [the protestors] have destroyed our homeland and on top of all you still claim to be women' (Koloğlu, Gençtürk, Kazaz, Mavituna and Şen, 2015: 254). The police chief's words to Gonca Arslan indicate that the women's massive participation in the protests was perceived as a denial of appropriate femininity, a subversive act against the politically acceptable gender roles. The police chief perceived women's participation in the Gezi Protests as an act against the essence of femininity, not because a woman is expected to stay aloof from political activism but because a woman is expected to engage in politics only for the sake of the centaur state's new ideology, the pan-Islamist nationalism.

It is for example also reported that the police accused the protesters of being paid by the Syrian government (Koloğlu, Gençtürk, Kazaz, Mavituna and Şen, 2015: 195). The Gezi women were constructed by the police as if they were the enemy within, the gender traitors who stab the government from its back. Another Gezi Protester, Ezgi Haberlioğlu reports that the police officers insulted and threatened them. They are reported to tell: 'We will bring you to extinction, the Alevi bastards' (Koloğlu, Gençtürk, Kazaz, Mavituna and Şen, 2015: 46). This connection established by the security personnel among women, political engagement, ethnic/confessional background and regional war in Syria became more complicated during the re-escalation of the conflict with the PKK and the PYD in Syria and in the aftermath of the failed Putsch attempt on 15 July 2016.

Right after the Gezi Events, on 5 October 2013, editor-in-chief of the pro-government Islamist daily *Yeni Şafak*, İbrahim Karagül wrote an article arguing that both the Islamist terrorist organization El-Kaide and the Revolutionary People's Liberation Party/Front (DHKP-C) are making part of the same international complot to ruin Turkey by way of creating an Alevi-Sunni conflict and provoking a *coup d'état* against the government. He composed this article just in the aftermath of a massive funeral of a young socialist man Hasan Ferit Gedik, who was shot to dead by members of a drug gang in the Gülsuyu district of Istanbul, a small shanty-town inhabited mostly by poor people from working-class and Alevi backgrounds. The funeral was in first place prevented from taking place by the police forces, who after circling the neighbourhood told to the principals of the Pir Sultan Abdal Cultural Association, an Alevi Community Organisation, to not let the funeral take place in *Cemevi* – Alevi place of worship in Turkey (Hasan Ferit Gedik Sonsuzluğa Uğurlandı, 2013).

Karagül resented that the funeral took place with the participation of parliamentary opposition figures and basically built his argumentation on the left-wing armed figures showing off in the funeral. Although the habitants of the neighbourhood have been complaining from the deliberative lack of attention given by the police forces to the growing clout of the drug gangs in the neighbourhood and explaining the rise of left vigilantism on this basis,[9] Karagül totally ignored this part of the story and tacitly claimed for the existence of a sovereignty deficit on the part of the state and assumed this to be part of an internationally backed preparation for an Alevi-based insurrection in Turkey. This conspiracy perspective has also been representative of the official position of the government and the state apparatus since the Gezi Protests (Nefes, 2017).

Leftist/revolutionary/socialist women who live in the outskirts of Istanbul – politically active women who are in touch with grass-root leftist organizations or who are claimed by police forces to be in touch with illegal organizations without any judicial evidence – have been considered as partakers of this international conspiracy against the ruling power. As the dialectical counterpart to the deradicalization strategy of the police reformers, where the main aim was to especially convince young men and women to dis-engage from their political activities, the police forces have chosen in the post-Gezi era to antagonize those figures who were resistant to deradicalization. By then onwards, the women participants of dissident political activities have been conceived as the *unwomen*: the woman who refuses to be put on a pedestal, to become part of the 'local and national' and thus ends up becoming a foreigner, always seeking to destroy the virtuous hand the state proposes to her.[10]

This approach has been further consolidated in the aftermath of the 15 June 2016 putsch attempt, when allegiance to President Erdoğan emerged as a central criterion of and for policing. Loyalty has since then been adopted as a virtuous principle for the requirements of state rehabilitation – mainly because the ruling bloc has fallen apart as a result of the clash between the Gülen Community and the pro-Erdoğan forces.[11] However, the discord and the crisis the putsch ignited within the state architecture have not outdated the state vision adopted in the reformist era. On the contrary, although the coalition between the Gülen Community and the pro-Erdoğan forces came to an end, the two dominant themes of the security sector reform era, populism and localism, continued to be promoted by Erdoğan and his entourage. Erdoğan accused those police and military figures who broke the alliance and participated in the putsch attempt as being not 'national and local' enough.

Indeed, the state apparatus has become more verbal about itself, started publishing plethora of documents and/or manufacturing newspaper articles, to underline that the state power cannot be otherwise but differential and selective and the provision of human security conditional on the loyalty accorded to President Erdoğan. Different from the case of the Gezi Protests, which they labelled 'as a tour de force against the state', the security bureaucracy framed the Putsch attempt as an attack against the persona of Erdoğan. In a 2017 dated report composed by the Police Academy on the infiltration of the Gülen Community to the state, it is stated that before the putsch attempt, 'over the course of the last seven years, FETÖ [Fethullahist Terrorist Organisation] has attempted to depose Recep Tayyip Erdoğan, whom they see as the most significant obstruction to their own interests several times' (Turkish National Police Academy, 2017: 20).

Women and their relation to the state power have mattered even more in this period. First, after the putsch attempt, there emerged a need for Erdoğan to replace the void emanating from the loss of the previous allies such as the Gülen Community and/or other liberal figures who supported the ruling bloc up until the Gezi Protests and its close aftermath. Second, the mobilization of Erdoğan's supporters during the putsch attempt against the putschists demonstrated the ever-rising centrality of the pro-Erdoğan women for the survival of the political power.[12] Therefore, in order to reconstitute an effective state power, the post-putsch attempt populist discourse re-posited women again over a pedestal. But of course, not all women. Those who were acting in accordance with the gender complementarity notion of the ruling power – according to which, gender division of labour not only in the household but in all fields of life including politics is a divine verdict – were considered as 'agreeable women'.

During the putsch attempt, high numbers of women participated in the anti-coup protests. The images of women shouting against the putschists and trying to convince them to give in have become iconic in the social media (Akınerdem, 2017). These 'local and national' women were constructed as women who are politically active without renouncing their essential work. They were women who looked after their family and who have become productive mothers for the future of the nation by deterring the 'enemies' of the nation. For this dual end of keeping women not only at home as mothers and wives but also as much politically active as possible so that they become guardians of Erdoğan's political power, the state apparatus has initiated a strategy of careful antagonism. It was careful in the sense that rather than enemizing all women, it was enemizing and antagonizing certain groups of (politically active) women.

The New Internal Security Law: The first official attempt to provide a social and legal basis to this selective functioning of the state was the introduction of the New Internal Security Law.[13] The government introduced in December 2014 a bill for changes in police powers, known by the general public as the 'New Internal Security Law'. The Law was ratified in the Parliament in March 2015. The state media represented it as an attempt to increase the preventive capacity of the public order policing.

As an extension of the reform era's expanding practice of administrative policing – at the expense of judicial policing – the new law gave the police the powers to act preemptively and conduct raids on intelligence of possible criminal activities without prior authorization by a public prosecutor or a court. The law indirectly accorded the police the right to use preventive detention as a mechanism of deterring 'violent mass incidents'. The police are also accorded the authority to detain a person without a warrant for up to 24 hours for certain crimes committed individually and to detain people for 48 hours 'when the spread of violent incidents poses a serious threat to public order during mass incidents'. Another significant component of the bill is the judicial right accorded to the provincial governors to instruct police to focus on particular crimes, a right previously owned only by the prosecutors and the judiciary.

The bill included measures which are building on the reform era's jargon and principles. For example, the Law includes an article on strengthening the civilian oversight of the gendarmerie, the semi-military policing organization responsible for policing outside the urban areas. It ties the previously semi-autonomous military organization of gendarmerie more closely to the Ministry of Interior. In fact, in line with the reform era's understanding of civilianization, this move is interpreted as extending the powers of the democratically elected executive in contradistinction to the appointed military bureaucrats. For the executive is thought to be the direct representative of a whole nation, of the legitimate embodiment of the people's will.

Indeed, even the human security notion sneaked itself into the justificatory attempts of the ruling party to expand the police powers. In the preamble of the security bill, it is stated that 'the recent popular events carry the risk to turn into propaganda opportunities for terrorist organizations. They threaten the livelihood of our citizens, damage public and private property, and even lead to looting attempts. Therefore, it is necessary to take new measures that will protect the freedom and security balance.' The Police Academy has also presented the new law as 'the most genuine and for a long time awaited step of Turkey's Security Sector Reform' (Arslan, 2016).

In his Security Sector Reform report published by the Police Academy, Ömer Arslan (2016) explains that this new Law should be conceived as a state response to social protest movements, 'which by exploiting the comfort-zones of liberal democracies become a threat for them'. From social protest movements, the report understands the rise of both 'far-right' and 'far-left'. Arslan further underlines the rationale of the police reform – the New Internal Security Law – as the indubitable need for forging new relations between *the state and society, society and politics* and *politics and the state.*

The report argues that some of the special articles included in the New Internal Security Law are especially in close track with 'people's expectations' in Turkey. These are the article on higher penalties for protesters who wear masks in public demonstrations and who use Molotov cocktails and the article which charges the protesters with the liability to compensate the losses arising from harms done to public and private property. 'The people's expectations', to which the report refers, basically cover the expectations of the *esnaf* [artisans, shopkeepers and small business-owning tradesmen], an indispensable social constituency for the AKP's political power. In the same days when the new security bill was in preparation, in a speech delivered to the 4th Council of Tradesmen and Artisans in Ankara, on 26 November 2014, Erdoğan said:

> In our civilization, in our national and civilizational spirit, tradesmen and artisans are soldiers when needed. They are 'alperenler' [the historical name given to Turkish Muslim knights]; they are martyrs, veterans and heroes defending their homeland when needed. They are the *policemen* who build order when needed; they are the judge and the referees who deliver justice when needed.
>
> (cited in Kandiyoti, 2016, italics added)

It is known that the AKP can mobilize tradesmen during political protests as irregular para-police forces and accords immunity to their vigilantism. In consideration of the social origins of the police powers in the aftermath of Gezi Protests in Turkey, the mutual dependency between the AKP and the *esnaf* is noteworthy. To illustrate, during the Gezi Protests, the *esnaf* of the Tophane district in Taksim brutally attacked the Gezi protesters. They targeted women protesters and attacked them with knives at hands. Their vigilant acts were tacitly approved by the authorities (Massicard, 2019).

One should remember that the pilot local security communities established during the pre-Gezi era with the help of the 'Civilian Oversight of the Policing Project' have also involved the *esnaf* as the local owners of the security plans to be developed in their residential and/or trading districts. In other words, the dialectical continuity regarding the formative power of the populist component involved into the SSR processes should not be underestimated when thinking about the crystallization phase of the centaur state in Turkey in the post-Gezi process.

Counter-insurgency policing and the birth of 'women avengers'

As the resolution process, the ruling party initiated with the PKK has crumbled under the course of events in 2015, the state violence in the Kurdish populated south-eastern region of Turkey reached severe levels. The community and development-based self-administration trials of the Kurdish political movement in the South-eastern Turkey evolved into armed self-defence when AKP decided to intervene to demolish the self-administration practices (Jorgenden, 2018). The state apparatus henceforth initiated military operations to urban settings such as Diyarbakır (the Sur district) and Cizre by deploying heavy armed troops of special police teams.

Following the political autonomy, the the Kurdish Democratic Union Party (PYD) acquired in Syria during the Syrian War and the self-governance experience of the Kurdish people in Rojava, the security bureaucracy considered these evolving self-administration practices as attempts to wear down Turkey's statehood in the region. In an article written by the students of the Police Academy, it is argued that contrary to the years-long denial of a separate Kurdish nation-state as their ultimate aim, the Syrian War provided the PKK leaders with the morale and international support to return to their struggle for territorial sovereignty (Şahin and İrdem, 2017). The authors, therefore, explain the military operations in the urban settings as the state's intervention to restore the political authority in the region. Relatedly, the security bureaucracy justifies the brutal and lethal state violence in the region as an attempt to bring the blurring lines between the political local administration and civil society in the region back into order. It is stated that the local municipalities were reluctant to set these limits and that they were permissive of 'the terrorist acts' (Arslan, 2016). A third sub-theme that accompanies the security bureaucracy's violent intercession is indeed resentment. The argument is built on the state's self-image. It reckons that despite the protectionist and caring policies of the reformist era in the region, the dislike of the state and disloyalty against it continued. To illustrate, during the operations, while special operation teams swore oaths of vindication by making use of Islamist motives and prays and shouted Allahu Ekber to cherish their victories, some of them sketched the following graffiti over the walls of the scattered towns: 'Don't betray the state. The people of Sur, you already have a state.'

This avenging mind-set of the security bureaucracy has first set free the gendered scripts of the special police teams. In the Sur operations, special police operation units continued drawing graffiti on the urban walls. On these graffiti, they used a sexualized language to undermine and demoralize the opposing side. Besides, police teams poked around in the sleeping rooms of the houses they raided during the operations and made fun of the women's underwear they found in drawers and scattered them around. On the one hand, this was supposedly a power message to the 'terrorists' who were hiding in the houses of the local habitants. On the other hand, it was a threat against the local habitants, against their 'honour'. Hence the state in fact redeployed a gendered script, that it never got rid of and restarted to use it for purposes of racketeering, for granting protection in return for full subjection. During the reform era, it was proudly declared that the people entrusted to the police 'their lives, their property and their honour'.

Nevertheless, it should be noted that transitioning from 'being entrusted with the protection of the honour of people' to racketeering them 'by threatening with violating their honour' is not that easy. This is more so especially after years of masculinist protectionism spread within the state apparatus both via programmes of deradicalization and via the Islamist gender ideology that commend men to become protectorates of 'women and children'. It is reported that many special operation troops wanted to quit the organization during and in the aftermath of the Sur operations, initiated by the government. However voluntary the recruits were, fighting is also a dissipating force, which requires constant reproduction of missionary policing via new tools. This has further led the government to augment the privileged status of the special operation teams and to find new ways of governmentalizing its selective patriarchy.

To this end, the Special Operations Department, which operates under the auspices of the Turkish National Police (TNP), accrued new autonomous powers. The department personnel, who are normally kept secluded from the entire TNP on the grounds that they are the last choice lethal forces, have been reinserted into the routine police and security personnel training processes as trainers. Since 2017, the Special Operations Department not only provides in-service training to the TNP in general, but also gives special training to foreign countries' police forces. Plus, the official status of the department within the overall TNP is uplifted by a regulation change, following the deployment of special operations teams to Syria in March 2017 along with the military forces. The latest video footage of the special operation teams serviced by the pro-government media also attests to the new modus special police teams are stationed within. During graduation, the new recruits sing the ancient army Marche, harkening back to the Ottoman Janissaries.

The 15 July 2016 putsch attempt gave the second biggest momentum to the power accruement of the Special Operations Department (see also the chapter on the philosophy of moral policing). Thereafter, special police teams have turned into folk heroes. Their mission has become idealized and along with the ever-rising recruitment numbers, their popularity captured a significant portion of the populace who associate themselves with President Erdoğan (10 Bin Özel Polis Harekat Alımı için 220 Bin Kişi Başvurdu, 2016). After 15 July, para-militarization along the role model of the Special Operations Department was evident in different attempts for organized vigilantism, publicized under names such as 'Peoples' Special Operations' (Resmi Kayıtlı Özel Harekat Derneği, 2017).

After 15 July, the political power has also had to find new ways for legitimation. To this end, it tried to restore the aesthetic of soldier-police as the figure of virtuous violence. This virtuous violence, asked the special police teams to be more delicate in choosing and differentiating the enemy, for instance, to be able to discriminate between the 'agreeable' and 'non-agreeable' women. The Department hereafter started to recruit more women into its ranks, framed them as symbols of 'agreeable women'. For the occasion of Women's Day on 8 March 2018, the state news agency AA publicized an interview made with a female special operations' team member, who argued that her mission is to fight for 'the mothers of the martyr and veteran soldiers'. Another female special operation team member declared that the rise of policewomen in the organization is closely related with the changing profile of the 'criminals' in recent times and with the augmenting desire among women to join the organization (Gemici, 2018).

This decision to recruit more women into the ranks of the Special Operations Department has in fact been designed as a response to the growing presence of women in the Middle East as agents of political violence and/or active in guerrilla movements. In other words, the ruling bloc has decided to move from the strategy of victimization and missionary policing initiated in the reform era – without necessarily leaving them out of the agenda – to a strategy of reciprocation. In the reform era and at least until 2017, the ruling bloc maintained a more generic understanding of femininity in political contexts.

It associated femininity with peace and vulnerability. In 2017, as the photos of Kurdish guerrilla women fighting against ISIS hit the headlines of global media, such as, *New York Times*, the Ministry of Interior composed international reports to argue for the dependent and vulnerable status of women in the PKK (Hülagü, 2020). However, this has hardly helped the AKP to legitimize its operations. This reform era victimization strategy has only to some extent helped the political power to get over the destabilizing effect the women's politicization in Turkey either via peaceful methods or in political organizations involved into political violence had on the gender stereotypes (Hülagü, 2020).

On the other hand, in the reform era, as also shown in the chapter on the philosophy of moral policing, victimization strategy of the state was accompanied by a parallel strategy, built on using gender as a governmental apparatus, that is, attacking politically active women as the security bureaucracy has come to the conclusion that women are the real forces that keep the 'terrorist organizations' such as the PKK and the DHKP-C intact. Following this logic, the security bureaucracy opted for enhancing patriarchal selectivity. In other words, women who antagonized the state and insisted on refusing the gadget of victimization have started to be coded as if they were *unwomen*, women who obstruct the state fulfilling its responsibility to protect.

The Ministry of Interior against Nuriye Gülmen: Constructing the 'unwomen'

The case of Nuriye Gülmen is illustrative for the centaur state's positioning vis-à-vis the women, who are claimed to be non-loyal dissidents. Nuriye Gülmen was expelled from the university following the 2016 failed putsch attempt, after which the political power declared a state of emergency (OHAL). During the state of emergency period, the government embarked on a massive purge of security officers and civil servants, who were allegedly members and/or supporters of the Gülen Community. The state apparatus has profited from this occasion to write down the names of leftist, socialist and/or dissenting names into the rules having force of law (KHKs) issued by the OHAL regime. According to a recent research, 20 per cent of the purged officers (a total number of 22,028) are women (KESK, 2018). Of these women, 1,069 were unionized workers of the KESK, the Public Employee's Trade Confederation. The research shows that following the loss of jobs, most of these women who are at the age of 40 or below had to return to dependency positions. Many of them had to change domicile and move back to their parents' home. Others become even deprived of their basic health insurance. Nuriye Gülmen is one of those purged civil servants during the OHAL period.

Before being purged, she had been teaching at the Selçuk University in Konya, a conservative city which is about 300 kilometres away from Ankara. She first faced allegations and was accused of being a member of the 'Fethullahçı Terrorist Organization/Gülenist Parallel State Structure' (FETÖ/PDY). On 9 November 2016, she initiated a protest with the motto 'I Want My Job Back' in front of the Human Rights Monument on Yüksel Street in Ankara. Every day she drew attention to her plight with hand-lettered signs. Gülmen's demands were not only limited to her own plight but also included 'the end of the emergency regime; of the unlawful and arbitrary dismissals and job security for all workers in the field of education including university research assistants' (CNN Shows Gülmen as One of 8 Leading Women of 2016, 2016). Every day, the police arrested Nuriye Gülmen for protesting in public and released her again a few hours later. Finally on 8 March 2017, she went on a hunger strike with her fellow teacher Semih Özakça. In May 2015, police raided the homes of Gülmen and Özakça in Ankara and detained them.

Nuriye and Semih's resistance to KHKs gathered considerable public support. On 25 May 2017, Interior Minister Süleyman Soylu claimed that Nuriye Gülmen and Semih Özakça were 'members of the DHKP-C terrorist organization' and that their actions were supported by this organization. In a press declaration, the Ministry of Interior Soylu added the example of Sıla Abalay, a young woman murdered during a police raid. Soylu argued that Sıla was captured by the terrorist organization despite her father's will and counter-efforts. In the case of Sıla, Soylu continued the reform era's policing ideology about women as victims of 'terrorist organizations'. He also refurbished the cop-sided thesis that police in fact help and/or work through families to deradicalize these women. He indeed said during his speech, 'We contacted their families and asked them to save their children from these organizations.' He tacitly justified the violent treatment of these women, one of which he claimed is Nuriye. He added that the state would not let these to confuse the public mind by 'looking sympathetic and good-humoured' (Bakan Soylu'dan Semih Özakça ve Nuriye Gülmen İle ilgili Açıklamalar, 2017).

Following the statements of Soylu, who linked Gülen and Özakça to DHKP-C, Gülmen and Özakça's lawyers and supporters declared that these accusations were unsubstantiated and that neither teacher has ever been charged or convicted of any link to that group. Nevertheless, the Ministry of Interior published in July 2017 a special report entitled 'The Repetitive Scenario of a Terrorist Organization – the Truth about Nuriye Gülmen and Semih Özakça' in both English and Turkish (Turkish Ministry of Interior, 2017). In the report, it is argued that 'Nuriye Gülmen's demands are neither innocent nor are they as simple as they sound like'. Although Nuriye Gülmen's link to DHKP-C and her political activities were not judicially fixated (and have not been since then), the report argued that the 'responsibility of statehood dictates to take preventive measures when so many doubts exist about the illegal acts of a person and this is so even if these are not judicially fixated'. Using the so-called liberal preventive/ administrative policing theses, the report showed how the police reform process meant in fact an expansion of police powers in Turkey. In fact, as the whole reform process was built on strengthening administrative policing rather than judicial policing, the result is not surprising. To recap, administrative policing signified for the police reformers, developing the preventive vocation of the police since it was argued that the essential task of a police service should be to act before the crime happens.

But beyond this straightforward reasoning, the report displays a more cunning reinterpretation of the notion of human security. Accordingly, Nuriye's bodily resistance aims to incapacitate the state to exercise its legitimate right to *make humans live*. In the report, it is argued that the hunger strike of Nuriye Gülmen (and Semih Özakça) aims at 'the seizure of the state will'. In the report it is repeated that 'the main desire seen here is to *seize the state* through hunger strike' (Turkish Ministry of Interior, 2017: 53, italics added). Moreover, it is also told that

> the main philosophy of our fight against terrorism is based on the holiness of the human life. However, some people are supporting this bloody organization on purpose or unwittingly; and lend himself/herself to the terrorist organization propaganda using these people. Our State shall maintain its stance in favour of rule of law and public order and shall stand straight against any kind of threat targeting sovereignty rights.
>
> (Turkish Ministry of Interior, 2017)

Nuriye's protest was built on the idea that being unrightfully sacked from her job – and even banned from an actual chance to find a decent job as a politically unfavourable individual – means that she is also banned from acquiring the basic means of self-subsistence. In other words, her position – as well as the position of many others who become unemployed within a day – was unveiling two essential characteristics of the capitalist social formation in Turkey: life is deeply dependent on work – on paid work – and defending decent work also means defending life and autonomy from dependency on traditional forms of power.

Nuriye's demand on returning to her job received broad acceptance by the public. Public intellectuals supported this specific demand by publishing a short petition, which stated that the right to work should be restored and the state should take the necessary steps so that Nuriye and Semih can go back to their schools and their lives. The Minister of Interior Süleyman Soylu immediately replied to this petition through his twitter account by sarcastically asking whether the signatories were aware of what they were signing. He was implying, indeed, that Nuriye and Semih were terrorists and that these public intellectuals were duped by them for their 'terrorist intentions'.

In fact, Soylu was claiming that the demand for right to work was not the real and sincere intention of the protesters. Thus, whereas the political society made Nuriye's and Semih's demands reach to greater social segments and pressurize the state to recognize their right to work, the state apparatus always replied via two narratives. One claimed that their intention is to gather public support for their hidden intentions. The other claimed that their hunger strike calls the state to make a justified intervention (when their hunger strike puts their lives in danger) as part of the human security responsibility of the state.

The state apparatus feared that 'their death' would gather further public support. In a disclosed communiqué sent by the security bureaucrats working in the Ministry of Justice to the Public Prosecutor of Ankara, it was recognized that the two were protesting because of their loss of jobs, and that their possible death would be instrumentalized by the political organizations who would claim the futility of legal ways of looking for justice in order to ignite mass street protests (Uludağ, 2017). Nuriye was especially targeted in the pro-government media and her being an academician was denied. 'She is actually a bomber not an educator', wrote many pro-government newspapers. Minister Soylu defined her as a 'crime machine' to whom nobody could entrust his or her child in the university.

In fact, all these attempts have pointed out a special strategy of the state apparatus, especially of the security bureaucracy and personnel: to deflect attention from the right to work demands of Nuriye. But the strategy did not only aim at discouraging the public support gathered around her demands. It also aimed at raising an antagonistic relation to annihilate all public legitimacy accorded to Nuriye's resistance, as a young woman who stubbornly asked for the recognition of her right to work. Her determinate resistance despite the regular police attacks, repetitive custodies and attempts at the isolation of her public protest via police shields primarily strived for detaining Nuriye due to the representative figure she became.

In a country like Turkey, where women's presence in formal employment is as low as 27 per cent (see the introductory chapter), the connections established by the wider public during Nuriye's resistance between the right to work, the right to live with a decent work, the right to be employed in the public sector without fearing precarity and to have a paid and secure job as a condition for (female) independence kept alive the spectre of Gezi Protests over the security bureaucracy.

Concluding remarks

This chapter tried to demonstrate the patriarchal selectivities of the state in Turkey and its crystallization during and after the Gezi Events with a focus on the growing policing powers of the state. The selective patriarchy of the centaur state in Turkey is itself a way of governing the two non-events the state has been trying to exclude from the range of possible in Turkey. On the one hand, the state tries to prevent any kind of radical transformation that would hamper the smooth functioning of the socio-economic order. On the other hand, it tries to prevent loss of popular support to the state project it tries to forge in Turkey. To do so, the political power both benefits from the legacy of the reformist era policing and evolves it into a new phase.

To compete with the ascendancy of women as a social force, the state constitutes categories of femininity. These provide the ruling power with an ability to deploy the rules of entitlement and identity adopted by the state in a very flexible manner. The state shows different faces to different groups in a very rapid and agile manner. Whereas the selective patriarchy prevents the establishment of collective identities, as was the case during the Gezi Uprisings, it also protects the state apparatus from plunging into a full-fledged misogyny with the danger of alienating its own women supporters. While it devalorizes certain forms of womanhood, it also upgrades the patriarchal dividend for certain women and men.

In fact, the devaluation of women in politics might even restore a general feeling of security, an under-the-radar form of brotherhood among men from opposing political ranks. This latter is especially the case regarding the women parliamentarians and mayors of the left-leaning pro-Kurdish People's

Democratic Party (HDP), who have been under a harsh political pressure since the late 2016. The case of women parliamentarians and mayors affiliated with the HDP exposes indeed how the gender has become a governmental apparatus for the centaur state in Turkey. Only in December 2016, about thirty female politicians of the HDP were imprisoned. The numbers have steadily increased since then. This has helped the ruling power to upgrade the patriarchal dividend as targeting these women-in-politics has also somehow pleased or at least possessed the potential to please certain men in the opposition – who were already not in ease with the idea of co-presidency system (Kışanak, 2018).[14] In other words, the ruling bloc has tried to buy in the shy consent of the male conservative opposition forces by imprisoning hundreds of women active from the ranks of the HDP.

Under the current socio-economic conditions that have been continuously fostering the expansion of a reverse army of male labour in Turkey, devaluation of (certain) women can also serve to sooth the masculine anger towards the state. Patriarchal selectivity does in fact help to enact a moral economy of labour. In a country of scarce employment opportunities and a wide reserve army of male labour, constructing the young and educated women who suffer from unemployment as *unwomen* could also serve to the AKP-led project of forced housewifization of women in Turkey.

Finally, by devaluing certain forms of femininity, the state does also try to dissipate the collective political identity the women have displayed since the Gezi Events. It is true that during the Gezi Protests, police officers used a gendered script – a sexual language – and gendered motives while attacking the women protesters. In short, the attacks were deploying verbal and/or physical sexual harassment and they were also motivated to dismiss women out of the political sphere.[15] But there is more to this police violence. The police violence, whatever the specific gendered form it takes, is also a political violence. In other words, gendered forms of police violence are not only 'crimes against women' but they also are political crimes, crimes targeting the *Political*.

Conclusion

This book has tried to contextualize the murder of a young woman by a special police operations team chief in Turkey in late 2015. Dilek Doğan was a young Alevi woman, in the beginning of her twenties. Before being killed, she was working as a shop assistant and living with her family in the outskirts of Istanbul. She was contributing to his younger sibling's schooling expenses as well as to his newly married brother's bank credit repayments. Although for many, I believe, the reasons behind this killing were not intriguing at all – if not totally apparent and clear – I still wanted to learn, 'why?'. I was motivated by an urge to understand the (lethal) police violence against politically active women in Turkey. Why were these women killed? Why have they been conceived as threats? Was the state violence against these women gendered? If so, how was it gendered? What does the gendered police violence tell about the character of the new state in Turkey?

But before responding to these questions, I felt it necessary to grasp the near history of the development of police powers in Turkey in relation to the question of gender. For many years, the ruling party has propagated for making a 'silent revolution' in Turkey. It was argued that the state and society reconciliation was fully achieved. And until the blatant exposure of its violent measures first in the Gezi Events and then following the 2015 general elections – when for the first time in its thirteen years of political history the party lost the general majority to establish the government on itself – the AKP was accorded both at home and abroad with a quite substantial credit for its democratic accomplishments. Even today, the separation between the reformist and authoritarian eras is assumed rather than explained. The dialectical continuity which this book tried to demonstrate is underestimated. Moreover, the existing bulk of the mainstream debates on authoritarianism in Turkey hardly includes the gender issue. The feminist analyses are omitted both by the political sociologists and political economists, who happen to vividly discuss the character of the new regime in Turkey. The relevance of gender is considered only in symptomatic manner.

In this book, I have tried to show that the lethal encounters between the state and politically active women in Turkey should be conceived as a microcosm reflecting the macrocosm of the whole AKP era. This microcosm displays the dialectic of coercion which condition Turkey's centaur state. It refutes the dichotomous perspective of the mainstream approaches, which explain the authoritarian turn in Turkey with a reified notion of power. The mainstream perspective reduces the state to a sovereign and the state power to a monolithic entity acting over another entity, called society. According to this perspective, the transition in Turkey from democratization to state violence is explicable with reference to the needs of Erdoğan's political survival. I argue, however, in this book that the democratic ethos of the so-called reformist era should not be taken for granted. This is not to say that there has been no difference in terms of the violence of the state powers that penetrate Turkey in these two respective periods. It is rather argued that the roots of the authoritarian turn were already present in the so-called reformist era.

These roots should not be conceived as evil intentions hidden under the liberal surface until the correct times come for their revelation. They were rather true to their nature and undeniably liberal. But it is now a well-established argument that liberalism is bound to reproduce illiberalism. Liberalism fails to leave up to its own promises in the absence of concurrent ideologies that force it towards the centre. The democratization of liberalism was a matter of concurrent ideologies – especially of the ideological struggles fought by the labouring classes for equal representation and egalitarian redistribution. It is therefore not a surprise that in the post-Cold War era, the de-democratization of liberalism has speeded up.

To display this dialectic of liberal state-building within the context of Turkey, I initially focused on the global manifestations and local adaptation of the liberal state-building agenda, namely of the security sector reform. This study focus demonstrated that the liberal reforms were from the start designed for the 'property-owner modest man', discursively constructed as the oppressed strata of the Kemalist state. The feminist contribution in the liberal reforms has potentially left untouched this core and tried to widen the state's inclusivity towards women. This contribution was formulated as 'working with the men in the state' to make a behavioural change in them so that they would/could consider women as rightful recipients of security. This, however, further smoothed the localist and populist adaptation of liberal reforms in Turkey.

Second, I tried to reconstruct the police science of the reformist police cadres. The research displayed that the reform process was designed as a process for widening the administrative police powers at the expense of the judiciary police powers. This was legitimated on the grounds that the police should become an organization for and by people. Judiciary intervention and therefore the application of legal measures by the police were conceived as a potential state alienation from the social. The social question for the reformist police cadres consisted of the falling of society to live up to its innate harmonious order because of a praetorian Kemalist state. Therefore, it was argued that the remedy should be looked at in the construction of moral policing – a local and popular solution to the question of statehood. This moralist police science incorporated the gender question in two different ways. First, practically speaking it stayed away from the criminalization of certain men – accused of violence against women – and opted for the victimization of women as noble recipient subjects of the state protection. Second, it made gender a governmental apparatus to be able to prevent the capitalist state in Turkey from sliding into another administrative crisis. Women-in-politics and women agents of political violence have become then a central object of police science, which came up with a variety of governmental techniques: a different visage for each different social group, caring or frowning, wild or mild.

To explain the making of this centaur state in Turkey, I benefited from a materialist-cum-feminist conception of the state, according to which the gendered nature of the state cannot be taken for granted but should be demonstrated or reconstructed each time it is brought under analysis. It is not possible to derive the gendered nature of the state from the concept itself. Based on this understanding, I first maintained that each state has gender selectivities that are shaped at the intersection of the requirements of capitalist accumulation with the political legitimation requirements. The necessities of capitalism force states to make strategic selections while trying to tackle with the social reproductive necessities of their populations. The political legitimation requirements operate in the form of 'non-events', telling the states not to do and what to prevent rather than what to do and how to do. The principle of anti-subversion refers, in this context, to the deterrence of emancipatory, revolutionary or anti-orderly events that might hamper the smooth functioning of the capitalist accumulation process and of the political power. The principle of non-failure, on the other side, refers to the deterrence of state weakness, disability or incapacity that might prevent the assimilation of demands of and for social security into the existing socio-political order.

I argued that the state apparatuses are active agents that interpret both clusters of requirements in their own ways and with the help of their ideological lenses. The requirements of capitalism have historically pressed the states to look for solutions to solve the contradictions between the needs for everyday survival or daily subsistence and the profit-oriented capitalist accumulation patterns. To this end, states have deployed different regimes of social reproduction, which have so far relied on unequally structured gender orders. These I describe as the capitalist-patriarchal gender selectivities of the state. In Turkey, this has to this day implied a patriarchal gender contract, where most women are responsible for household-based social reproduction. The bureaucratic-ideological gender selectivities of the state apparatuses, on the other hand, try to rebalance the problems emanating from these patriarchal gender contracts, as their sustainability requires constant patriarchal bargains with women and men. In Turkey, the reform era's attempt to include women into the state protection schemes can be a pertaining example.

On the other hand, the principle of anti-Subversion, one of the two non-events that limit the capitalist state, encourages the bureaucratic-ideological apparatuses to deploy gender itself as a governmental apparatus and construct models for 'agreeable' femininity and masculinity. In Turkey, the AKP era's promotion of a protective/paternalist masculinity with the help of an Islamist conception of gender complementarity is also a relevant example. These facilitate the state to have nuanced strategies for each social group of men and women. Whereas certain women conditionally benefit from the state protection, certain others are more violently treated. Even within the group of women who are subjected to state violence, there are groups whose acquiescence to the power of the state is more prized than others. This differential treatment does also help to seal in the depreciated value of female labour – either domestic or waged – in Turkey. In other words, devalorization and revalorization are ingrained in the centaur state's selective patriarchy.

Table I can be helpful to better summarize the state theoretical perspective I endorse in this study and its application to the empirical material I presented throughout the chapters.

I also maintained in this study that a materialist-cum-feminist state analysis cannot be non-relational. In other words, state forms are rooted in social and political struggles. However, the translation of the formative impacts of social forces into concrete state practice is a complex phenomenon. In the case of feminist movement, for example, the engagements of the feminists with the state are filtered through the gender selectivities of the state. Depending on the nature of these selectivities, the formative interventions in the state are re-signified, distorted and/or refused. But compromises and the conditional empowerment of women are also possible.

Table I Gender Selectivities of the State in the AKP Era with a Focus on the Field of (Human) Security

Gender Selectivities of the State	Non-Event I: The Principle of Anti-Subversion	Non-Event II: The Principle of Anti-Failure
Capitalist-patriarchal	➤ The state in Turkey had to introduce certain *entitlement rights* to improve gender equality. ➤ In the field of (human) security, the state in Turkey has tried to ameliorate the patriarchal protection (e.g. prevention of violence against women) as a way of convincing women into the housewifization, for example marrying and mothering.	➤ The state in Turkey has tried to find *new rules of identity* after years of economic-cum-political crisis. ➤ In the field of (human) security, this principle meant improving the participation of 'people' into the production of security itself. In short, the principles of localism and populism have been adopted.
Bureaucratic-ideological	➤ The moralist and missionary policing instrumentalized gender as a governmental apparatus. This helped it to refine its *selective patriarchy*, the differentiated treatment and inclusion of women (and men). ➤ The post-2013 process speeded up the unfolding of the violent character of human security in Turkey. The transition from moral policing to virtuous violence happened as a *difference-in-identity*.	➤ The populist perception based on the ideal of a harmonious-authentic society prioritized men and especially 'the property-owner modest man' as the real subject recipient of state protection. ➤ The post-2013 process prioritized the policiarization of this 'property-owner modest man', for example, the *Esnaf*, while trying to accord a role of political vengeance to certain loyal women.

Table II summarizes the relational perspective this study embraced to understand some of the limits and promises of the feminist interventions in and against the state during the so-called reformist era of the AKP rule.

The final part of this book displays the sharpening of the gender selectivities of the state with a specific focus on the legal, institutional and ideological changes which have taken place in the security sector in the aftermath of the Gezi Protests. When Gezi Protests outbroke, the state was already on the road to become a centaur state – a state which benefits from gender as a governmental apparatus. Despite the feminist interventions during the reformist era, and despite the introduction of some 'counter-hegemonic rules' into the legal-

Table II The Power-Effects of Feminist Interventions in and against the State

Feminists Interventions in and against the State	Equal Rights Feminism	Governance Feminism	Anti-Militarist Feminism
Mechanisms of State Power (I)	Compromising	Re-signifying	Distorting
Some results	Equal Rights Feminism focuses on the reform of Criminal Law to make women recognized as individuals.	Governance Feminism focuses on changing the conduct of 'the men in the state'.	Peace Feminism focuses on making the state recognize women in their differences, that is women's special needs.
	The reforms were to a great extent realized and yet the implementation of them remained even in the best cases only partial.	The state cadres inserted this to their populist-moralist project based on changing police conduct and behaviours.	The state retaliated against this gender difference perspective by distorting these demands, for example by recruiting more policewomen.
Mechanisms of State Power (II)	Refusing	Refusing	Refusing
Some results	Feminist interventions insist on an effective punishment policy vis-à-vis the male perpetrators of gendered violence.	Feminist interventions want to foster welfarist public policies for women's protection.	Feminist interventions ask for the recognition of the agency of Kurdish women in peace-making process.
	The state apparatus under-criminalizes men perpetrators due to its gender selectivities.	The state apparatus prioritizes restoring the 'honour' of men due to its gender selectivities. It also depicts itself as 'power-less' before the immensity of social question.	The state apparatus refuses to recognize the agency of Kurdish women unless they present or construct themselves as victims of 'terrorist organizations'.

institutional apparatus of the state, these changes have rather stood short of being translated into effective practice. The security bureaucracy has either resignified these interventions to upgrade their own authoritarian agenda or refused to translate them into state practice. It has also distorted the feminist interventions against the militarist-nationalist character of the state. Therefore, even before the full-blown transition from moral policing based on populist and localist state formation schemes to virtuous violence, the state was on the road to become a centaur state – a state which adopts hybrid mechanisms of administration for different social groups.

Feminist interventions could not hamper this process. The false cooperation between the so-called reformist state cadres and the feminists withered away even before the eruption of Gezi Protests. Since then, the gendered state violence has become not only symptomatic but also constitutive of a new society-state nexus in Turkey. In other words, the change of political atmosphere in Turkey within a decade from one of democratization (2006) to that of full authoritarianism (2016) displays a dialectical character.

This, however, does not mean that the centaur state is devoid of any contradictions. On the contrary, the centaur state is itself a state-in-crisis. On the one hand, it sharpens the selective patriarchy to be able to govern women (and men). On the other hand, it faces various cul-de-sacs as not only governing the non-agreeable women but also governing the so-called agreeable women becomes a challenging job.

During this era, feminists have continued struggling against the state in Turkey. They have transitioned from an 'in the state' politics to a more confrontational 'against the state' politics. Nevertheless, the feminist political horizon appears to remain quite similar. Human security continues to be central to feminist politics even though the previous period has displayed the political power's ability to instrumentalize human security as part of its own state project. The concept of human security itself does not provide immunity from co-optation and/or resignification. On the contrary, the concept itself is very anti-Political. But the question of how the feminist politics can effectively challenge the centaur state in Turkey needs to be further discussed. Below, I propose some hypotheses that need further research and scholarly analysis. But before discussing the possible strengths and weaknesses of the feminist interventions in and struggles against the state, I suggest giving a very rapid look at the post-Gezi era feminist politics.

Feminists against the centaur state?

In the post-Gezi era, the discursive strategy of the feminist contenders certainly moved to a new style. The state has been widely called a 'masculine-state'. The feminist strategy about the state form, on the other hand, has been displaying a continuity with the previous period's strategy to benefit from the contradictions of the bourgeois state form. It tries to pressurize the state to abide by the rule of law, to prevent the impunity accorded to police violence and to protect women from male violence.

Women, who participated in the neighbourhood forums – established after the Gezi Protests so that the Gezi movement does not lose momentum – immediately initiated protests against the gendered police violence.[1] Feminists portrayed the police violence against women protestors of Gezi movement as an instrument of state torture used in a systematic way to intimidate women – to discourage them from pursuing oppositional political activity. In a declaration made under the title of 'Women mobilize against sexual harassment and violence under police custody', for example, it is mentioned that the women are determinate to reveal the harassment under police custody and to explain to the public that 'it is not the women who should be ashamed of these harassments'. In a late 2013 public declaration made under the title of 'We call to account for the police violence and harassment. Women's rebellion continues!', feminists asked the state to punish the police involved in harassment and whoever further is involved in 'this crime against humanity'.

The anti-militarist feminism analysed the evolving structure of gendered state violence in the Gezi with reference to the 1990s. One of the members of the Women's Peace Initiative, Feyza Akınerdem reasoned that 'there is a link between the state violence that we experience today during the Gezi Uprisings and the fact that the 1990s have not been called into account and that we have not come into terms with it, yet' (Aşan, Uncu and Kutluata, 2014). Accordingly, the legacy of the past harms done by the state has determined the AKP era's state violence.[2]

After the introduction of the New Internal Security draft bill, feminist struggles against the state continued this antagonistic discursive style but also held onto the political horizon of human security. In early December 2014, just after the introduction of the New Internal Security draft bill to the parliament by the government, one of the umbrella organizations in Turkey, which hosts more than hundred organizations, Women's Coalition made a quick declaration.[3] The declaration questioned the legitimacy of the proposed bill. It asked 'The Government prepared a draft bill for security reform. Whom did it consult?' The statement mentioned that the bill is prepared outside the democratic procedures and that the changes proposed in the law cannot be qualified as reform as it does not secure the liberty and security of individuals. It qualified the government as an oppressive regime, and the bill as a regressive law for and of insecurities.

Accordingly, the security reform draft bill aimed at creating a protective shield for the government and sacrificed human security for the sake of state security (Women's Coalition, 2014). Later, the Coalition published a detailed analysis of the draft bill and posted it in English under the name of 'Assessment of Women's Coalition on the Draft Bill to Amend the Law on the Powers and Duties of the Police' (Women's Coalition, 2015). In the detailed Assessment, it is shown that the new police powers contradict the very principles embraced in the Turkish Constitution and indeed nullifies the very constitutional safeguards.

Amid debates on the internal security law and the growing authoritarian character of the state in 2015, a brutal case of femicide, the murder of Özgecan Aslan, made the opposition forces including women's organization further question the security understanding of the ruling party.[4] The women's organizations were indeed voicing their concerns about the rise of public violence against women and accusing the state of non-enforcing laws that had been enacted to protect women's human rights and the government of failing to pursue its agenda of zero tolerance against violence against women. Basically, women's organizations were accusing the state of three things: one is of failing to fulfil its responsibility to protect; the second is of expanding the police powers with an aim to crush the political opposition; and third, they were arguing that violence against women, including the brutal murder of Özgecan Aslan, cannot be conceived as an act done by some evil villain – as argued to be so by the representatives of the ruling party – but is itself an act of 'male violence'.[5] In the same big rally organized to protest the murder of Özgecan Aslan, women's organizations also protested the new internal security law and shouted 'No!' against the new law and they wrote on the banners: 'The Internal Security Law means insecurity for women. No!' (Kadınlar Özgecan ve katledilen tüm kadınlar için yürüdü, 2015). In August 2015, another feminist organization *Eşitiz* (Equality Monitoring Women's Group) made a declaration regarding the ruthless police operations in the Sur district of Turkey. In this declaration, it is stated that 'women's security of life' is in danger due to war, which is a 'male game'. Same year, on the World Day of Peace, the women's and LGBTI+ organizations made a common declaration of peace, where it was argued that women are on the side of life and not death. In these declarations, state power is associated with death and counter-posited to the women's politics that are deemed as politics of and for life.

As very quickly exemplified, the feminist struggles against the state has since the Gezi Protests leaned on constructing an antinomy between the masculine lethal state and the peaceful life-giving women. They do however also resolutely repeat what the state should do to protect women. It is true that remembering the state about its failure to protect women citizens can be an effective strategy. It can constitute a serious challenge to 'the principle of non-Failure', which the capitalist state in Turkey tries to prevent at all costs. However, as effective as it can be, this strategy also prevents moving to a new question like 'what kind of state should we [the feminists] be attempting to construct?' (Curthoys, 1993: 36). In other words, even if it challenges the state power and causes many cul-de-sacs for it, the feminist politics in and against the state risks of reproducing the existing state form. Why?

A first reason appears to be the risk of essentialism. However radical is the confrontational strategy of the feminists – that is equating women with life and the state with death – it does also possess the risk of reproducing essentialist/biologically determinist conceptions of femininity. It fosters the idea that women are by virtue of their subjective position within the oppressive gender relations more prone to peace. Although this perspective had empowered women's movements around the world in different historical periods (Cockburn, 2010), it is also known that this perception might end in reproducing myths about praiseworthy femininity. These myths, however, have been so far skilfully inserted into the global gender regime without necessarily deranging the structures of inequality (Prügl, 2012). In short, it risks speaking into the 'agreeable women' categorization of the centaur state.

Second, the confrontational strategy, if it stays short of bringing back the *Political*, the debate on 'what kind of state should we build?' also risks leading to antagonistic encounters with the state forces. In the absence of *the Political*, the idea of being anti-statist by virtue of being a woman (woman as life) indirectly invites a vicious circle of (violent) encounters: gendered state violence against women using their bodies as means of and for resistance and vice versa. This is indeed what the centaur state strives to do: to prevent its contenders from focusing on anything other than the sovereign, himself.

As previously mentioned, the centaur state's primary strategy to deal with the politically active women is to victimize them, as detailed down in the second chapter. However, those who refuse to abide by this paternalist human security understanding of the state are invited by the state to a non-political encounter. The state sometimes leaves no place to women activists other than a tragic confrontation strategy. In other words, the state makes its selective method of administration obvious and targets certain 'non-loyal women', who reply with self-annihilating antagonistic methods like indefinite hunger strikes or death fasts. In short, the selectivity of the state creates a spiral of violence. And women of subaltern classes become more open to adopt antagonism as a way of politicization. By antagonism, in this context, it is also meant a strategy which includes suicidal and non-suicidal violent attacks against police forces. To this, the state fiercely and antagonistically responds. The deployment of the special operations teams in the Alevi and poor neighbourhoods of Istanbul points to that strategy. Indeed, the special operations teams are designed as lethal forces. They are trained to kill. 'Being a hunter' and 'hunting' are the two commonly used markers by the team members. They argue that their task is to intervene to 'hunt militants' when things get 'out of control'.

Third, a single strategy of naming and shaming or singling out the police behaviours to expose their masculinist character risks of being resignified by the centaur state as an imperative to employ more female officers – but of course to do the very same job – and deepen the segregationist gender policies. The very latest developments in the Turkish National Police follow this direction. Either to prevent violence against women or to respect the sex of women protestors, the state has started recruiting more and more female officers. As a policy to which feminists should and could not oppose, the strategy of increasing policewomen displays the intertwining of the violent and caring visages of the centaur state in Turkey.

All in all, the post-Gezi feminist struggles against the centaur state risks reproducing the state paradox. No matter how much radicalized they are, the concentration on a dichotomy of women's human security vs. state security does not challenge the continuum of violence and paternalism through which the centaur state operates. This dichotomy skips the gender selectivities of the state which operate at the intersection of gender, class, ethnic background, and political affiliation/intention/activity/militancy. It prioritizes the gendered outcomes – as the core of feminist politics – at the expense of destabilizing these selectivities, which are indeed the root causes of these outcomes.

Against the gendered state violence but beyond human security?

One of the staunch critics of the human rights perspective, Susan Marks invites the social scientists and activists alike to reconsider their methodology and their ontological assumptions when they deal with human suffering (Marks, 2011). She argues that to get over the moralistic stance of human rights, we should get rid of the constraining power of the 'what should governments do?' question. We should rather first ask 'why governments are doing what they are doing?'. This would, according to Marks, also prevent us from the illusion of voluntarism, the state of human forgetting or underestimating the structural factors behind the human misery. Applying this warning to the case of Turkey might help to bring back a discussion on the nature of the capitalist state in Turkey beyond an excessive occupation with the gendered outcomes. Plus, this might push us to work on a feminist theory of the social and of the social question in Turkey. How does feminism conceive the problems of Turkey's capitalist social formation?

Second, she invites us to change the intransitive formulation of social harms. She says that we should be using transitive concepts, for example exploitation instead of discrimination. Thus, Marks argues, the fact that human misery is planned and indeed necessary for the reproduction of the systemic order becomes more visible. Third, she argues that a perspective that limits itself to victims and perpetrators and thus to the immediate encounter in the crime scene is not actually a relational perspective that fulfils its mandate. To be relational, one should demonstrate how deprivation and privilege interrelate and thus who the beneficiaries are. Following these suggestions might force to rethink the alliance politics the feminists follow in Turkey. Which kind of social groups and classes do exactly benefit from the devalorization of female body and labour?

Fourth, Marks insists on the need for materialist analysis in the sense that the ideas, including the idea of human rights, develop and gain influence within certain socio-economic conditions. This has been the case with the idea of human security, as shortly explained in the first chapter. Even transitioning from the politics of human rights to politics of human security denotes a material-cum-ideational transformation in the hegemonic liberal world order. As implied throughout the analysis in this book, the concept of human security has led the feminist contenders to misconstrue the gender selectivities of the state and/or to stop the uncovering of them too soon. In other words, human security has obscured the feminist vision and become a catalyser of 'false contingency' (Marks, 2011).

According to Marks (2009: 10), the activists of human rights tend to forget that 'the current [human rights] arrangements are not simply arbitrary or accidental [hence contingent], but belong with the logics of a system which must also be brought within the analytical frame'. In other words, voluntarism, which constitutes the core of human rights activism, paradoxically risks of underestimating the structural determinants of a process. Yet, Marks is very subtle in her critique of human rights' voluntarism for neglecting structural causes and processes. Indeed, she argues that 'false contingency is generally true so far it goes, but false as to what it excludes; *true in what it says but false in what it leaves unsaid, in its unarticulated assumptions, implications and effects'* (2009: 17, italics added). To put it very simply, for Marks it is not the actual demands of the human rights activists and the very practical interests which they advocate that are false. What is false is the effect this advocacy creates. It obscures the resignification of these (abstract) demands within and by the historically determinate conditions and the discrepancy between the legal changes and actual implementations.

I argue that human security has become a blinder, a false object of misconception. It is mainly because, although maintaining in appearance a common aim – providing women with their individual and non-alienable right to protection from violence – the historical and political references of the human security concept actually significantly differed for the feminist movement and for the reformist state cadres. Whereas the feminist movement's political horizon was shaped after an ideal of a bourgeois modern state, the AKP-led transformation in Turkey was already moving towards a post-modern, a centaur state.

The vision of state possessed by different agents are symptomatic of their stance vis-à-vis the question of *the Political*: 'What kind of a political horizon does the feminist/liberal politics have?' or 'What kind of an ideal political community animates their specific politics?' The vision of state is a *Political* anchor that animates the politics each group pursues. It is both latent and reproduced within daily politics. However, it is also distinct from it, from a notion of politics as a process of struggle for power including different mechanisms such as negotiations, lobbying, daily protests etc.

In line with this line of thought, I would argue that even when the temporal unevenness between the feminist movement's vision of a modern bourgeois state form and the post-modern state vision of the political power left its place to a more synchronic and radical confrontation with the centaur state after the Gezi Protests, the liberal geoculture – specifically the politics of human security – has continued to determine the political horizon of the feminists. However, it appears that whereas in the making of the bourgeois modern state, the protection of human life was a rule limiting the patriarchal power of the state; in the making of the centaur state, it re-empowers it.

By temporality, I mean the historical time of different social and political forces. Here certainly temporalities – of different social and political forces – do not differ in terms of the very vague signifiers of progress vs regress; but rather in terms of the sets of ideas and predispositions that determine the political horizon (past, present and future) – and hence the material power – of different societal agents within a *longue durée*. The struggle which reproduces or shapes the state form within a social formation does not happen among agents situated in the exact same time-space continuum. As Saskia Sassen (2000) argues, globalization or the post-Cold War liberal order as the concept preferred in this study has produced different temporalities existing alongside each other. Unevenness among different social and political agents which struggle to put their prints on state form is therefore a major factor in the specific way the state is reproduced within a polity. The temporal unevenness between the police reformers and the feminist contenders, in that respect, might be another ground for false cooperation.

The complex and differential temporality of the feminist movement and that of the ruling bloc has ended in the unevenness of the women's (partial) integration to the institutional order and of the institutional transformation. For the feminist movement's envisioning of the state form and the dominant political forces' envisioning of the state-in-the-making were so structurally different that the populist-patriarchal roots of the reform process have been ignored, especially in the early years of the AKP rule. Whereas women's organizations saw a political opportunity moment to appropriate the bourgeois modern state, the state form under the yoke of the ruling bloc – which included the AKP, the Gülen Community, the police organization, different factions of capital but also the internationalization belts of these actors – was in fact becoming more and more intransient to such demands – or transient so long as they were adjusted to their own gender selectivities. Whereas women's organizations detected a strategic moment for transformative intervention into the state, the state had been becoming more and more de-rationalized, anti-Political and selectively patriarchal.

Alain Badiou criticizes the human rights perspective on the grounds that its political horizon is too limited and indeed restricted by the mission to identify the Evil. According to this French philosopher, 'the only content of the good is to identify an Evil that is defined a priori (as violation of life, body, or cultural identity) and to prevent it from occurring' (cited in McLoughlin, 2016). This critique, I would argue, is also valid for the politics of human security. Yet, there is also need for further elucidation in the case of human security as besides detecting the Evil, it does also point out to a potential 'Good'. The human security turn goes beyond identifying abuses. It is both normative and prescriptive. This makes the hegemonic power of the human security concept more difficult to counter. Therefore, there is an urgent need for an alternative vocabulary with which to challenge political domination and re-imagine women's emancipation.

Notes

Introduction

1 The latest happened in 2017 (İstanbul'da 18 Yaşındaki Sıla Abalay Öldürüldü, 2017).

2 A recent exception to this is the case of Dilan Kortak, a young woman murdered in Istanbul during the police operations in December 2015. Despite the dismissal of the case by the criminal courts of peace, the Constitutional Court decided for the breach of legal procedures, which normally dictates an effective investigation by the public prosecution (AYM Dilan Kortak Davasında Gerekçeli Kararını Açıkladı, 2020).

3 President Tayyip Erdoğan repeatedly uses the following expressions in his public appearances since the early days of the AKP rule in Turkey: 'We love the creature because of the creator. We do not discriminate against anyone. We love everyone for Allah' (President Erdoğan Attends the Opening Ceremony of Sıdıka Tayyar Hatun Mosque, 2014).

4 This is another motto Erdoğan frequently uses in his public speeches (Erdoğan: Let People Live So the State Will Live, 2019).

5 Due diligence is defined by the United Nations Declaration on the elimination of violence against women (1993) as the state obligation 'to prevent, investigate and, in accordance with national legislation, punish acts of violence against women, whether those acts are perpetrated by the State or by private persons'.

6 As an emblematic example of this discourse, see Insel (2008).

7 This formulation once popularized in the field of Middle Eastern studies focusing on the question of democratic transition in authoritarian countries has also been frequently used in the left-liberal popular media discussions of the early AKP era. For the origin of the term, see Waterbury (1994).

8 For a recent critical evaluation of the liberal peacekeeping and state-building processes implemented in the Global South, see Mustafa (2015).

9 There are many other political moments in Turkey which testify the becoming of women a collective agents of resistance and transformation in Turkey. For an illuminating discussion on the case of ecological dispossession in Turkey and the resistance of women against it, see Yaka (2017).

10 On the crisis of neoliberal state and the gendered implications of this situation, see LeBaron and Roberts (2010).

11 On the political economy of punishment in the Global South, see Amar (2011) and Wright (2011).

12 It is interesting to note that the right to an active resistance to the privatization of state power was also recognized in the Preamble of the Universal Declaration of Human Rights: 'It is essential, if man is not to be compelled to have recourse, as a last resort, to rebellion against tyranny and oppression, that human rights should be protected by the rule of law.'

13 When I refer to the modern bourgeois form of the capitalist state, I do basically refer to the impersonal power of the modern state. From impersonality, I basically understand the revolutionary dethroning of the political classes and the end of the monarchical legitimation of the private possession of state apparatus by aristocratic classes. For an elaborate discussion on the bourgeois state form, see Gerstenberger (2007).

14 A similar argument is made by Christos Boukalas (2014) who focuses on the homeland security measures and practices of the state in the United States. Having demonstrated the co-existence of constitutional democracy with the ever-expanding power of the executive and the transformation of the judiciary into an executive body, Boukalas (2014: 17) argues that what we see in the United States is the making of a 'double polity: a normal-democratic state for dominant capital and an exceptional-dictatorial state for everyone else'.

15 There are also other significant differences between the processes which have been making the centaur state in the Global North and Global South. These processes, however, will not be further discussed here as they would require another line of argumentation and discussion.

16 I name Turkey's new state form, for want of a better term, centaur state. The book however is not a detailed study on every aspect of the centaur state in Turkey. Rather, it tries to excavate some key internationally driven political and ideological processes whose formative roles have been under-recognized in the existing literature.

17 This victimization strategy is also discussed by Babül (2015).

18 The definition of the state as a 'material condensation of the relationship of social forces' is further developed in the Poulantzasian school of state theory. For a detailed discussion on perceiving the state apparatus and the state institutions as the material condensation of social struggles, see Kannankulam and Georgi (2014).

19 For the details and for an elaboration on the categorization of social contention over these three Rs: representation, redistribution, and recognition, see Fraser (1997).

20 The 2009 World Bank report on the 'Status and Progress of Women in the MENA' states: 'While women's labour force participation in the Middle East and North Africa (MENA) increased from 28 to 32 per cent between 2000 and 2006, it remains the lowest in the world (world average is 58 per cent).' In its 'Women in

Statistics 2018' report, Turkish Statistical Institute said the rate of employment among women above the age of fifteen was 28.9 per cent while it was 65.6 per cent for men. Turkey can therefore be considered as one of the most resilient countries in this sense when compared with some selected group of countries in the region (Algeria, Tunisia, Morocco, Egypt, Saudi Arabia and Iraq), for Turkey still displays lower than average levels of female labour force participation and a much more persistent pattern of housewifization among different generations of women within MENA (World Bank, 2009; Memiş, Öneş and Kızılırmak, 2011).

21 Housewifization does mean not only relegating women to the role of housewife but also appropriating their means and resources that would otherwise make women independent from patriarchal control (Mies, 1986). Therefore, participation into the labour force does not guarantee women a direct exit from housewifization as many proletarian women's incomes are appropriated by their male relatives. Still, many women who are home-based workers do earn money but only below the self-subsistence levels (Bair, 2010).

22 It is important to note that this housewifization process has been sustained not only through oppressive practices such as forced seclusion but also by protection accorded to women (Hunnicutt, 2009). Hence, the capitalist patriarchal protection includes the promise of physical protection (from alleged or real threats such as sexual harassment and rape), the promise of status protection (from loss of 'dignified women' status) and also economic protection (from hardships that emanate as a result of divorce and/or loss of spouses). Since the promise of protection has been indeed one of the strategies of the capitalist patriarchal states in the MENA region to secure the hierarchical continuation of the gender order and hence of the gendered division of labour, the weakening of this protection system today, as identified in the increasing numbers of domestic violence, constitutes a threat to both the social reproduction processes in general and the reproduction of the capitalist-patriarchal states in particular. Furthermore, patriarchal protection is not immune to the historical changes in the development of capitalism. It is constantly negotiated, challenged and reproduced (Kandiyoti, 1987). In the context of MENA, from the late nineteenth century, feminism has developed as an oppositional consciousness (Fleischmann, 2018).

23 In the case of the Middle Eastern countries, the early and mid-twentieth-century state feminism(s) can be considered such a strategic gender selectivity historically forged to attenuate the dependence of women on male kin-based patriarchal protection. Although not challenging the basic relation of dependence and hierarchy between the sexes, in Egypt the 'state feminism' has made the social reproduction issue a less private concern for women and opened the public sphere to them (Hatem, 1992). State strategies, which are named as 'public patriarchy' on the other hand, can be conceived as attempts to provide women with preferential

social entitlements – such as allowances paid to women who take care of elderly at home – that paradoxically reproduce the dependent status of women (Dedeoğlu and Elveren, 2012).

24 Indeed, the gender equality in the field of educational attainment in Turkey is remarkably close to parity. However, the gender equality in the field of economic participation and opportunity is less than half of the parity. This gap can be considered as emblematic of the contradictory tendencies in Turkey's capitalist social formation. For recent data on gender equality in Turkey, see World Economic Forum (2019).

25 One of the fiercest bureaucratic struggles in the Turkish state apparatus, causing a deep state crisis, happened just after the Gezi Protests which have completely changed the political atmosphere in Turkey since 2013. From the last day of May 2013 to early July 2013, about 10 million people took to the streets in different urban centres of Turkey to protest the government due to its neoliberal and neoconservative policies giving deep harm to nature, work life, social life, gender equality and societal peace. The common rallying cry was the resignation of the Turkish Government. Just in the aftermath of these protests, during 17–25 December 2013, the Financial Crime Unit of the Istanbul Security Directorate – most of which were Fethullah Gülen community-associated police officers – detained forty-seven people, including high-ranked public officials and three sons of the then Turkish ministers, Muammer Güler (Minister of the Interior), Zafer Çağlayan (Minister of Economy) and Erdoğan Bayraktar (Minister of Environment and Urban Planning) for allegations of corruption and money-laundering. The fight within the state continued until 16 July 2016, when a group of security personnel – assumedly linked to the Fethullah Gülen community – initiated a putsch attempt, suppressed by the government. These bureaucratic struggles in Turkey were not fought necessarily on how to monopolize and validate one's own expertise on the social question. But it was certainly not independent from it, as the timing of the events is self-telling. After the Gezi Protests, the very much internationalized Gülen-affiliated state cadres, who had also for years parcelled the state including the higher-echelons of security bureaucracy, feared of a loss of power stemming from societal upheaval and tried to compensate the loss of state legitimacy by way of persecuting certain AKP cadres.

26 'Patriarchal dividend' is a concept used by Raewyn Connell (2009: 142) who defines it as 'the advantage to men as a group from maintaining an unequal gender order'. The benefits range from money income to access to institutional power. The dividend, I would maintain, can be extended to certain women under certain conditions – especially in cases where conservative political regimes are also supported by a non-negligible number of women, such as in the case of AKP's Turkey.

27 Of course, what is this excess and how it is determined is a highly struggle-laden issue and it is the feminist movement which has so far successfully pressurized the state in this matter.

28 The fact that the great majority of the state officers in Turkey are men is an important factor in the shaping of the gendered scripts of the state. Only 6 per cent of the police personnel in Turkey are women. This is a decisive fact in the making and reproduction of a sub-culture of masculinity within the police organization. Although excluded from the research scope of this study, this sub-culture certainly has an impact on the gender selectivities of the state in the job of policing. On the hegemonic masculinity in the police organization in Turkey, see Eksi (2019).

29 For many Western Marxists, including Claus Offe, the legitimation strategies of the capitalist state are causally linked and/or explained by reference to liberal-democratic practices. However, I maintain that there is no historical and structural necessity which ties the legitimation needs of capitalist social formations to democratic politics. The expansion of democratic inclusion has historically been only one of the ways the capitalist state could prevent state and system failure. Legitimation of the capitalist system or of the social contract does not have to be democratic.

30 From 2009 until its violent collapse in the aftermath of the June 2015 general elections, the AKP governments conducted a political process to resolve the long-lasting 'Kurdish question' of the Turkish Republic (Yegen, 2015). Named by the public as 'the resolution process', the state in Turkey conducted negotiations with the jailed PKK leader Öcalan mediated by the social-democrat and pro-Kurdish Peoples' Democratic Party. The AKP governments have also introduced some reforms seemingly ensuring democratization and recognition of the cultural and individual – but not collective – rights of Kurds (Yegen, 2015; Cicek, 2018).

31 One of the essential challenges the feminist activism has been facing in Turkey has been this 'in or against the state' dilemma. Although more will be told on this dilemma in the coming chapters, it would now suffice to say that the feminist movement both needs the state's legitimate monopoly of violence in order to struggle against the gendered violence and fears from being co-opted by the very same state, whose institutional and financial contribution in women's protection could and would come at significant costs for gender emancipatory goals. For a study in relation to state-run women's shelters and the question of compromised feminist autonomy in Turkey, see Toktaş and Diner (2011).

32 By state fetishism, I refer first (1) to a deterministic idea that there is no way for progression or amelioration of the human condition other than to work with the existing state form and second (2) to the act of desiring the attention of the state. On the one hand, this deterministic idea and desire for state attention help to reproduce the existing order. On the other hand, it relieves the desiring subject

from the burden of feeling responsible for the reproduction of the existing order. This fetishism mostly results from separating politics with a small 'p' from the Political or the politics of security-seeking from the politics of emancipation.

Chapter 1

1   During the reform era, the centre-periphery analogy was widely espoused to make sense of the political history of modern Turkey. This analogy proposes that the foundational cleavage in Turkish society lies between two groups of conflicting cultural worlds: the state elites at the centre and the religious masses on the periphery. The model enabled its adherents to condemn the anti-religious state policies of Turkish modernizers, especially the Kemalists, for alienating 'the pious Muslims', whose values are assumed to be the authentic values of not only a section of but of the whole society at large. In the same token, the educated urbanized sectors of the Turkish society were accused of being the privileged class, 'White Turks', favoured by the state against the pious people of Anatolia from the beginning of Turkish modernization (Örnek and Hülagü, 2018). The rise of the Muslim businessmen during the AKP era has also been considered as the decentring of the old guards like the Istanbul-based capital groups by pious capital owners from Anatolia. For an analysis see, Buğra and Savaşkan (2012).

2   This had also facilitated the becoming of liberalism a cornerstone of global political thought because when liberalism started to make its journey from Latin America to Asia, it was already wrapped into the ideology of nationalism – organic nations posited against corrupt rulers (Bayly, 2011).

3   On the middle-class ideal of liberal internationalism and why it has been to this day conceived as the security valve of the international system, see Smith (2017).

4   In the *Human Security Now* report previously mentioned, it is argued that 'states built powerful security structures to defend themselves – their boundaries, their institutions, their values, their numbers. Human security shifts from focusing on external aggression to protecting people from a range of menaces' (2003: 6). In the *same* report, Amartya Sen (2003: 9) explains the difference between human rights and human security perspectives and argues that 'human security can make a significant contribution [to the normative framework of human rights] by identifying the importance of freedom from basic insecurities – new and old'. Besides all emphasis put on the need to empower people so that they can fend for themselves, human security accords the guiding role in the prevention of these insecurities to some form of *humanitarian authority* – be it state or any other legal or non-legal entity. Amartya Sen explains this as the 'duties of other people or institutions'.

5   Although the reformist police cadres were more open to working with the feminists for reasons that will be discussed in detail in the following chapter, there were also incidents of police resistance. Many training anecdotes that the project members/trainers tell demonstrate that the police officers were feeling uncomfortable either with the notion of gender (the idea that femininity and masculinity are social constructs) or with the idea of empathizing with feminist demands, especially those that are voiced in street demonstrations. Some of them had also a hard time understanding the seriousness of domestic violence, which they tended to reduce to 'one single slap in the face'.

Chapter 2

1   The community-based policing projects included projects specialized in children, for example, projects on improving the life chances of children under risk. The police organization cooperated with several non-governmental organizations and in the case of children with the Union of Chambers and Commodity Exchanges of Turkey (TOBB). This business organization was asked to provide children with vocational training so that they stay away from 'crime'.

During the 2000s, the police organization was highly active in re-making the social tissue in the Kurdish-populated regions of Turkey. Police chiefs were organizing community activities especially targeting Kurdish children. Instituting after-school classes to help poor children in their homework, organizing city trips for them, playing football with them were among the central activities of the reformist police cadres. During these activities, children were taught by the police on the merits of concentrating on their individual careers and selecting some role models for themselves from within the Kurdish politicians and celebrities affiliated with the AKP. During this era, religion has also been proficiently instrumentalized by the police organization to redefine Kurdish children as Muslim children. On an expanded discussion, see Hülagü (2016, 2017).

2   One of the important components of the police reform process in Turkey was ensuring 'secure cities'. To this end, the police organization underlined the need for surveillance and intelligence-based policing. The performance criteria for this type of policing was positively correlated with the rate of 'crime reports' received from the public. To secure the effectiveness of surveillance, many undercover police officers have been patrolling the cities in Turkey. They are mostly disguised as local salesmen and/or street vendors.

3   During the police reform process, the Kurdish-populated regions of Turkey received special attention. The introduction of community-based policing in this region was also devised as a reconciliation between the state and society following years

of violent conflict with the PKK. It was argued that through community-policing security would be co-produced with the citizens. Thus, they would own the state and not resent against it. On this missionary style of policing, see Hülagü (2016).

4 On this conservative sensibility about shoes and about police entering home or any other private area with shoes, see Cantek (2019).

5 The police reformers are also known to be highly active in the preparation of Balyoz and Ergenekon cases in Turkey. Balyoz (sledgehammer) was the name of an alleged coup plan initially surfaced by *Taraf* newspaper, once the primary voice of liberalism and left liberalism in Turkish media, and in response to which a court case was opened in 2010 persecuting hundreds of people. Ergenekon operations started in 2008 with the persecution of high-ranking army officers and some prominent Kemalists for allegedly being members of a clandestine organization named Ergenekon, which, according to the prosecutors, was preparing a military coup plot against the government.

6 Mustafa Şen (2010) defines the Turkish-Islamist synthesis as "'a form of ideologized Islam that not simply focuses on Qur'anic values" but also highlights "the idea of return to the Turkish 'national culture' which is seen as a product of the synthesis between Turkishness and Islam'". According to Şen, the Gülen Community is one of the staunchest followers of this synthesis, which also involves an ideal and project of state whose 'grandeur would be reminiscent of the Ottoman Empire'.

7 Among a plethora of others, see Berberoğlu (1997).

8 The 28 February 1997 military intervention to politics in Turkey is usually discussed with a preponderating emphasis on the military's envy to tame the growing Islamization of Turkey by taking under control the governmental and parliamentary representatives of the political Islam in Turkey and to define the political Islam and Kurdish separatism as the two essential internal threats. As an example, see Jenkins (2007).

9 One of those reform proposals was prepared under the auspices of the then President Tansu Çiller, who worked with a US team headed by Jay L. Kriegel, an international mentor to Çiller in between 1994 and 1997. Among others, the most underlined measure of this reform proposal was about curbing down the numbers of high-ranked police officers, who were considered as corrupt and overly politicized. For further details on this and on the 1990s' tit-and-tat between the police and the military and between the police and the political establishment, see Özdemir (2009).

10 During this reformist era, several other twinning projects were introduced by the European Union to strengthen the police capacity in Turkey. On these twinning projects and their general impact on the TNP, see Bahçecik (2014).

11 For a detailed study on the social bases of political Islamism in Turkey, see Gülalp (2001).

12 Wives are not criticized for being non-submissive to male authority, as would be expected from a classical patriarchal perspective, but rather for being inconsistent about their positions vis-à-vis their abusive husbands. Police officers argue that 'when women [subjected to violence] do behave in a consistent manner and pursue their [judicial] complaints without hesitation, the mindfulness level of the men [husbands] augments' (cited in Demir, Fidan and Nam, 2013: 53).

13 In the welfarist era during the mid-twentieth century, for example, crime was a deviation 'from normal civilized conduct and was explicable in terms of industrial pathology or else faulty socialization' (Garland, 1996: 450). In the mid-twentieth century, 'the consensus among professionals in the criminal field was that the prison is an outdated and discredited institution' (Weis, 2017: 152). The good policing was back then identified with scientific expertise and objective knowledge. The crime was defined as a welfare problem requiring therapeutic or social-remedial interventions than as a law and order problem requiring a punitive response (Palmer and O'Mally, 1996).

14 This apologetic attitude towards male violence against women is also visible in the attitudes of other constituents of the ruling bloc, of which the reformist police cadres were once a central group. In 2006, the Security General Directorate that governs the TNP published a report on the violence against women in Turkey with a specific focus on the cases that are categorized as 'honour crimes'. The report was hotly debated in the mainstream media and the establishment newspapers communicated the results of this study under headings which gender-wash the honour crimes: 'Men are as much victims of the honour crimes as women are'; 'More men are victims of honour crimes than women' (Töre daha çok erkekleri vurdu, 2006).

15 During the police reform era, the UNFPA Turkey organized different gender trainings in cooperation with the police organization in Turkey (for the details, see Chapter 1, 'New Liberal Geoculture'). Following the second round of these trainings, the participant police officers were asked to write some short stories to elaborate on their experiences regarding domestic violence. These short stories brought together in an edited book, *Bilindik Bilinmez Hikayeler*, are published by the international partner UNFPA Turkey in 2011.

16 This Undersecretariat was specifically established in 2010 in order to develop policies and programmes that would help the state to strengthen the project of 'National Unity and Brotherhood' declared in 2009 in order to end the armed conflict with the PKK and establish a conflict resolution process. It was assigned as the main coordinating body of the 'Resolution Process' in 2014. The Undersecretariat is abolished in 2018.

17 It is possible to argue that this perspective represents today more than ever the official position of the state in Turkey. Recently, the Minister of Interior Süleyman

Soylu argued that 'the PKK is a women's organisation' and that 'in all activities of the PKK, more than half of the militants are female'. He added that 'the PKK's propaganda of women's rights ... create a cultural terrorism that attacks religion, nation, family, love and respect for parents' (Soylu: Olası Büyük İstanbul Depremi için Hazırlanıyoruz, 2020).

18 On the emergence of international discussions about the 'Turkish Model' for Middle Eastern democratization, see Altunışık (2005).

19 One should also remember the fact that this return to the militarized policing strategy via SPO came just after the abrogation of the EMASYA Protocol in 2010, a nation-wide celebrated decision as an essential step for the civilianization process of politics in Turkey. Before becoming ineffective, the EMASYA Protocol or the Protocol on Security, Public Order and Assistance Units had provided soldiers with the possibility of intervention in civilian events. According to TESEV, the EMASYA Protocol was one of the most privileged devices of the military tutelage system in Turkey. The then Prime Minister Erdoğan said in a live broadcast on TRT on 31 January 2010: 'There is nothing like the EMASYA protocol and there will not be. We will take measures accordingly to close this issue' (Korkut, 2010).

Chapter 3

1 While categorizing the feminist interventions in and against the state in Turkey via making a differentiation between the equal rights feminism and the gender mainstreaming feminism, I am inspired by the heuristic categorization made by Elisabeth Prügl (2009) in her study on the feminist interventions in the German Agricultural State.

2 On the waves of feminism and feminist movement in Turkey, see Diner and Toktaş (2010).

3 Establishing such a link between state violence and domestic violence was also a political method used by the feminists during the 1980s because they were ferociously criticized by the traditional leftist groups on the grounds that they prioritized private sphere in the middle of an ongoing state fascism and thus did a political wrong by changing the target of political struggle from the 1980 fascist regime to men. The First Woman's Congress which convened in 1989 was home to such discussions where violence against women and especially the struggle of feminists against domestic violence was despised by traditional leftist groups. State violence was considered by these groups essentially as violence against revolutionary men. However, women revolutionaries were also subject to state violence, especially in forms that directly targeted their bodies and sexualities.

4	Feminists joining this campaign originally initiated by the magazine *Feminist*
	were trying to challenge the acceptability of domestic violence by way of
	augmenting women's solidarity and independence from male institutions. The
	magazine *Feminist* was in that regard pointing out the need for the establishment
	of women shelters, as centres protecting women from abusive relatives and
	especially from husbands (Ayşe, 1987). Apart from mentioning getting some help
	from local municipalities, feminists were arguing for complete self-sufficiency.
	Women were invited to take care of themselves and have a distinct politics for and
	by women.
5	Nevertheless, feminists were also formulating the following question: including
	the state, women are deprived of the many apparatuses of and for political power;
	then, should they leave men to enjoy these tools on their own or ask for equal
	participation and rights in order to shake the male domination and destroy its
	comfort zones? Although answered in positive terms many times, the fear of being
	co-opted, pacified by the male dominance system was always there, looming in the
	backyard of each political decision.
	In the socialist-feminist magazine *Kaktüs*, feminists were warning against
	the possibility that establishing women's shelters can also be tolerated by the
	capitalist system. It was, however, also further explained that this toleration
	would only be to some definite extent as shelters are indeed threats to the
	traditional family structures on which the capitalist system of (re)production
	depends in Turkey. Therefore, it was argued, the only guarantee of being not
	assimilated to the requirements of the system and possessing some power for
	effective negotiation is the existence of an independent women's movement
	(Paker, 1988).
6	This bold strategy, despite the suffocating anti-feminist atmosphere within the
	state and society, worked very well. The Article 438 of the Criminal Code could be
	abolished in the National Assembly (Kardam, 2005: 112).
7	In one such letter, it is stated for example that women prisoners could not profit
	from the infirmary on the grounds that it was located over the corridors used by
	men (Bayrampaşa Cezaevinde Kalan bir Siyasi Tutuklunun Mektubu, 1990).
8	State feminism refers to the political projects usually initiated by the anti-colonialist
	reformist/revolutionary elite male in the MENA region, for alleviating social
	discrimination against women through legal changes and public policy measures.
	In relation to that, state feminism has always had a double legacy. While partially
	emancipating women from patriarchal domination rooted in the private sphere, it
	has built up a public version of patriarchy, sustained the dependence of women on
	elite men and hindered their liberation. Moreover, the beneficiaries of the reforms
	have strongly varied in accordance with the socio-economic contexts where they
	are introduced. Whereas in Turkey, the upper middle-class women have historically

been the main beneficiaries of these reforms, in Egypt, working-class women have also benefited from state feminism up until the economic liberalization of the 1970s (Kandiyoti, 1987; Hatem, 1992). Moreover, whereas some forms of state feminism were more successful in making egalitarian changes in personal status laws like in Turkey, others like in the case of Egypt were less powerful in doing so but more determinate in lessening the social reproduction burden of women. In other words, state feminism is a historically and geographically changing phenomenon. Its central character, however, is its being a top-to-down transformation, instrumentalized by state elites, lacking grassroot ownership and therefore possessing paradoxical implications for gender liberation.

9 The statist turn of the women's organizations is not limited to Turkey. For a more detailed insight see Rai (1996).

10 Feminists also criticize state feminism as being an apparatus of newly emerging political regimes, which by instrumentalizing women's rights try to acquire international recognition and prestige, see Kandiyoti (1987).

11 In the 1980s, Turkey transitioned to low-cost, labour-intensive export-based production. The driving industry of this newest trend was the textile industry, which benefited from feminization of labour in two main ways: through high value-added sub-contracting and through cheap standardized production. For the former, women homeworkers and indeed 'housewives' were employed. This has also permitted the firms to profit from informality and flexibility. For the latter, women workers usually came from the poorest families, freshly migrated to urban settings from rural areas, with extremely limited education. For further details, see Eraydın and Erendil (1999).

12 The increasing dialogue with the state has not yet meant a complete outdoing of the initial principles of the feminist movement of late 1980s. The principle of establishing an independent, self-sustaining women's movement persisted in the early 1990s, even in the struggle against violence against women (Işık, 2002: 46). To sustain both independence and consistency in the struggle against violence, feminists decided to institutionalize their voice in different types of organizations. As Işık (2002) tells, the need to make the campaign against battering endurable and to find ways to support women who need sustenance encouraged them to build legal entities that can establish women's shelters and/or counselling centres. The first organization was the Purple Roof Foundation (Mor Çatı), founded in 1990, in Istanbul, and the second was Women's Solidarity Foundation (Kadın Dayanışma Vakfı), established in 1991, in Ankara.

13 Interestingly, in the mentioned Congress, a *femocrat* who worked by then in the Ministry of Women and Family Affairs, Halime Güner (Mor Çatı Kolektifi, 2002: 81) pointed out that the state policies with regard to women in Turkey had always been cosmetic policies to impress the international community and especially

to sustain the prestige of the Turkish state in the West. Her speech implied that connecting with these or those men in the state, however good they may be, was at some point senseless and determined at the last instance with the political agenda of those men.

14 This strategy of pressurizing the public authority to act true to its image first started with the struggle to make the Law 4320 applied in practice. Especially the efforts of women's movement to make the Law 4320 actively enforced activated women lawyers, who gave voluntary legal aid to women either who need professional support or, for example, who trained the police rank-and-file so that they become aware of the nuances of the new law and how it should be implemented in real life. In other words, during this process women lawyers organized in bar associations were mobilized.

15 For an extended discussion on this gap, see GREVIO (2018).

16 Many women who felt more empowered to speak up their stories also tried to restore justice by using international mechanisms. One prominent example is Asiye Zeybek Güzel who wrote a book titled *Rape during Torture* (1997) and sued the Turkish state in the European Court of Human Rights, which in turn, found Turkey guilty of not providing people whose rights and freedoms are violated with the right to make an effective application to a national mechanism.

17 The United Nations Security Council Resolution (2000) expresses concern that the 'civilians, particularly women and children, account for the vast majority of those adversely affected by armed conflict' and reaffirms 'the important role of women in the prevention and resolution of conflicts and in peace-building' and therefore urges states to take appropriate action.

In the feminist literature, it is highlighted that despite its gender sensibilities, the functions and aims of the resolution should be conceived within the general context of the post-1995 Beijing backlash, where various international actors including the Vatican coalesced to suppress the growing power of the transnational women's movement with the help of biologism or biological determinism. The post-1995 decisions taken by the international organizations, including the UNSC, have all bore the mark of this backlash through difference. In other words, by putting women on a pedestal because 'they are biologically reproductive' and hence naturally different from men and hence in need of special diligence, the backlash forces defeated various feminist demands. The concentration of the post-UNSC 1325 era on sexual crimes and on the victimization of women, as a human category represented only with reference to their reproductive capacity and sexuality, veiled other significant forms of gender discrimination (Ertürk, 2015). Laura Sjoberg and Caron Gentry (2007: 223) define this process as 'the evolution of a new, under-the-radar sort of gender subordination in global politics'.

Chapter 4

1 According to a KONDA (2014) survey realized in 2013, women constituted 51 per cent of the Gezi protesters.

2 For a detailed analysis of the politics of intimacy of the AKP governments, see Acar and Altunok (2013).

3 Erdoğan himself has accused feminists and women's rights activists many times by being non-national. He has in fact put into work a generic political Islamist reflex about feminism framed as a 'Western-specific ideology'.

4 However, the reverse is also possible. For example, the Islamic Republic in Iran had to restore some of the rights women enjoyed in the pre-Revolutionary era, within six years of the 1979 Revolution. The regime could not afford to totally discard women because the economic and social necessities resulting from the Iran-Iraq War made the exclusion of women from the public sphere impossible (Moghadam, 2002).

5 On an expansive study done for the years 2015–16 on the availability of abortion at state hospitals in Turkey, it is found that 'only 7.8% of state hospitals provide abortion services without regard to reason which is provided for by the current law, while 78 per cent provide abortions when there is a medical necessity ... There are two regions, encompassing 1.5 million women of childbearing age, where no state hospital provides for abortion without restriction as to reason' (O'Neil, 2017).

6 The daughter of Recep Tayyip Erdoğan, Sümeyye Erdoğan Bayraktar, leads the pro-government women's organization KADEM (Women and Democracy Association). In order to differentiate their perspective with regard to the 'woman issue', Sümeyye Erdoğan tells that they are in peace with their natural constitution or original and divine disposition [*fitrat*]. According to this women's rights activist, current feminism is individualist and therefore constitutes a threat to the generational reproduction (Kadem Başkan Yardımcısı Sümeyye Erdoğan Bayraktar'ın III. Olağan Genel Kurulu Açılış Konuşması, 2019).

7 For an analysis of the government-organized non-governmental women's rights organizations which help to foster the anti-feminist gender politics of the AKP, see Diner (2018).

8 Gezi Events are full of episodes on the violent encounters between the police and the women protesters. Mücella Yapıcı, the then representative of the Taksim Solidarity Platform, which was established in 2012 to prevent governmental urban projects to transform the Taksim Square and the Taksim Gezi Park into a neo-Ottomanist structure, describes the police attitude towards the female detainees who were taken into custody on 8 July 2013 with the following words: 'We encountered serious torture as if in a narcotic search... When the other young women detainees woke up at night, they realized that their photos were taken...

Cameras in the hands of male cops… What is this? … One day we outrageously noticed that there are cameras in the toilets. We went to the toilet without noticing those cameras. I do not forgive this; I will not forgive… I saw those young women, I witnessed them. That testimony requires me to continue struggling. I won't die without asking accountability for this' (Yapıcı, 2013). One of the strategies used by the police to intimidate young women was to conduct strip-searches. Another one, for example, was the use of human excreta by the police officers.

9   It is also reported that the police forces frequently intervened in the Gülsuyu district to detain the DHKP-C members who were accused of pressuring the drug dealers in the neighbourhood (Gökaçtı, 2012)

10 In the 'Handmaid's tale', the dystopian novel of the acclaimed feminist writer Margaret Atwood (1985), freshly composed during the neoliberal-neoconservative backlash under the auspices of Ronal Reagan against the rise of second wave feminism in the United States, tells the story of an ultra-patriarchal authoritarian regime (Gilead) that categorizes women according to their fertility and compliance status. Those women who are not biologically fertile and/or who resist the regime at all force are profiled as unwoman. These women are punished with forced labour in the camps built on and around toxic wastes. The novel displays a meticulous hierarchy of women, who are both constructed and governed by a patriarchy which selectively works at the intersection of class, gender and political stance.

11 In the aftermath of the 15 July Failed Coup, the AKP government and President Erdoğan have started a complete reshuffling of the state apparatus, with thousands of state employees dismissed from jobs, a mass purge indeed. Many measures were taken via State of Emergency Decree Laws. All military schools are shut down (A new National Defence University is built up). Thousands of soldiers are dismissed from the army over suspected links to the 15 July Failed Coup attempt. Nearly 44 per cent of Land Force Generals, 42 per cent of Air Force Generals and 58 per cent of Navy Admirals were dismissed. The AKP government has argued that the Gülen-affiliated bureaucrats constituted a parallel state within the state and staged a coup against the government. The government with the help of a New Internal Security Bill (see below), issued in March 2015, closed the Turkish Police Academy with the assumption that many graduates were affiliated with the Gülen movement. The police vocational high schools are converted into vocational training centres with the approval of the Ministry of Interior. The ex-minister of Interior Efkan Ala argued that out of the 7,000 police members of the police intelligence department linked to the General Security Directorate, 6,500 were Gülenists.

12 The female constituency behind Erdoğan's political power has been a significant component of the new patriarchal face the authoritarian state in Turkey has acquired. In different studies, it is demonstrated that women who are active in the ranks of the AKP trust Erdoğan better than their male kin, feel empowered

and honoured by Erdoğan's presence. Sezen Yaraş (2018) keenly demonstrates in her study on the female local politicians of the AKP that the pro-Erdoğan women adamantly desire to become active in the construction of a new womanhood and a new moralist political spirit in Turkey.

13   But even before the Gezi Protests, the changes introduced into the Criminal Law were facilitating the selective enforcement of law against the politically active women. The introduction of probation as a new criminal execution procedure is important in that regard. Accordingly, the women who are convicted with three or less years of prison sentence can benefit from the probation procedure if they have children between zero and six years old. However, as probation law strictly forbids the political detainees from benefiting from this regulation, women who are sentenced due to cases such as 'Crimes against the Security of the State', 'Crimes against the Constitutional Order and the Functioning of This Order', and 'Crimes against National Defense' fall outside the scope of law.

14   The HDP operates a co-presidential system of leadership, with one chairman and one chairwoman. This rule is also applied in municipality administrations, albeit unofficially. In the latest, 2019 local elections, thirty-seven women mayors were elected in Turkey, with twenty-four from the HDP. An additional thirty-four women co-mayors also run for office, through the co-presidency system implemented by the HDP.

15   On the heuristic differences between gendered forms, gendered motives and gendered outcomes of violence targeting politically active women, see Bardall, Bjarnegard and Piscopo (2019).

Conclusion

1   In their call made to women and to transwomen, they declared that 'we are afraid neither of the AKP nor of its harassing police. We defy the misogynists and tell them: It is actually you who should be afraid of us' (Yoğurtçu Parkı Forumu, 2013).

2   Akınerdem cites the example of the then Mayor of Istanbul Hüseyin Avni Mutlu, as one of the state cadres directly or indirectly involved in the state atrocities of 1990s continuing his job without having to face any judicial process. The impunity accorded to those state cadres has also been a trademark of the AKP era despite the cases of Ergenekon and Balyoz, where the political power made as if there was such a reckoning.

3   Coalition is a platform with a stated mission to act as a transformative movement primarily aiming to change the dominant political culture that discriminates against women. Among others, the principles of the coalition include to support peace, equality and freedom; to condemn all forms of violence; to be against all

forms of oppression and domination and be for human rights and women's human rights.

4   Özgecan Aslan was a university student who was ferociously murdered while resisting attempted rape on 11 February 2015. In the following days, thousands of protesters took to the streets, in several provinces. Vast majority of them were women, shouting slogans like 'We are not mourning but revolting'.

5   In 2015, after the violent murder of Özgecan Aslan that sparked an unprecedented mobilization of women through public protests, the Islamist press also condemned the murder and made calls for bringing back capital punishment in order to retaliate and to prevent further sexual violence. Some others including the Ex-Minister of Family Betül Sayan Kaya proposed chemical castration as a way of deterring sexual harassment of women and children. Not only feminists reacted strongly against this penalization strategy and condemned it as a totally misleading approach to deal with gender inequality and gender based violence, the Islamists themselves finally opted for another strategy: to put the blame on feminists and women in general rather than on men and male offenders in particular.

Bibliography

10 Bin Özel Polis Harekat Alımı için 220 Bin Kişi Başvurdu. (2016, November 15). T24. Retrieved from: https://t24.com.tr/haber/10-bin-ozel-harekat-polisi-alimi-icin-220-bin-kisi-basvurdu

Acar, F., and Altunok, G. (2013). The 'Politics of Intimate' at the Intersection of Neo-liberalism and Neo-conservatism in Contemporary Turkey. *Women's Studies International Forum*, 41, 14–23.

Acuner, S. (2002). 90'lı Yıllar ve Resmi Düzeyde Kurumsallaşmanın Doğuş Aşamaları. In A. Bora, and A. Günal (Eds.), *90'larda Türkiye'de Feminizm* (pp. 125–59). İstanbul: İletişim.

Ağduk, M. (2019, July 30). (F. Hülagü, Interviewer).

Aguilar, D. (2015). Intersectionality. In S. Mojab (Ed.), *Marxism and Feminism* (pp. 203–20). London: Zed Books.

Akıncı, S. (2013). *Yerel Güvenlik Komisyonları*. Ankara: UNDP.

Akınerdem, F. (2017). Are There Women Out There? Democracy Vigils and the Political of Representation after the Failed Coup Attempt in Turkey. *Journal of Middle East Women's Studies*, 13(1), 189–94.

Akkaya, G., and Demir, B. (2005). Gülnur Acar Savran: Sistemin Temeli Kadının Görünmeyen Emeği. *Pazartesi*, (99), 10–14.

Alagüney, A. H. (2011). Umut. In *Bilindik Bilinmez Hikayeler* (pp. 51–88). Ankara: UNFPA.

Alkan, N. (2011). *Özgürlükten Araçsallığa: PKK'da Kadınlar*. Ankara: Polis Akademisi Yayınları.

Alkan, N., and Çitak, C. (2007). Youth and Terrorism. In H. Durmaz, B. Sevinç, A. S. Yayla and S. Ekici (Eds.), *Understanding and Responding to Terrorism* (pp. 285–306). Amsterdam: IOS Press.

Altunışık, M. B. (2005). The Turkish Model and Democratization in the Middle East. *Arab Studies Quarterly*, 27(1–2), 45–63.

Altunok, G. (2016). Neo-conservatism, Sovereign Power and Bio-power: Female Subjectivity in Contemporary Turkey. *Research and Policy on Turkey*, 1(2), 132–46.

Amar, P. (2011). Turning the Gendered Politics of the Security State Inside Out? Charging the Police with Sexual Harassment in Egypt. *International Feminist Journal of Politics*, 13(3), 299–328.

Andersen, L. (2012). The Liberal Dilemmas of a People-centred Approach to State-building. *Conflict, Security and Development*, 12(2), 103–21.

Anderson, L. (1987). The State in the Middle East and North Africa. *Comparative Politics*, 20(1), 1–18.

Aradau, C., and Blanke, T. (2010). Governing Circulation: A Critique of the Biolopolitcs of Security. In M. D. Larrianaga and M. Doucet (Eds.), *Security and Global Governmentality: Globalization, Power and the State* (pp. 44–58). Basingstone: Palgrave.

Arın, C. (1996). Kadına Yönelik Şiddet. *Cogito*, (7), 305–12.

Arruzza, C. (2016). Functionalist, Determinist, Reductionist: Social Reproduction Feminism and Its Critics. *Science and Society*, 80(1), 9–30.

Arslan, Ö. (2016). *Türkiye'de Güvenlik Sektörünün Dönüşümü: Polisliğin Yeniden Yapılandırılması*. Ankara: Polis Akademisi.

Arslan, Z. (2006). 11 Eylül Sonrasında Yeni Güvenlik Anlayışı, İnsan Hakları ve Demokratik Kolluk. *Polis Bilimleri Dergisi*, 8(2), 121–36.

Arslan, Z. (2008). The Fragile Balance between Security and Human Rights. In Ü. Cizre and İ. Cerrah (Eds.), *Security Sector Governance: Turkey and Europe* (pp. 25–43). İstanbul: TESEV/DCAF.

Aşan, E., and Aslan, Ö. (2009, June). *Nazan Üstündağ ile Söyleşi: 'Türkiye'de Devlet Sorunu Üzerine'*. Feminist Yaklaşımlar. Retrieved from: http://www.feministyaklasimlar.org/sayi-08-haziran-2009/turkiyede-devlet-sorunu-uzerine/

Aşan, E., Uncu, Ü., and Kutluata, Z. (2014, March). *Barış Sürecinde Kadın Politikası Üzerine Barış İçin Kadın Girişimi'nden Feyza Akınerdem, Filiz Oğuz ve Nükhet Sirman İle Söyleşi*. Artizan. Retrieved from: http://arsiv.art-izan.org/toplumsal-cinsiyet-dosyalar-1/baris-surecinde-kadin-politikasi-uzerine-baris-icin-kadin-girisiminden-feyza-akinerdem-filiz-oguz-ve-nukhet-sirman-ile-soylesi

Atwood, M. (1985). *The Handmaid's Tale*. Toronto: McClelland and Stewart.

Ayata, A., and Dogangün, G. (2017). Gender Politics of the AKP: Restoration of a Religio-conservative Gender Climate. *Journal of Balkan and Near Eastern Studies*, 19(6), 610–27.

Ayata, A., and Tütüncü, F. (2008). Party Politics of the AKP (2002–2007) and the Predicaments of Women at the Intersection of the Westernist, Islamist and Feminist Discourses in Turkey. *British Journal of Middle Eastern Studies*, 35(3), 363–84.

AYM Dilan Kortak Davasında Gerekçeli Kararını Açıkladı. (2020, February 24). T24. Retrieved from: https://t24.com.tr/haber/aym-dilan-kortak-basvurusunda-gerekceli-kararini-acikladi-ekspertiz-raporunun-istenmemesi-kesif-yapilmamasi

Ayşe. (1987). Dayak Aileden Çıkmadır. *Feminist*, (2), 6.

Aytaç, Ö. (1997). *Medyanın Gözüyle Çeteler ve Susurluk*. İstanbul: Sam Yayınları.

Aytar, V. (2008). Preface: How to Normalize the Security Sector Debate: TESEV's and This Book's Contribution. In Ü. Cizre and İ. Cerrah (Eds.), *Security Sector Governance: Turkey and Europe* (pp. 12–14). İstanbul: TESEV.

Babül, E. (2015). The Paradox of Protection: Human Rights, the Masculinist State, and the Moral Economy of Gratitude in Turkey. *American Ethnologist*, 42(1), 116–30.

Bahçecik, O. (2014). European Union Twinning Projects and the Turkish Police: Looking beyond Europeanization. *New Perspectives on Turkey*, (51), 69–96.

Bahçecik, O. (2015). The Power Effects of Human Rights Reforms in Turkey: Enhanced Surveillance and Depoliticization. *Third World Quarterly*, 36(6), 1222–36.

Bair, J. (2010). On Difference and Capital: Gender and the Globalization of Production. *Signs: Journal of Women in Culture and Society*, 36(1), 203–26.

Bakan Atalay Kürt Açılımını Kadınlara Sorsun. (2009, August 24). Bianet. Retrieved from: http://bianet.org/bianet/print/116610-bakan-atalay-kurt-acilimi-ni-kadinlara-sorsun.

Bakan Soylu'dan Semih Özakça ve Nuriye Gülmen'le ilgili Açıklamalar. (2017, May 25). NTV. Retrieved from: https://www.ntv.com.tr/turkiye/bakan-soyludan-semih-ozakca-ve-nuriye-gulmenle-ilgili-aciklamalar,Jg2i0I634EyPWqK_cXdIbg

Bardall, G., Bjarnegard, E., and Piscopo, J. M. (2019). How Is Political Violence Gendered? Disentangling Motives, Forms, and Impacts. *Political Studies*, 00(0), 1–20.

Barış İçin Kadın Girişimi. (2013a). *Barış Konferansı Sonuç Metni*. Sosyalist Feminist Kolektif. Retrieved from: http://www.sosyalistfeministkolektif.org/web-yazilari/bar-s/baris-konferansi-sonuc-metni/

Barış İçin Kadın Girişimi. (2013b). *Barış İçin Kadın Girişimi Çözüm Süreci Raporu*. Sosyalist Feminist Kolektif. Retrieved from: https://www.sosyalistfeministkolektif.org/web-yazilari/bar-s/bar-s-icin-kad-n-girisimi-coezuem-suereci-raporu

Barış İçin Kadınlar Girişimi. (2014). *Karakol Gölgesinde Barış Umudu*. Sosyalist Feminist Kolektif. Retrieved from: https://www.sosyalistfeministkolektif.org/web-yazilari/bar-s/bikg-lice-ziyaretini-anlatt/

Barton, C. (2004). Global Women's Movements at a Crossroads: Seeking New Definition, Alliances and Greater Impact. *Socialism and Democracy*, 18(1), 151–84.

Baştuğ, M., and Evlek, U. (2016). Individual Disengagement and Deradicalization Pilot Program in Turkey: Methods and Outcomes. *Journal for Deradicalization*, (8), 25–45.

Bayat, A. (2013). *Life as Politics: How Ordinary People Change the Middle East*. Stanford: Stanford University Press.

Bayhan, K., and Vural, E. (2013). 6284 Sayılı Kanun Çerçevesinde Aile İçi Şiddetle Mücadelede Kolluğun Rolü. In S. K. Gül (Ed.), *Aile İçi Şiddet ve Polis* (pp. 261–77). Ankara: Polis Akademisi.

Bayley, D., and Sheaford, C. (2001). *The New Structure of Policing: Description, Contextualization, and Research Agenda*. Washington: Research Report Prepared for National Institute of Justice.

Bayly, C. (2011). European Political Thought and the Wider World during the 19th Century. In C. Bayly, G. S. Jones and G. Claeys (Eds.), *The Cambridge History of 19th Century Political Thought* (pp. 835–63). UK: Cambridge University Press.

Bayrampaşa Cezaevinde Kalan bir Siyasi Tutuklunun Mektubu. (1990). *Kaktüs*, (10), 78–80.

Bekdil, B. (2014). *Erdoğan's Egyptian Nightmare*. New York: Gatestone Institute, International Policy Council. Retrieved from: www.gab-ibn.com.

Benhabib, S. (2013, June 3). Turkey's Authoritarian Turn. *New York Times*. Retrieved from: https://www.nytimes.com/2013/06/04/opinion/turkeys-authoritarian-turn.html

Berberoğlu, E. (1997, July 9). *Polis Partisi İktidara Yürürken İşine Gelen Hükümeti Kullanıyor*. Hürriyet. Retrieved from: https://www.hurriyet.com.tr/polis-partisi-hayirli-olsun-39254302

Berksoy, B. (2013). *Türkiye'de Ordu, Polis ve İstihbarat Teşkilatları: Yakın Dönem Gelişmeler ve Reform İhtiyaçları*. İstanbul: TESEV.

Bernstein, E. (2012). Carceral Politics as Gender Justice? The 'Traffic in Women' and Neoliberal Circuits of Crime, Sex and Rights. *Theor Soc*, 41(3), 233–59.

Bora, A. (1996). Kadın Hareketi: Nereden Nereye. *Birikim* (83). Retrieved from: https://www.birikimdergisi.com/dergiler/birikim/1/sayi-83-mart-1996-sayi-83-mart-1996/2281/kadin-hareketi-nereden-nereye/5031

Bora, A. (2005). DYP Kadın Stratejisi Arıyor. *Pazartesi*, (105), 22–3.

Borchert, J., and Lessenich, S. (2016). *Claus Offe and the Critical Theory of the Capitalist State*. New York: Routledge.

Boukalas, C. (2014). No Exceptions: Authoritarian Statism. Agamben, Poulantzas and Homeland Security. *Critical Studies on Terrorism*, 7(1), 112–30.

Brown, W. (1992). Finding the Man in the State. *Feminist Studies*, 18(1), 7–34.

Brown, W. (2015). *Undoing the Demos: Neoliberalism's Stealth Revolution*. New York: Zone Books.

Bu Süreçten Hepimiz Değişerek Çıktık. (2000, February). *Pazartesi*, (59), 16–17.

Buchanan, E. (2015, February 10). Turkey: PM Pledges Dowry of Gold to Young Women to Have Children. *International Business Times*. Retrieved from: https://www.ibtimes.co.uk/turkey-pm-pledges-dowry-gold-young-women-have-children-1487426

Buğra, A., and Savaşkan, O. (2012). Politics and Class: The Turkish Business Environment in the Neoliberal Age. *New Perspectives on Turkey*, 46, 27–63.

Çağlayan, H. (2013). *Kürt Kadınların Penceresinden: Resmi Kimlik Politikaları, Milliyetçilik, Barış Mücadelesi*. İstanbul: İletişim.

Çakmak, K. Ç. (2013). Eşleri Tarafından Şiddet Gören Kadınlar ve Bu Kadınlara Yönelik Alınan Tedbir Kararları: Aydın Örneği. In S. K. Gül (Ed.), *Aile İçi Şiddet ve Polis* (pp. 57–89). Ankara: Polis Akademisi.

Çalı, H. H. (2013). Kamu Politikası Analizi Çerçevesinde Aile İçi Şiddet. In S. K. Gül (Ed.), *Aile İçi Şiddet ve Polis* (pp. 103–33). Ankara: Polis Akademisi.

Candan, Filiz, and Kamile. (2013). Hewler'in Ötesindeki Kadınlar. *Feminist Politika*, (20), 51–2.

Canlı, E., and Umul, F. (2015). Bodies on the Streets: Gender Resistance and Collectivity in the Gezi Revolts. *Interface: A Journal for and about Social Movements*, 7(1), 19–39.

Cantek, F. (2019, December 6). *Ayakkabıyla Eve Girmek*. Gazete Duvar. Retrieved from: https://www.gazeteduvar.com.tr/yazarlar/2019/12/06/ayakkabiyla-eve-girmek

Çelik, A. (2019, October 21). Genç ve Kadın İşsizliği Korkutucu Düzeyde. *Birgün*. Retrieved from: www.birgun.net.

Çelik, O. (2011). Orhan ve Diğerleri. In UNPFA Turkey (Ed.), *Bilindik Bilinmez Hikayeler* (pp. 19–49). Ankara: UNPFA.

Cerrah, İ. (2011). *Demokratik Toplumlarda İç Güvenlk*. Ankara: Polis Akademisi
Yayınları.

Chanaa, J. (2002). *Adelphi Paper 334: Security Sector Reform: Issues, Challenges and
Prospects*. London: The International Institute for Strategic Studies.

Chandler, D. (2006). *Empire in Denial: The Politics of State-building*. London: Pluto.

Chandler, D. (2010). *International State-building: The Rise of Post-liberal Governance*.
London: Routledge.

Çicek, C. (2018). The Failed Resolution Process and the Transformation of Kurdish
Politics. *MERIP 288*. Retrieved from: https://merip.org/2018/12/the-failed-
resolution-process-and-the-transformation-of-kurdish-politics/

Cizre, Ü. (2005a). *Almanak Türkiye 2005: Güvenlik Sektörü ve Demokratilk Gözetim*.
İstanbul: TESEV/DCAF.

Cizre, Ü. (2005b). New Horizons in the Parliamentary Oversight of the Security Sector:
Relevance for Turkey. In Ü. Cizre (Ed.), *Democratic Oversight of the Security Sector:
Turkey and the World* (pp. 65–9). İstanbul: TESEV.

Cizre, Ü. (2006a). Giriş ya da 'İtaat' Kültürü yerine Bilimsel 'İtiraf' ve 'İtiraz'. In Ü. Cizre
(Ed.), *Almanak Türkiye 2005: Güvenlik Sektörü ve Demokratik Yönetişim* (pp. 8–12).
İstanbul: TESEV.

Cizre, Ü. (2006b). Güvenliğin Yönetimi Sivil, ancak 'Demokratik' Olmalı. *Amargi*, (2),
30–4.

CNN Shows Gülmen as One of 8 Leading Women of 2016. (2016, December 28). Bianet.
Retrieved from: https://bianet.org/english/women/182160-cnn-shows-gulmen-as-
one-of-8-leading-women-of-2016

Cockburn, C. (2010). Gender Relations as Causal in Militarization and War.
International Feminist Journal of Politics, 12(2), 139–57.

Coleman, L. M., and Rosenow, D. (2016). Security (Studies) and the Limits of the
Critique: Why We Should Think through Struggle. *Critical Studies on Security*, 4(2),
202–20.

Connell, R. (2009). *Gender: In World Perspective*. Cambridge: Polity.

Coşar, S., and Özkan-Kerestecioğlu, İ. (2017). Feminist Politics in Contemporary
Turkey: Neoliberal Attacks, Feminist Claims to the Public. *Journal of Women, Politics
and Policy*, 38(2), 151–74.

Curthoys, A. (1993). Feminism, Citizenship and National Identity. *Feminist Review*,
44(1), 19–38.

DCAF. (2009). *DCAF Backgrounder: Police Reform*. Geneva: Geneva Centre for
Democratic Governance.

DCAF, and TESEV. (2005). *Democratic Oversight of the Security Sector: Turkey and the
World*. İstanbul: TESEV.

Dedeoğlu, S. (2012). Türkiye'de Refah Devleti, Toplumsal Cinsiyet ve Kadın İstihdamı.
In S. Dedeoğlu, and A. Elveren (Eds.), *Türkiye'de Refah Devleti ve Kadın*
(pp. 211–30). İstanbul: İletişim.

Dedeoğlu, S., and Elveren, A. Y. (Eds.). (2012). *Gender and Society in Turkey: The Impact of Neoliberal Policies, Political Islam and EU Accession.* London: I.B. Tauris.

Delice, M. (2013). Polis Kayıtlarına Yansımış Kadına Şiddet Olaylarının İncelenmesi: Erzurum Örneği. In S. K. Gül (Ed.), *Aile İçi Şiddet ve Polis* (pp. 13–41). Ankara: Polis Akademisi.

Delice, M., and Teymur, S. (2012). Gündeydoğu Bölgesindeki İntihar Olaylarının İncelenmesi: Batman İli Örneği. *Atatürk Üniversitesi Sosyal Bilimler Enstitüsü Dergisi*, 16(1), 57–80.

Delice, M., and Teymur, S. (2013). Kadına Yönelik Şiddet Olaylarında Failin ve Mağdurun Özelliklerinin İncelenmesi ve Karşılaştırması. *EKEV Akademi Dergisi*, 54(17), 225–50.

Delice, M., and Yaşar, M. (2013). Examination of Knife Crimes against Women. *European Scientific Journal*, 9(34), 370–90.

Demir, B. (2001a, December). Evdeki Devlete Karşı. *Pazartesi*, (80), 7.

Demir, B. (2001b, October–November). Herkes Acıklı Öykü Peşinde. *Pazartesi*, (79), 18–19.

Demir, B. (2004, Mart). Mezar değil Sığınak. *Pazartesi*, (88), 4.

Demir, B. (2005, February). Tecavüz Erkeklerin Sorunudur. *Pazartesi*, (99), 2.

Demir, S. A., Fidan, F., and Nam, D. (2013). Sakarya'da Kadına Yönelik Aile İçi Şiddet: Görünümü, Nedenleri ve Önlenmesine Yönelik Yaklaşımlar. In S. K. Gül (Ed.), *Aile İçi Şiddet ve Polis* (pp. 41–57). Ankara: Polis Akademisi.

Diner, C. (2018). Gender Politics and GONGOs in Turkey. *Turkish Policy Quarterly*, 16(4), 101–8.

Diner, Ç., and Toktaş, Ş. (2010). Waves of Feminism in Turkey: Kemalist, Islamist and Kurdish Women's Movements in an Era of Globalization. *Journal of Balkan and Near Eastern Studies*, 12(1), 41–57.

Ebo, A. (2011, November 25). (F. Hülagü, Interviewer).

Eisenstein, H. (2015). *Feminism Seduced: How Global Elites Use Women's Labor and Ideas to Exploit the World.* London and New York: Routledge.

Eisenstein, Z. (1981). Antifeminism in the Politics and Election of 1980. *Feminist Studies*, 7(2), 187–205.

Eksi, B. (2019). Police and Masculinities in Transition in Turkey: From Macho to Reformed to Militarized Policing. *Men and Masculinities*, 22(3), 491–515.

Ellison, G., and Pino, N. (2012). *Globalization, Police Reform and Development: Doing It the Western Way?* UK: Palgrave Macmillan.

Eraydın, A., and Erendil, A. (1999). The Role of Female Labour in Industrial Restructuring: New Production Processes and Labour Market Relations in the Istanbul Clothing Industry. *Gender, Place and Culture: A Journal of Feminist Geography*, 6(3), 259–72.

Ercan, F., and Oğuz, Ş. (2015). From Gezi Resistance to Soma Massacre: Capital Accumulation and Class Struggle in Turkey. *Socialist Register*, 51(1), 114–35.

Erdoğan: Let People Live So the State Will Live. (2019, October 20). Anadolu Agency. Retrieved from: https://www.aa.com.tr/en/turkey/erdogan-let-people-live-so-the-state-will-live/1589700

Ergil, D. (2005). Q and A Session. In Ü. Cizre (Ed.), *Democratic Oversight of the Security Sector: Turkey and the World* (pp. 54–9). İstanbul: TESEV.

Ertürk, Y. (2015). *Sınır Tanımayan Şiddet: Paradigma, Politika ve Pratikteki Yönleriyle Kadına Şiddet Olgusu.* İstanbul: Metis.

Esen, B., and Gümüşçü, Ş. (2016). Rising Competitive Authoritarianism in Turkey. *Third World Quarterly,* 37(9), 1581–606.

European Code of Police Ethics. (2001). *European Code of Police Ethics.* Strasbourg: Council of Europe.

European Comission. (2006, May). *A Concept for European Community Support for Security Sector Reform.* Retrieved from: https://eur-lex.europa.eu/LexUriServ/LexUriServ.do?uri=COM:2006:0253:FIN:EN:PDF

Federici, S. (2005). *Caliban and the Witch: Women, Capitalism and Primitive Accumulation.* New York: Autonomedia.

Federici, S. (2009). The Reproduction of Labour-power in the Global Economy, Marxist Theory and the Unfinished Feminist Revolution. *UC Santa Cruz.*

Ferguson, S. (2016). Intersectionality and Social Reproduction Feminisms: Toward an Integrative Ontology. *Historical Materialism,* 24(2), 38–60.

Filiz, K. (1987). Kadınlar Dayağa Karşı Dayanışmaya. *Feminist,* (2), 6–8.

Fleischmann, E. (2018). The Other 'Awakening': The Emergence of Women's Movements in the Modern Middle East, 1900–1940. In M. L. Meriwether (Ed.), *A Social History of Women and Gender in the Modern Middle East* (pp. 89–139). New York: Routledge.

Fraser, N. (1997). *Justice Interruptus: Critical Reflections on the Postsocialist Condition.* New York: Routledge.

Fraser, N. (2009). Feminism, Capitalism, and the Cunning of History. *New Left Review,* (56), 98–117.

Fraser, N. (2015). Legitimation Crisis? On the Political Contradictions of Financialized Capitalism. *Critical Historical Studies,* 2(2), 157–89.

Fraser, N. (2017). Crisis of Care? On the Social-Reproductive Contradictions of Contemporary Capitalism. In T. Bhattacharya (Ed.), *Social Reproduction Theory: Remapping Class, Recentering Oppression* (pp. 2–36). London: Pluto.

Frazer, E., and Hutchings, K. (2011). Virtuous Violence and the Politics of Statecraft In Machiavelli, Clausewitz and Weber. *Political Studies,* 59(1), 56–73.

Fukuyama, F. (2006). *Nation Building: Beyond Afghanistan and Iraq.* Baltimore: Johns Hopkins University Press.

Garland, D. (1996). The Limits of the Sovereign State: Strategies of Crime Control in Contemporary Society. *The British Journal of Criminology,* 36(4), 445–71.

Gemici, O. O. (2018, March 6). *Kadın Özek Harekatçıların Lügatinde Pes Etmek Yok.* Anadolu Ajansı. Retrieved from: https://www.aa.com.tr/tr/dunya-kadinlar-gunu/kadin-ozel-harekatcilarin-lugatinde-pes-etmek-yok/1081040

Genel-İş. (2019). *Kamuda İstihdam Raporu*. Retrieved from: www.genel-is.org.tr

Gerstenberger, H. (2007). *Impersonal Power: History and Theory of the Bourgeois State*. London: Brill.

Gökaçtı, M. A. (2012, November 19). *Uyuşturucu Çetesine DHKP-C baskısına polis operasyonu*. Radikal. Retrieved from: http://www.radikal.com.tr/turkiye/uyusturucu-cetesine-dhkp-c-baskisina-polis-operasyonu-1108474

Göktaş, K. (2014, April 10). *İçişleri'nin Gezi Raporu*. Vatan Gazetesi. Retrieved from: http://www.gazetevatan.com/icisleri-nin-gezi-raporu-625797-gundem/

GREVIO. (2018) Baseline Evaluation Report: Turkey. Retrieved from: https://rm.coe.int/eng-grevio-report-turquie/16808e5283

Gülalp, H. (2001). Globalisation and Political Islam: The Social Bases of Turkey's Welfare Party. *International Journal of Middle East Studies*, 33(3), 433–48.

Günay, E. (2015). Kadınların Gözüyle Çözüm Süreci. In N. Alpay and H. Tahmaz (Eds.), *Barış Açısını Savunmak: Çözüm Süreci'nde Ne Oldu?* (pp. 173–81). İstanbul: Metis.

Gürdan, E. C., and Peker, E. (2014). Turkey's Gezi Park Demonstrations of 2013: A Marxian Analysis of the Political Moment. *Socialism and Democracy*, 28(1), 70–89.

Hall, S. (1978). *Policing the Crisis: Mugging, The State and Law and Order*. London: Macmillan.

Halley, J. (2006). *Split Decisions: How and Why to Take a Break from Feminism*. New Jersey: Princeton University Press.

Halley, J., Kotiswaran, P., Rebouché, R., and Shamir, H. (2018). *Governance Feminism: An Introduction*. Minnesota: University of Minnesota Press.

Hançerli, O., and Nikbay, S. (2007). *Understanding and Responding to the Terrorism Phenomenon: A Multi-dimensional Perspective*. Amsterdam: IOS Press.

Hasan Ferit Gedik Sonsuzluğa Uğurlandı. (2013, October 1). Sol Haber. Retrieved from: https://haber.sol.org.tr/devlet-ve-siyaset/hasan-ferit-gedik-sonsuzluga-ugurlandi-haberi-80404

Hatem, M. (1992). Economic and Political Liberation in Egypt and the Demise of State Feminism. *International Journal of Middle East Studies*, 24(2), 231–51.

Hinton, M., and Newburn, T. (2009). *Policing Developing Democracies*. New York: Routledge.

Hobson, J. (2012). *The Euro-centric Conception of World Politics: Western International Theory, 1760–2010*. Cambridge: Cambridge University Press.

Hoodfar, H., and Sadeghi, F. (2009). Against All Odds: The Women's Movement in the Islamic Republic of Iran. *Development*, 52(2), 215–23.

Hülagü, F. (2016). Global Lineages of the Police Violence against Kurdish Population in Turkey in the 2000s. *Praksis*, 40(1), 153–85.

Hülagü, F. (2017). Post-Cold War Police Reform and the Modern Political Field: Reflections from Turkey. *Science and Society*, 81(1), 98–123.

Hülagü, F. (2019). 'Ruling-bloc's search for a host ideology? Counter-gender Narrative and Anti-feminism in Turkey', paper presented at the workshop, 'Blurring boundaries? Re-articulations of feminisms and gender politics in the context of right-wing mobilizations in Europe', 23–25 May 2019, University of Marburg, Germany.

Hülagü, F. (2020). Domesticating Politics, Degendering Women: State Violence against Politically Active Women. In P. Bedirhanoglu, C. Dölek, F. Hülagü and Ö. Kaygusuz (Eds.), *Turkey's New State in the Making: Transformations in Legality, Economy Management and Coercion* (pp. 245–60). London: Zed Books.

Human Rights Watch. (2008). *Closing Ranks against Accountability: Barriers to Tackling Police Violence in Turkey*. Retrieved from: www.hrw.org

Hunnicutt, G. (2009). Varieties of Patriarchy and Violence against Women: Resurrecting 'Patriarchy' as a Theoretical Tool. *Violence against Women*, 15(5), 553–73.

Huntington, S. (1968). *Political Order in Changing Societies*. New Haven: Yale University.

Huysmans, J. (2008). The Jargon of Exception- On Schmitt, Agamben and the Absence of Political Society. *International Political Sociology*, 2, 165–83.

Ikenberry, J. (2009). Liberal Internationalism 3.0: America and the Dilemmas of Liberal World Order. *Perspectives on Politics*, 7(1), 71–87.

İlkkaracan, P. (2007). *Reforming the Penal Code in Turkey: The Campaign for the Reform of the Turkish Penal Code from a Gender Perspective*. Sussex: Institute of Development Studies.

İlkkaracan, P. (2012). Why So Few Women in the Labour Market in Turkey? *Feminist Economics*, 18(1), 1–37.

Insel, A. (2008). Cet État n'est pas sans propriétaires!: Forces prétoriennes et autoritarisme en Turquie. In O. Dabène (Ed.), *Autoritarismes démocratiques. Démocraties autoritaires au XXIe siècle* (pp. 133–53). Paris: La Découverte.

Işık, N. (1999). *Türkiye'de Aile İçinde Şiddete Uğrayan Kadına Yönelik Polis Hizmetlerinde Durum ve Sorunlar*. Ankara: Polis Akademisi.

Işık, N. (2002). 1990'larda Kadına Yönelik Aile İçi Şiddetle Mücadele Hareketi İçinde Oluşmuş Bazı Gözlem ve Düşünceler. In A. Bora and A. Günal (Eds.), *90'larda Türkiye'de Feminizm* (pp. 1–73). İstanbul: İletişim.

Işık, N. (2006). *Kadına Karşı Şiddetin Önlenmesinde Polisin Rolü ve Uygulanacak Prosedürler Eğitici Eğitimleri Kitabı*. Ankara: UNFPA.

Işık, N. (2019, August 16). (F. Hülagü, Interviewer).

İstanbul'da 18 Yaşındaki Sıla Abalay Öldürüldü. (2017, May 6). Evrensel. Retrieved from: https://www.evrensel.net/haber/318585/istanbulda-18-yasindaki-sila-abalay-olduruldu

Jahn, B. (2013). *Liberal Internationalism: Theory, History, Practice*. London: Palgrave Macmillan.

Jenkins, G. (2007). Continuity and Change: Prospects for Civil-Military Relations in Turkey. *International Affairs*, 83(2), 339–55.

Jessop, B. (2002). Time and Space in the Globalisation of Capital and Their Implications for State Power. *Rethinking Marxism*, 14(1), 97–117.

Jessop, B. (2004). The Gender Selectivities of the State. *Journal of Critical Realism*, 3(2), 207–37.

Jorgenden, J. (2018). Looking beyond the State: Transitional Justice and the Kurdish Issue in Turkey. *Ethnic and Racial Studies*, 41(4), 721–38.

Kadem Başkan Yardımcısı Sümeyye Erdoğan Bayraktar'ın III. Olağan Genel Kurulu Açılış Konuşması. (2019, March 8). KADEM. Retrieved from: https://kadem.org.tr/kadem-baskan-yardimcisi-sumeyye-erdogan-bayraktarin-iii-olagan-genel-kurulu-acilis-konusmasi

Kadın Sığınakları ve Dayanışma Merkezleri 4. Kurultayı Sonuç Bildirgesi. (2001, November 24–25). Retrieved from: http://www.siginaksizbirdunya.org/tr/kurultaylar/sonuc-bildirgeleri/4-dorduncu-kurultay-sonuc-bildirgesi

Kadının Statüsü Genel Müdürlüğü. (2007). *Kadına Yönelik Aile İçi Şiddetle Mücadele Ulusal Eylem Planı: 2007–2010.* Ankara: TC. Başbakanlık KSGM.

Kadınlar Özgecan ve katledilen tüm kadınlar için yürüdü. (2015, February 23). Halkevleri. Retrieved from: http://www.halkevleri.org.tr/guncel/kadinlar-ozgecan-ve-katledilen-tum-kadinlar-icin-yurudu-isyanimiz-buyuyor

Kandiyoti, D. (1987). Emancipated but Unliberated? Reflections on the Turkish Case. *Feminist Studies*, 13(2), 317–38.

Kandiyoti, D. (1988). Bargaining with Patriarchy. *Gender and Society*, 2(3), 274–90.

Kandiyoti, D. (2016). Locating the Politics of Gender: Patriarchy, Neoliberal Governance and Violence in Turkey. *Research and Policy on Turkey*, 1(2), 103–18.

Kannankulam, J., and Georgi, F. (2014). Varieties of Capitalism or Varieties of Relationships of Forces? Outlines of a Historical Materialist Policy Analysis. *Capital and Class*, 38(1), 59–71.

Kantola, J. (2006). *Feminists Theorize the State.* London: Springer.

Kara, H., Ekici, A., and İnankul, H. (2014). The Role of Police in Preventing and Combatting Domestic Violence in Turkey. *European Scientific Journal*, 10(20), 1–21.

Karakuş, F. (2006). Resmi İdeoloji ile Hesaplaşan bir Feminizm İçin. *Amargi*, (2), 84–6.

Karakuş, Ö. (2013). Aile İçi Şiddet ve Sosyal Kontrol: Kadına Karşı Aile İçi Şiddetle Mücadelede Polisin Rolü. In S. K. Gül (Ed.), *Aile İçi Şiddet ve Polis* (pp. 249–61). Ankara: Polis Akademisi.

Kardam, N. (2005). *Turkey's Engagement with Global Women's Human Rights.* Aldershot: Ashgate.

Kardam, N., and Ertürk, Y. (1999). Expanding Gender Accountability? Women's Organisations and the State in Turkey. *International Journal of Organisational Theory and Behaviour*, 2(1–2), 167–97.

Kaygusuz, Ö. (2018). Authoritarian Neoliberalism and Regime Security in Turkey: Moving to an 'Exceptional State' under AKP. *South European Society and Politics*, 23(2), 281–302.

Keohane, R. (2002). The Globalization of Informal Violence, Theories of World Politics, and the 'Liberalism of Fear'. *Dialogue International Organisation*, 1(1), 29–43.

KESK. (2018). *Kesk'li Kadın İhraçlar Çalışması*. Ankara: KESK.

KHU Gender and Women's Studies Center. (2020). *Research on Perception of Gender and Women in Turkey*. İstanbul: Kadir Has University.

Kışanak, G. (2018). *Kürt Siyasetinin Mor Rengi*. Ankara: Dipnot.

Kızıltan, Ö. (2019, 6 July). *Bir Milyondan Fazla Kadın Çocuk Bakımı Nedeniyle İş Bırakıyor*. Birgün. Retrieved from: https://www.sosyalistfeministkolektif.org/web-yazilari/bar-s/bar-s-icin-kad-n-girisimi-coezuem-suereci-raporu/

Klein, N. (2007). *The Shock Doctrine: The Rise of Disaster Capitalism*. Canada: Random House.

Koçali, F. (2000, February). Eren Keskin: Herkesin İlk Düşündüğü Babası Oluyor. *Pazartesi*, (59), 4–5.

Koğacığoğlu, D. (2006). Orada bir fon var, uzakta (mı)? *Amargi*, (01), 38–40.

Koloğlu, D., Gençtürk, D., Kazaz, G., Mavituna, İ., and Şen, S. (2015). *Polis Destan Yazdı: Gezi'den Şiddet Tanıklıkları*. İstanbul: İletişim.

KONDA. (2014). *Gezi Report: Public Perception of the 'Gezi Protests'; Who Were the People at the Gezi Park?* İstanbul: Konda Araştırma ve Danışmanlık.

Korkut, T. (2010, February 8). *EMASYA Protokol Abrogated*. Bianet. Retrieved from: https://m.bianet.org/english/human-rights/119903-emasya-protocol-abrogated

Küçükalioglu, E. G. (2018). Framing Gender-based Violence in Turkey. *Les Cahiers du CEDREF*, (22), 128–57.

LeBaron, G., and Roberts, A. (2010). Toward a Feminist Political Economy of Capitalism and Carcerality. *Signs: Journal of Women in Culture and Society*, 36(1), 19–44.

MacInnes, J. (1998). *End of Masculinity: The Confusion of Sexual Genesis and Sexual Difference in Modern Society*. UK: McGraw-Hill Education.

Mann, M. (1999). The Dark Side of Democracy: The Modern Tradition of Ethnic and Political Cleansing. *New Left Review*, (235), 18–45.

Mannitz, S., and Reckhaus, S. (2016). Competing Gender Perspectives in Security Sector Reforms in Turkey. *Working Paper*. Retrieved from: https://gencen.isp.msu.edu/files/6314/7889/2002/1066_Mannitz_FINAL.pdf

Marenin, O., and Caparini, M. (2005). Crime, Insecurity, Post-Socialist Police Reform in CEE. *The Journal of Power Institutions in Post-Soviet Societies*, (2), 1–12.

Marks, S. (2009). False Contingency. *Current Legal Problems*, 62(1), 1–21.

Marks, S. (2011). Human Rights and Root Causes. *The Modern Law Review*, 74(1), 57–78.

Massicard, E. (2019). Quand Les Civils Maintiennent L'Ordre: Configurations Vigilantes à Istanbul. *Revue des Mondes Musulmans et de la Méditerranée*, 145, 229–56.

Mazower, M. (2006). An International Civilisation? *International Affairs*, 82(3), 533–66.

Mazower, M. (2013). *Governing the World: The History of an Idea*. New York: Penguin.

McLoughlin, D. (2016). Post-Marxism and the Politics of Human Rights: Lefort, Badiou, Agamben, Ranciere. *Law and Critique*, 27(3), 303–21.

Melzer, P. (2011). 'Death in the Shape of a Young Girl': Feminist Responses to Media Representations of Women Terrorists during the 'German Autumn' of 1977. *International Feminist Journal of Politics*, 11(1), 35–62.

Memiş, E., Öneş, U., and Kızılırmak, A. B. (2011). Housewifisation of Women: Contextualising Gendered Patterns of Paid and Unpaid Work. In Saniye Dedeoğlu and Adem Yavuz Elveren (Eds.), *Gender and Society in Turkey: The Impact of Neoliberal Policies, Political Islam, and EU Accession* (pp. 87–102). London: I.B. Tauris.

Mies, M. (1986). *Patriarchy and Accumulation on a World Scale: Women in the International Division of Labour*. London: Zed Books.

Moghadam, V. (2002). Islamic Feminism and Its Discontents: Toward a Resolution of the Debate. *Signs: Journal of Women in Culture and Society*, 27(4), 1135–71.

Moghadam, V. (2008). Feminism, Legal Reform and Women's Empowerment in the Middle East and North Africa. *International Social Science Journal*, 59(191), 9–16.

Molyneux, M. (1985). Mobilization without Emancipation? Women's Interests, the State, and Revolution in Nicaragua. *Feminist Studies*, 11(2), 227–54.

Mor Çatı Kolektifi. (2002). *Kadın Sığınakları Birinci ve İkinci Kurultayları*. İstanbul: Mor Çatı Yayınları.

Mustafa, T. (2015). Damning the Palestinian Spring: Security Sector Reform and Entrenched Repression. *Journal of Intervention and State-building*, 9(2), 212–30.

Nalla, M. K., and Boke, K. (2011). What Is in a Name? Organizational, Environmental and Cultural Factors on Support for Community Policing in Turkey and in the US. *European Journal on Criminal Policy and Research*, 17(4), 285–303.

Nash, K. (1998). Beyond Liberalism? Feminist Theories of Democracy. In G. W. Vicky Randall (Ed.), *Gender, Politics, and the State* (pp. 45–57). London: Routledge.

Nefes, T. S. (2017). The Impacts of the Turkish Government's Conspiratorial Framing of the Gezi Park Protests. *Social Movement Studies*, 16(5), 610–22.

Negron-Gonzales, M. (2016). The Feminist Movement during the AKP Era in Turkey: Challenges and Opportunities. *Middle Eastern Studies*, 52(2), 198–214.

Neocleous, M. (2000). *The Fabrication of Social Order: A Critical Theory of Police Power*. London: Pluto.

O'Neil, M. L. (2017). The Availability of Abortion at State Hospitals in Turkey: A National Study. *Contraception*, 95(2), 148–53.

OECD DAC. (2009). *Security Sector Reform: What We Have Learned?* Paris: OECD.

Offe, C. (1994). Structural Problems of the Capitalist State: Class Rule and the Political System. On the Selectiveness of Political Institutions. In C. Offe (Ed.), *The State-Critical Concepts. First Volume* (pp. 104–29). London: Routledge.

Offe, C., and Ronge, V. (1975). Theses on the Theory of the State. *New German Critique*, (6), 137–47.

Ogata, S., and Sen, A. (2003). *Human Security Now*. New York: UN Commission on Human Security.

Oğuz, E. (2007). Family Case Approach in Understanding and Combatting Crime in General and Specifically Terror. In H. Durmaz, B. Sevinç, A. S. Yayla and S. Ekici (Eds.), *Understanding and Responding to Terrorism* (pp. 271–85). Amsterdam: IOS Press.

Onar, N. F., and Paker, H. (2012). Towards Cosmopolitan Citizenship? Women's Rights in a Divided Turkey. *Theory and Society*, 41(4), 375–94.

Önder, N. (1998). Interacting with the Global Market: The State and the Crisis of Political Representation. *International Journal of Political Economy*, 28(2), 44–84.

Örnek, C., and Hülagü, F. (2018). Idiocy or Ideological Fallacy? The Left-liberal Intelligentsia in Turkey and the Allure of Islamists. Unpublished Article.

Örnek, G. (2019, 26 May). TYP'li Kadınlar: Her İş Bitiminde Depresyona Girmek İstemiyoruz. Retrieved from: https://ekmekvegul.net/.

Ovadia, S. (1987). SHP'nin Kadın Bakanlığı Yutturmacası. *Feminist*, (3), 20–1.

Özdemir, C. (2009). *Önemli İşler Dairesi: Derin Devletin Yeni Sahibi*. İstanbul: Doğan Kitap.

Özdilek, Z. (2016, April 21). Ensar'dan Gezi Çıkar Korkusu. *Cumhuriyet*. Retrieved from: http://www.cumhuriyet.com.tr/haber/ensardan-gezi-cikar-korkusu-520015

Özel Harekat Polisinin Ağlatan Mektubu. (2012, December 25). Haber7. Retrieved from: http://www.haber7.com/guncel/haber/969308-ozel-harekat-polisinin-aglatan-mektubu

Öztürk, S. (1988). Saadet Akkaya'ya Emniyette Şişeyle Tecavüz Ettiler. *Kaktüs*, (3), 66–9.

Özyurt, A. (2016, June 10). Bir PÖH Röportajı: Nusaybin'de Özel bir Yürek. *Milliyet Gazetesi*. Retrieved from: http://blog.milliyet.com.tr/bir-poh-roportaji–nusaybin-de–ozel–bir-yurek/Blog/?BlogNo=533711

Paffenholz, T. (2015). Unpacking the Local Turn in Peacebuilding. *Third World Quarterly*, 36(5), 857–74.

Paker, B. (1988). Kadın Örgütlenmesinde bir Dönüm Noktası: Dayağa Karşı Kampanya. *Kaktüs*, (1), 25–8.

Palmer, P., and O'Malley, D. (1996). Post-Keynesian Policing. *Economy and Society*, 25(2), 137–45.

Pantev, P. (2005). *Civil-Military Relations and Democratic Control of the Security Sector*. Sofia: ProCon.

Paris, R. (2001). Human Security: Paradigm Shift or Hot Air? *International Security*, 26(2), 87–102.

Pichio, A. (1992). *Social Reproduction: The Political Economy of the Labour Market*. New York: Cambridge University Press.

President Erdoğan Attends to the Opening Ceremony of Sıdıka Tayyar Hatun Mosque. (2014, October 17). Presidency of the Republic of Turkey. Retrieved from: https://www.tccb.gov.tr/en/news/542/3345/president-erdogan-attends-to-the-opening-ceremony-of-sidika-tayyar-hatun-mosque

Prime Minister: 'Every Abortion Is Uludere'. (2012, May 28). Bianet. Retrieved from: http://bianet.org/english/english/138659-prime-minister-every-abortion-is-uludere

Prügl, E. (2009). Does Gender Mainstreaming Work? Feminist Engagements with the German Agricultural State. *International Feminist Journal of Politics*, 11(2), 174–95.

Prügl, E. (2011). Diversity Management and Gender Mainstreaming as Technologies of Government. *Politics and Gender*, 7(1), 71–89.

Prügl, E. (2012). 'If Lehman Brothers Had Been Lehman Sisters': Gender and Myth in the Aftermath of the Financial Crisis. *International Political Sociology*, 6(1), 21–35.

Puechguirbal, N. (2010). Discourses on Gender, Patriarchy and Resolution 1325: A Textual Analysis of UN Documents. *International Peacebuilding*, 17(2), 172–87.

Rai, S. (1996). Women and the State in the Third World. In H. Afshar (Ed.), *Women and Politics in the Third World* (pp. 25–40). London and New York: Routledge.

Randall, V. (1998). Gender and Power: Women Engage the State. In V. Randall and G. Waylen (Eds.), *Gender, Politics, and the State* (pp. 185–205). London: Routledge.

Reiner, R. (2010). *The Politics of the Police*. London: Oxford University Press.

Resmi Kayıtlı Özel Harekat Derneği. (2017, December 12). Birgün. Retrieved from: https://www.birgun.net/haber/resmi-kayitli-ozel-harekat-dernegi-195099

Roché, S. (2010a, March 12). (F. Hülagü, Interviewer).

Roché, S. (2010b). *Setting Up Local Prevention and Security Partnerships at the Local Level*. Ankara: UNDP.

Sağırlı, O., and Demir, A. (2011, October 10). Özel Harekatçılar Hakkari Temizliğini Anlattı. *Türkiye Gazetesi*.

Şahin, B. (2015, December 4). *Polis son 5 ayda ev baskınlarında 3 kadını öldürdü*. Diken. Retrieved from: http://www.diken.com.tr/polis-son-bes-ayda-ev-baskinlarinda-uc-kadini-oldurdu/

Şahin, İ. N. (2013). Önsöz. In S. K. Gül (Ed.), *Aile İçi Şiddet ve Polis* (pp. 5–6). Ankara: Polis Akademisi.

Şahin, Y., and İrdem, İ. (2017). PYD-YPG: Suriye'deki PKK. *Journal of Security Studies*, 19(1), 21–45.

San, S. (2018). Counterterrorism Policing Innovations in Turkey: A Case Study of Turkish National Police CVE experiment. *Policing and Society*, 30(5), 583–98.

Sancar, S. (2011). Türkiye'de Kadın Hareketinin Politiği: Tarihsel Bağlam, Politik Gündem ve Özgünlükler. In S. Sancar (Ed.), *Birkaç Arpa Boyu: 21. Yüzyıl'a Girerken Türkiye'de Feminist Çalışmalar* (pp. 61–117). İstanbul: Koç Üniversitesi Yayınları.

Sassen, S. (2000). Spatialities and Temporalities of the Global: Elements for a Theorization. *Public Culture*, 12(1), 215–32.

Sassen, S. (2000b). Women's Burden: Counter-geographies of Globalization and the Feminization of Survival. *Journal of International Affairs*, 53(2), 503–24.

Savran, G. (1989). Kadınların Kurtuluşu Manifetosunun Düşündürdükleri. *Kaktüs*, (7), 8–13.

Şen, M. (2010). Transformation of Islamism and the Rise of Justice and Development Party. *Turkish Studies*, 11(1), 59–84.

Shepherd, L. (2008). Power and Authority in the Production of United Nations Security Council Resolution 1325. *International Studies Quarterly*, 52(2), 383–404.

Simon-Kumar, R. (2004). Negotiating Emancipation: The Public Sphere and Gender Critiques of Neo-Liberal Development. *International Feminist Journal of Politics*, 6(3), 485–507.

Sjoberg, L., and Gentry, C. (2007). *Mothers, Monsters, Whores: Women's Violence in Global Politics*. London: Zed Books.

Slaughter, A. M. (2009). *A New World Order*. Princeton: Princeton University Press.

Smith, T. (2017). *Why Wilson Matters: The Origins of American Liberal Internationalism and Its Crisis Today*. New York: Princeton University Press.

Soylu: Olası Büyük İstanbul Depremi için Hazırlanıyoruz. (2020, February 27). Sputnik news. Retrieved from: https://tr.sputniknews.com/turkiye/202002271041489582-soylu-olasi-buyuk-istanbul-depremi-icin-buyuk-istanbul-plani-hazirliyoruz/

Tekeli, Ş. (1987). Kadın ve Yaşam. *Feminist*, (2), 10–11.

Teymur, S. (2007). *A Conceptual Map for Understanding the Terrorist*. Texas: University of North Texas.

Teymur, S. (2013). *İdeallerimizdeki Yarınlar: 110 İdeal, 11 Gerçek Hayat*. İstanbul: Bahçeşehir Üniversitesi Yayınları.

Teymur, S., Günbeyi, M., and Özer, M. (2010). Kültür-odaklı polislik. *TÜBAV Bilim Dergisi*, 3(3), 282–91.

Tilly, C. (1985). War Making and State Making as Organized Crime. In P. Evans, D. Rueaschmayer and T. Skocpol (Eds.), *Bringing the State Back In* (pp. 169–86). Cambridge: Cambridge University Press.

Toksöz, G. (2012). The State of Female Labour in the Impasse of Neoliberal Market and the Patriarchal Family. In A. Y. Elveren and S. Dedeoğlu (Eds.), *Gender and Society in Turkey: The Impact of Neoliberal Policies, Political Islam and EU Accession* (pp. 47–64). London: I.B. Tauris.

Toktaş, Ş., and Diner, Ç. (2011). Feminists' Dilemma – with or without the State? Violence against Women and Women's Shelters in Turkey. *Asia Journal of Women's Studies*, 17(3), 49–75.

Töre daha çok erkekleri vurdu. (2006, July 7). *Yeni Şafak*. Retrieved from: https://www.yenisafak.com/gundem/tore-daha-cok-erkekleri-vurdu-2700086.

Tuğal, C. (2002). Islamism in Turkey: Beyond Instrument and Meaning. *Economy and Society*, 31(1), 85–111.

Turkish Ministry of Interior. (2017). *The Repetitive Scenaria of a Terrorist Organization – the Truth about Nuriye Gülmen and Semih Özakça*. Ankara: İçişleri Bakanlığı.

Turkish National Police Academy. (2017). *A New Generation of Terrorism: An Analysis of FETÖ*. Ankara: Turkish National Police Academy.

Türkiye'de Polis Devleti Endişesi. (2015, February 17). *T24*. Retrieved from: https://t24.com.tr/haber/turkiyede-polis-devleti-endisesi.

Uludağ, A. (2017, November 28). Bakanlığa göre hüküm belli: Gülmen ve Özakça'nın "ölmesi" durumunda … *Cumhuriyet*. Retrieved from: http://www.cumhuriyet.com.tr/haber/bakanliga-gore-hukum-belli-gulmen-ve-ozakcanin-olmesi-durumunda-875690

UN Declaration on the Elimination of Violence against Women (1993). General Assembly resolution 48/104 of 20 December 1993. New York. Retrieved from: https://www.ohchr.org/Documents/ProfessionalInterest/eliminationvaw.pdf

UNFPA. (2008). *UNFPA at Work: Six Human Rights Cases*. New York: UNFPA.

UNFPA. (2009). *Partnering with Men to End Gender-based Violence: Practices That Work from Eastern Europe and Central Asia*. New York: UNFPA.

United Nations Security Council (2000). Resolution 1325 on Women and Peace and Security, New York. Available from: https://www.un.org/ruleoflaw/blog/document/security-council-resolution-1325-2000-on-women-and-peace-and-security/

Ünlü, Ü. (2010, July 15). *Hüseyin Çelik 'özel ordu'yu tarif etti*. HaberTürk. Retrieved from: https://www.haberturk.com/polemik/haber/532747-huseyin-celik-ozel-orduyu-tarif-etti

Üstün, İ. (2019, June 11). (F. Hülagü, Interviewer).

Valasek, K. (2008). *Security Sector Reform and Gender*. Geneva: DCAF, OSCE/ODIHR,UN-INSTRAW.

Valbjorn, M. (2012). Upgrading Post-democratization Studies: Examining a Re-politicized Arab World in a Transition to Somewhere. *Middle East Critique*, 21(1), 25–35.

Walby, S. (2002). Feminism in a Global Era. *Economy and Society*, 31(4), 533–57.

Walby, S. (2009). *Globalization and Inequalities: Complexity and Contested Modernities*. London: Sage.

Wallerstein, I. (1995). *After Liberalism*. New York: The New Press.

Wallerstein, I. (2011). *The Modern-World System IV: Centrist Liberalism Triumphant, 1789–1914*. Berkeley: University of California Press.

Wacquant, L. (2010). Crafting the Neoliberal State: Workfare, Prisonfare and Social Insecurity. *Sociological Forum*, 25(2), 197–220.

Waterbury, J. (1994). Democracy without Democrats? The Potential for Political Liberalization in the Middle East. In G. Salamé (Ed.), *Democracy without Democrats* (pp. 23–47). London: I.B. Tauris.

Waylen, G. (1996). Analysing Women in the Politics of the Third World. In H. Afshar (Ed.), *Women and Politics in the Third World* (pp. 7–25). London and New York: Routledge.

Weis, V. V. (2017). *Marxism and Criminology: History of Criminal Selectivity*. New York: Brill.

Women's Coalition. (2014). *Hükümet, güvenlik reformu kanunu tasarısını Meclise sundu. Kime sordu?* Retrieved from: http://kadinkoalisyonu.org/

Women's Coalition. (2015, March 27). *Assessment of Women's Coalition on the Draft Bill to Amend the Law on the Powers and Duties of the Police*. Retrieved from: http://kadinkoalisyonu.org/womens-coalition-on-the-draft-bill/

World Bank. (2009). *Female Labour Force Participation in Turkey: Trends, Determinants and Policy Framework*. Retrieved from: http://siteresources.worldbank.org/TURKEYEXTN/Resources/361711-1268839345767/Female_LFP-en.pdf

World Economic Forum. (2019). *Global Gender Gap Report 2020*. Retrieved from:
    https://www.weforum.org/reports/gender-gap-2020-report-100-years-pay-equality

Wright, M. (2011). Necropolitics, Narcopolitics, and Femicide: Gendered Violence
    on the Mexico-US border. *Signs: Journal of Women in Culture and Society*, 36(3),
    707–31.

Yaka, Ö. (2017). A Feminist-Phenomenology of Women's Activism against Hydropower
    Plants in Turkey's Eastern Black Sea region. *Gender, Place and Culture*, 24(6),
    869–89.

Yapıcı, M. (2013, September 16). *Söyleşi: Evet, mesele üç-beş ağaç değil*. Retrieved from:
    https://haber.sol.org.tr/devlet-ve-siyaset/evet-mesele-3-5-agac-degil-haberi-79708

Yaraş, S. (2018). The Making of the 'New' Patriarch in Women's Self-narrations of
    Political Empowerment: The Case of Local Female AKP Politicians in the Aftermath
    of 2009 Elections. *Turkish Studies*, 20(2), 273–96.

Yeğen, M. (2015). *The Kurdish Peace Process in Turkey: Genesis, Evolution and Prospects*.
    Istanbul: Istanbul Policy Centre.

Yılmaz, İ. (2009). *Patterns of Differential Involvement in Terrorist Activities: Evidence
    from DHKP/C and Turkish Hezbollah*. (Unpublished PhD Thesis). Virginia: Virgina
    Commonwealth University.

Yılmaz, Z. (2015). 'Strengthening the Family' Policies in Turkey: Managing the Social
    Question and Armoring Conservative–Neoliberal Populism. *Turkish Studies*, 16(3),
    371–90.

Yoğurtçu Parkı Forumu. (2013). *Kadınlara ve Translara*. Retrieved from: http://www.
    sosyalistfeministkolektif.org/

Index